CONFESSIONS
OF A HERETIC

A Jawbone book
First English-language edition 2015
Published in the UK and the USA by
Jawbone Press
2a Union Court,
20–22 Union Road,
London SW4 6JP,
England
www.jawbonepress.com

Originally published as *Spowiedz Heretyka* by
Gruner & Jahr
www.guj.pl

ISBN 978-1-908279-75-0

EDITOR Tom Seabrook
DESIGN Maciej Szymanowicz

Printed in the Czech Republic by PB Print UK

2 3 4 5 19 18 17 16

CONFESSIONS OF A HERETIC

ADAM NERGAL DARSKI
WITH MARK EGLINTON
AND KRZYSZTOF AZAREWICZ & PIOTR WELTROWSKI

CONTENTS

INTRODUCTION
BY KRZYSZTOF AZAREWICZ
& PIOTR WELTROWSKI

The book you are holding in your hands took over six months to complete. It is, however, the result of a long-standing friendship between Nergal and us. During the interviews, we always tried to capture Nergal in his natural habitat and to present him in the way we know him to be in everyday life.

For the purposes of this book, we engaged in over a hundred conversations. These took place in various places: our houses; during long walks by the Baltic Sea or Old Town part of Krakow; in many restaurants in London; and during Behemoth's tours. Various emotions accompanied our conversations, which sometimes took the form of a lazy and long chitchat over a cup of coffee. Occasionally we turned the Dictaphone on impulsively, just to record one or two sentences, and then there were other occasions when Nergal didn't even realise we had been recording the conversation at all …

Throughout the process of preparing *Confessions Of A Heretic*, however, we always did our best to ensure that our own views and opinions would not cast a shadow on what Nergal had to say. In fact, oftentimes we assumed a position that was directly opposite to his view of the world—the sole aim being to provoke him into speaking his mind. As a result, we often felt that working on the book was a test of our friendship. Regardless, we always did our best to keep the conversations honest and uncompromising. There were jokes, smiles, guitar playing, but also serious stares and even some tears.

We hope that this emotional kaleidoscope inspires your own reflections and gives your worldview a bit more colour.

ABOUT THIS EDITION
BY MARK EGLINTON

The English edition of this book came about by pure chance. Of course—as a fan of Nergal and his music—I'd been aware of his illness and also the existence of the Polish edition, published in late 2012, but what I didn't fully appreciate at that time was the strength and depth of character that lay behind what was, frankly, a very intimidating public persona. Personas can be misleading, however, and in dealing with adversity, Nergal displayed a humanity that surprised anyone who might have been quick to judge someone whose lyrical stances are considered extreme, to put it mildly.

Let's face it, though: whether you're a fan of Behemoth or not, Nergal's story and approach to life generally—not just those aspects that deal with him overcoming life-threatening illness—surely deserve to be read and enjoyed in all languages. So, with that in mind, I sent the man an email asking if, by chance, he needed help to bring an English edition to life. I was surprised to receive a response within thirty seconds. 'Let's do it,' he said.

Confessions Of A Heretic is the result. It should be said straightaway that this edition does differ in some ways—most of them subtle—from the original, Polish equivalent. What we had to work with was a raw translation, painstakingly undertaken by Piotrek Niesluchowski. It was good, and brutally accurate, but my feeling was that—in order to really capture the imagination of a potentially large English speaking audience—the text needed to be edited, enhanced, and generally moulded to fit its new purpose. The core meaning was never altered, and the often-raw nature of the dialogue was also preserved, but in the process of *anglification*, for want of a better word, a few inevitable departures from the Polish version were necessary—all of which make this an extremely engaging book. What mattered most to me was that Nergal's unique voice shone through, regardless of language. As someone who captures voice—from all walks of life—as my day-to-day job, it was vital that this extraordinary man's character was preserved for all to read.

FOREWORD
BY D. RANDALL BLYTHE

Adam Nergal Darski is a survivor. But as most people in civilized countries never face any real life-threatening situations (and survival is, after all, the primary human instinct) that overused term of respect doesn't really hold much weight with me these days. It doesn't say much about the man, other than the fact that—as of this writing—he is alive, but so are approximately seven billion other humans on the planet. *Big fucking deal.*

All humans—unless they are mentally ill or suicidal—are, at their innermost core, driven to safeguard their existence. In fact, *all* life forms strive to survive, so it's really nothing extraordinary at all, as everything wants to live and will attempt to do their damnedest to do so, often at the expense of everything else if need be. People have survived horrific occurrences since we first rose from four legs to two, so survival isn't inherently special. If we weren't able to persevere through adversity, none of us would be here today.

But what differentiates humans from, say, seagulls or rattlesnakes or houseplants, is the ability to consciously choose the manner in which we handle certain crisis situations based on our individual code of ethics. True, sometimes we have to do what we have to do; it's not pretty, and we just get by. But in a world gone soft—a world that seems to grow more and more self-centred with each passing day—the concept of self-preservation at any cost is king (although I would consider self-*promotion* a more accurate term). Entitlement and compromised ethics seem to be the norm now: everyone whining about their woes as they step on others in the scrap for money, prestige, and the ludicrous 1.5 seconds of virtual fame most people seem to think they are entitled to in this sorry-ass modern age.

For survival to impress me these days, it has to be *real*, and it has to be done with panache. There are simply too many motherfuckers on this planet for me to be impressed by your mere continuing existence: making it through your girlfriend dumping you without hanging yourself, or a tough week at the office without having a meltdown, is not 'surviving'. If I am going to call someone a survivor, that person has to hold on to their convictions in the face of *real* adversity, and to emerge from whatever crisis they faced with their inner directive intact and their head held high. It helps even more if they are a snazzy dresser. Nergal is one of these people—he survives with *style*.

I do not always agree with Nergal. Some of his beliefs taste a bit extreme for my palate, and I certainly wouldn't handle some things the way he does. But I always, always, always respect those beliefs and the man who holds them, for they are well thought out and logical, and Ner holds steadfastly true to them, even when doing so could result in possibly very unpleasant circumstances for him. I witnessed the intersection of belief, action, and possible consequence first hand during an event he very briefly describes early on in this book.

In 2007, my band, Lamb Of God, was on tour with Behemoth as part of the Sounds of the Underground tour. The tour had made a stop on the grounds of Waverly Hills Sanatorium, an abandoned and reputedly haunted treatment centre for tuberculosis (and, later, elderly/mentally ill patients) located in the woods outside Louisville, Kentucky. There were twenty or so bands on the bill that day, one of which happened to be a Christian 'metalcore' band who apparently thought it would be a good idea to give Nergal a Bible before Behemoth took the stage. Whether this was an evangelical attempt to save Nergal's immortal soul or a passive-aggressive snipe at the man, I do not know. What I do know is that it backfired on them in a big way.

My wife and I were standing at the side of the stage with a friend to watch Behemoth's set when I saw Nergal stride to the front of the stage, Bible in hand, and address the crowd of seven thousand or so people. The venue had a capacity of four thousand, and the show had sold out well in advance. Another three thousand or so ticketless metal-heads, curious Louisville locals, and just plain old drunken rednecks with nothing better to do, had simply walked through the woods to check out the show. The festival wasn't going as planned: everyone's set was running late, there weren't nearly enough port-a-johns, and the vendors had sold out of water early due to the unexpectedly large turnout. It was a blazingly hot and humid afternoon, and a noticeably foul mood hung over the sweaty crowd. Security wasn't the tightest that day (to put it lightly), and as I saw Nergal hold the Bible aloft, I remember thinking, *Whatever is about to happen, I bet it's not going to go over well.*

'How many of you believe in this man called Jesus?' Nergal barked into the microphone.

About half of the crowd's hands went into the air.

'And how many of you read this book, and believe it holds the true words of this Jesus, your Lord and saviour?' he said, waving the Bible in front of the crowd. The same 3,500 hands went back into the air.

'Well, I've got some bad news for you,' he growled. 'This book you love so much … I say it is a book of *lies!*'

Then Nergal began ripping the Bible apart, spitting on the torn pages and throwing them into the audience. As the pages fluttered into the audience, he said into the microphone, 'This next one is for all of you believers of the false Christ, this one you call Jesus. This song is called "Christians to the Lions".' Then Behemoth tore into it, and chaos ensued.

Holy fuck, I thought. *We're all going to die.*

This wasn't a show in some Los Angeles art-house where bearded hipsters would make smarmy remarks later on the internet about how 'edgy' the front man of the Polish metal band had been. This wasn't a televised Sinéad O'Connor ripping apart a picture of the Pope on *Saturday Night Live* in New York fucking City (although I'm sure Nergal loved that), prompting a totally pussified network apology the next week. This was a barely restrained crowd of several thousand intoxicated people, many of whom were not metal fans. Deep in the woods. In Kentucky. In the *Bible Belt*. Where people have guns. *Lots* of guns. If it was going to go wrong, it was going to go *really wrong*.

That took balls. No, that took *style*.

Somehow a full-scale redneck massacre of the entire tour didn't occur, but there were plenty of very, very unhappy people in the audience. As Behemoth left the stage, I walked up to Nergal and said, 'Damn man, whoever gave you that Bible really pissed you off, huh?'

'You know, I try to be nice to everyone,' he said, still visibly angered, 'but obviously some people will not let me.' With that, he stomped off to his dressing room.

After knowing him for several years, I can say with no small amount of confidence that Nergal *is* a super-nice guy. While I certainly do not hold the same disdain for religious belief that Nergal does, I do have a huge problem with what many people do in the name of whatever God it is they worship. Like the old bumper sticker says: *God save me (from your crazy followers)*. My band, although taking our name from the Christian bible, has exactly zero lyrics that are either pro or anti any religion, and I don't have a problem with anyone believing in whatever God they want to (as long as that belief doesn't cause them to harm or infringe upon the rights of others). But Lamb Of God have been picketed and banned from venues. Hell, we've been banned from entire *countries* by religious zealots who have absolutely no concept of what we are about at all. On more than one occasion I've had the screaming religious loonies in my face outside our gigs telling me I'm going to hell because of the 'devil music' I make.

In contrast, while Nergal obviously despises Christianity (the dude *did* release an album entitled *The Satanist)*, I've never once seen or heard of him running around in front of a fundamentalist church in corpse paint, screaming blasphemous curses at the faithful, and trying to shove his views down their throats while waving a sign in their face that says 'Satan Saves' (although that would be pretty funny to witness). In fact, I've never once seen him randomly abuse anyone, physically or verbally. Despite his onstage presence, I've always known Nergal to be a kind-hearted, well-mannered man. He's a lot of fun to hang out with, and a truly nice guy—honestly, he really is.

He's also exceedingly intelligent, able to articulately explain his beliefs, and has no qualms about defending them publicly. After he was diagnosed with leukaemia, Nergal encouraged his fans to sign up for a bone-marrow donation organisation in order to help save the lives of others who may be suffering from the same disease as himself. But as well, in his first public statement since his diagnosis, he soundly dispelled any rumours that he might change his scornful views of religion and convert to Christianity because he faced a life-threatening illness.

'Why should the illness change my point of view? It is true this is a difficult time for me and the thoughts of ultimate matters are hard to chase away. But the idea that I will change my opinions, priorities, and values as a consequence of my illness sounds as if someone regards my head, and not my body, ill … so, I say to those, who see some chances to break my rules, and myself because of the illness: over my dead body!'

Now that's surviving with *style*.

Like my own sorry self, Nergal is also no stranger to controversy and legal woes, as the readers of this book will come to understand. He's faced down courtroom adversity with pretty severe repercussions (a former Eastern Bloc prison is *not* a nice place—just trust me on that one) on more than one occasion, clung to his beliefs, and once again, survived the battle with *style*. Ner's a complex guy who has walked an intriguing path, one full of unexpected twists and turns—his life makes for a great story. Throughout the telling of his story, he doesn't take it easy on himself, nor does he try to paint a picture of himself as something greater or more glamorous than what he is. It's a good read, an honourable book, and I was proud to be asked to write the introduction for the English edition. As I highly value intelligence, ethics, and inner strength in the people I choose to associate with, I'm even prouder to call the man my friend.

Beyond just enjoying the book, I hope the reader will find a passage or two that will give them pause, make them take a moment to reflect on the circumstances of their own life, and consider the course of their actions within their daily existence. I certainly did.

Be without fear!

D. Randall Blythe
Richmond, VA
December 1, 2014

I

I AM YOUR BLIND FATE,
WHO DELIVERED YOU
FROM THE LAND OF
HIGH~RISE BLOCKS

When was the last time you actually went to confession?
I don't know. I don't remember. It's been ages.

Every Polish child goes to confession, though.
I might have been about fourteen. I was preparing for the sacrament of confirmation but I never actually received it. I demanded that I be removed from that circus. Religion itself started to turn me off. It stank somewhat. I had been aware of the smell even prior to that, when I had felt Catholic and thought I believed. There was such a time in my life. Seriously. But it was a momentary faith. There was nothing profound about it. I was a kid, so I was more interested in having fun than anything to do with the church.

Try to think. Maybe you *can* recall the moment when you confessed your sins for the last time?
No. I remember only the feelings that accompanied me when going to the confessional, not the act itself. You just stand there, wait in the queue, and it's all sad and cold around you. I hated it and I still do. Churches may be beautiful, but they're always sad and cold.

Adam Darski fled from confirmation and the heavens didn't shed so much as a tear …
The only thing special about my birth was the place. Even though my family lived in Gdańsk, I was born in a hospital in Gdynia so, technically, I'm a 'herring' (the town's emblem has a herring in it). Apart from that, it was quite normal. The three kings were not there; there was no bright star. Just another ordinary birth. My childhood was similar. We were just a typical Polish family.

Adam is such a nice biblical name, though.
Yeah, it's nice.

Were traditions important in your household?
Only as decoration. There was a crucifix on the wall, and we let the priest

come to our house, but I felt that it was all just ornamental. There was an obvious discord between things that hung on walls and what we actually practiced. My father was in the PZPR (the Polish United Workers' Party). I knew he was at the crossroads, and he tried to find a compromise between his own worldview and these traditions. He took part in all the celebrations, but he would never actually kneel—he always stood aside. He kept up appearances and manoeuvred around …

What about your mother?
She attached more weight to religion, but I don't actually think her faith was very deep. She might be angry with me for saying it, but that's the way I saw it. But there was a period in her life when she genuinely did seek help from God.

I was eight years old and my brother, Paweł, was sixteen when he brought home an unexploded shell. There were no computers back then, and there were only two channels available on the TV, so kids had to find fun in different ways. My brother was always interested in old military stuff. It wasn't difficult to find it, after all. All you had to do was go into the forest.

Paweł started tinkering with a piece he found, it exploded, and he lost his eyesight for quite some time. He was in hospital for a few months. The doctors didn't know if he would ever see again. *That* was when my mother Irena started praying. She attended the church, sought help from the crucifix. But when my brother got better, she gave it up. Fortunately for her and I, she didn't become a zealot.

The age difference between you and Paweł is quite a lot—eight years. What was your relationship like?
We had the same mother, but—half-seriously—I am not so sure about our father. We were polar opposites. We differed in every way, starting with our characters and finishing with how we lived our lives generally. I was a good student; I didn't cause major problems either at home or at school.

My brother was a proper hooligan. He caused a lot of trouble and he barely finished primary school. He just didn't want to continue his education. He went to a vocational school and after that he found a job. His ambitions veered radically away from education. He was mainly interested in parties, girls, and the gym. He even set up a gym in the attic.

One day I found a set of syringes and some strange vials in the cupboard. Of course I had no idea what they were. Only later—when Paweł gained some impressive musculature in a short period of time—did I connect the dots. Not that it bothered me. We lived in one room, but we spent our time *beside* each other, not with each other—there is a distinction. But having said all that, it was largely thanks to him that I discovered music, so you could say he changed my life …

Did you go to church at Easter?

Never! Even when I considered myself to be a Catholic—I hated churches. That was the way my instinct worked. I started lying to my parents. As a kid, I had to tell my mother that I had been to the church. Every Sunday my brother would, of course, steal away in the morning; my father would go to take care of his allotment and I would stay with mom. Sunday mass for the youth took place at eleven o'clock, so that was when I left home.

Was your mother standing in the doorway waiting for you to return and to ask you what the mass was about?

No, she never played the Gestapo role. But yes, some of my friends would have to wait for their buddies coming back from the church to ask about the mass. It didn't concern me. I was not forced to do anything; it was more like a silent kind of pressure.

I don't even remember how my Sunday trips ended. One day I just didn't go to the church and that was it. It was uneventful. There was no punishment—nobody took my pocket money away.

How did your parents make their living?

My father used to work in the Lenin Shipyard as a shipbuilding technician. He would spend most days in his office. He took me there a few times, but it was boring for me. My mother, on the other hand, worked her whole life at Bimet, a bearings factory. She also worked in an office. As a young girl she wanted to become a nurse, but once, during classes, when she saw blood, she almost fainted and she changed her mind. I always had something to eat and wear. We weren't rich, but we didn't struggle either, and even if we did, my parents did their best for me not to notice it.

Did they pamper you?

To this day I feel stupid because of one particular incident. In the 80s, the shops were practically bereft of stock. But there were markets where you could get all kinds of interesting stuff. There was one such market in the Wrzescz neighbourhood of Gdańsk. I liked going there, both with my parents and later with my friends. Once, I saw a computer—a ZX81, probably the most primitive machine of its type. It looked like a big calculator, but it did let you play games. It was a forerunner of the ZX Spectrum, Atari, or Commodore.

Oh, to have something like this was every young boy's wet dream. I didn't care about the price; I just wanted to have one. At first, my parents refused, because it was quite expensive. But they could see a fire in my eyes, so we brought the salesman to our house; he explained to me how the computer worked, and then we did a deal.

I never turned the thing on after that. It just sat there and collected dust. Those were difficult times, and the money could have been used in a better way. This is what my parents were like, and still are. They fulfilled all my demands. They lacked character …

And you lacked discipline?

Every pot has two handles.

Come on—answer the question.

I am really grateful to my parents for how they brought me up. But even as a child I could take life into my own hands. I learned responsibility and self-reliance. I didn't have to take piano lessons or ballet classes. I studied languages because I felt like it, not because somebody forced me to. I could take up martial arts, play the guitar; nobody was depriving me of that—on the contrary, my parents made things easier for me.

Were you beaten?
No, but my brother was. He often took a beating. Thanks to his excesses, my ass was covered. My parents knew that being rough didn't pay with me anyway. They had other more educational methods for me.

So you never actually took a beating?
Maybe twice in my entire life.

Did you deserve it?
Once I did, for sure. I was six years old and we were spending the holidays in the countryside. Our house was on a hill, and there was a steep road next to it that led to a footbridge over a river. On the side of the hill there was a tractor. I climbed up to the driver's seat; I pressed the clutch and the machine started and was soon headed straight toward the water. I tried to drive, but the engine was not running. There was no way a little boy could gain control over such a large vehicle. Luckily, my uncle was not too far away, together with my father, and they stopped the machine a few metres from the river. For that, I got a solid beating. I had to stay in bed for two days, and it hurt so much.

Do you hold a grudge against your father for that?
No, I deserved it. There were always children playing by that road. It was pure luck that on that day there was nobody there when I started the tractor. Even today, I get chills when I think about it. We do a lot of dumb stuff when we're young.

You didn't become a tractor operator, then!
What about martial arts?
My father took me to a judo lesson. I was really into it. Martial arts became a part of my life, almost as important as music. I had one more passion:

19

drawing. I would spend hours filling whole notebooks with drawings—I even created my own comic books. Mostly I drew battle-pieces. Every boy loves war.

Did you play with plastic soldiers?
My neighbour from the seventh floor, Piotrek, used to come over. We waged wars by throwing marbles at the enemy's army. He was fucking good at it! Much better than me—so I usually lost. It made me furious.

Did you stamp your feet and throw the soldiers off the table?
No, but my friend's winning was extremely frustrating. I never knew how to lose—I couldn't be second to anybody. Other kids played football. I knew I was no match for the best of them, so I let that pass. I was much better at judo; I was a really scrupulous student, so I would never miss any practice. And there was a prize to fight for, too: the best competitors got tickets to the swimming pool. That was really exclusive entertainment. Today, you just turn up, buy yourself a season ticket, and you go whenever you want. Back then, there were just a couple of swimming pools in the Tricity district, and it was not easy to get in. I was there every Saturday.

Were you interested in girls at that time?
I discovered the gentle sex as early as in kindergarten. I attended three of them … I wasn't thrown out of any of them, but my first kindergarten experiences were traumatic. I was really close with my parents; I just didn't understand why my mother would leave me in some strange place. I would just stand by the window with tears streaming from my eyes as I watched my parents leave the building. Then I would go to the toilet, close the door, and keep crying.

The other kids didn't react like that, but I really hated it. The worst thing about it was the so-called 'pork chop'. I say 'so-called' because it had nothing in common with a real pork chop. Some ligaments, gristle, and tendons connected with tiny bits of meat that stayed intact only because of the hideous coating. That was the kindergarten pork chop. It was just impossible to eat it. The problem was that they wouldn't let us leave the table if there was food left on our plate.

Did you clench your fists and eat?
I tried. Once I didn't manage it. I think that was my biggest childhood trauma. While I'm chewing this damn piece of pork, I'm trying from each possible angle, keeping bits of meat in my cheeks like a hamster. At the same time, I felt that my bowels had something important to announce but I couldn't leave the table to go to the toilet because my plate was still full. For a few moments I fought valiantly with nature.

I kept fidgeting, and I deluded myself that someone finally would let me go to the toilet, but nothing happened. When the critical moment finally arrived, I jumped to my feet and ran to the shitter. I could hear somebody yelling at me, but I completely ignored it.

There's one more thing you need to know: in the same kindergarten there was this girl from the other class, a little blonde called Bożenka. All the boys were crazy about her—and me, too. It was purely platonic of course; I had no actual contact with her. She was a very kind girl: calm, quiet, and beautiful. Just perfect. I loved staring at her, but that was all I did.

What was her role in the pork chop story?
I ran out of the room. I went into the shitter at high speed, but it was already too late. I didn't even manage to close the door and take my pants off. It was all there. So there I am, covered in my own shit, trying to wipe it up with toilet paper, when the door opens and Bożenka appears. She stared at me; I stared at her. My shit was just everywhere.

I gave her a sheepish smile, opened my mouth, and asked her not to tell on me. Of course, the first thing she did was call the tutor. It all ended up with a good deal of embarrassment and a bath in the paddling pool. My tutor held my hand like a rag while she cleaned me with a hose. I got a reprimand and some bonus naptime. Well, that and the feeling that my unfulfilled love snitched on me that I shat my pants.

Was that your first girl/boy experience?

No. The first one was much more pleasant. I did something bad—I don't even remember what it was, but I got punished. That meant more naptime, of course. I had to wear my pyjamas and lie in the 'penalty bed' in the middle of the room. I did my time, so my tutor came to me and said that I could get up. But I distinctly felt that something else had also 'got up'. It was the first erection that I remember.

Did you have a real girlfriend in the kindergarten?

I even got my first blowjob! I remember it in detail. The girl's name was Magda, and she was definitely not my type. She had a hooked nose and hair that stood on end, like a hen or something. But during the sleeping time she was lying in the bed next to me. We started whispering. Suddenly she made an offer I couldn't refuse. She wanted to lick me down there if I licked her there, too. I was curious, so I said, 'I'm in.' When she got under my blanket, though, I didn't feel the fire … I just shrugged.

What about your part of the deal?

I got cold feet. I put my head under the blanket, but halfway there I decided I didn't really want it. I moved back and announced with all seriousness that I couldn't reach. I turned my back and went to sleep.

You broke the poor girl's heart. When did you find out what that dangling thing down there is for?

It's hard to say. Quite early, I suppose. I received my first proper sexual education when I was eight. My guide was Cezar, my brother's buddy. He liked to party; he was a kind of a local badass but he always treated me OK.

My brother threw a party. Our parents weren't at home, and I was supposed to keep my mouth shut in my room. So there I was, lying in my bed reading, while the other room was hosting quite a party: cigarettes, alcohol, loud music. Suddenly Cezar, hammered as fuck, came into my room; he sat on my bed and began this drunken monologue. After a while, he gave me a VHS cassette and told me that he was lending it to me; that I didn't have to give it back any time soon, but I was to watch it when I was alone in the house. I got to it the next day.

It wasn't a Disney cartoon, then?

There were cartoons on it, too, but they were not exactly suitable for children. It was three hours of hardcore porn. I didn't give the tape back for a few *months*—it was that inspiring. Had it not been for Cezar, I would have waited a few more years before I saw movies like that.

Let's go back to kindergarten. Were you a bad boy?

More of a rebel. I made all kinds of plans and then made them happen. Once, I even managed to run away. The reason was so mundane. I couldn't understand why I had to be in some strange place when the house was empty. So I came up with a plan. Nothing complicated; I decided that when we went to play outside, I would head toward the gate, avoid all the obstacles, and somehow I'd make it. And that's what I did, but Mrs Jadzia chased me. She wasn't too fast, and her running was rather clumsy, so I made it to the gate before her with no problem.

So that was your first truancy.

My brother was the one playing truant. I met him when I was running home. He noticed me and was really surprised. 'What are you doing here?' he asked. I said that I had run away. He took me home and I didn't go back to school that day. You could say that I had made the plan come true.

And after kindergarten, there was school …

I attended the 93rd Comprehensive School in Gdańsk. It was right beside my house—about 300 metres away. That was convenient, because I never liked to get up early.

Did you feel that you were different from your friends?

Not really. Not back then. I only stood out because I could draw nicely. That had its consequences, too: I had to draw for the school magazine.

Did you finish school with honours?

I was a better student than my brother was, but not that good.

What was your best subject?

PE. I was always fond of physical activities. For me, it was an antidote for all the subjects I didn't like that much. I was allergic to exact sciences; my biggest enemy was mathematics, and it still is today. I always have my calculator with me.

An artist, a musician, a humanist …

Those talents showed up later, in high school. Before that, I didn't really have the best association with books. There were books that were mandatory to read, and we all know that if you are forced to do something, you don't really feel like doing it. A few years passed before I discovered that there are books you can read because you want to and be happy about it.

But you watched movies?

There was a VHS player in the house and I used it. As I mentioned before, I was really drawn in by martial arts, so I absorbed karate movies. Every Saturday, I would go to the market and buy two. They were recorded on one tape. You could buy one tape and then just come back and trade it for another one for a small fee. Of course, these were all rather 'Z-class' movies with crude plots, primitive dubbing, and so on. But the action was there, and I didn't need anything else.

Did you enjoy studying Russian?

I was pretty good, but I don't remember much today. Shame.

Your father was in the Party, and now you're sorry you didn't study Russian more scrupulously. And yet you don't understand why some people call you a Bolshevik … didn't you rebel against communism?

My brother did. I cared only for the yard, my friends, and having fun.

The only contact with politics I ever had was when I went through Paweł's drawers. There were brochures and leaflets by Solidarność, the Polish trade union. I flicked through them—don't confuse that with actually *reading* them.

There were two rooms in the house: one was my parents', the other was for my brother and I. Sometimes, when our father watched debates on the TV in his room and there were some Party discussions, my brother would play some songs by Perfect, who were one of the most popular Polish rock bands of the time, and tell me that 'we want to be ourselves' *really* meant 'we want to beat ZOMO'.

Did your father and brother ever have political arguments?

Not really. My father didn't bring politics home. He signed up for the Party, but he wasn't an active member. He just had his ID in his pocket; that's it. He didn't bash Paweł for his views either. Of course, today I know that communism actually meant *constrain*, but back then I just didn't give a shit.

Didn't your brother's stories incite anything in you?

He was really fascinated by Solidarność, and I cared for Perfect's music much more than for their lyrics. The sounds, to him, were just a carrier of content.

So what's the story with you and music? How did it start?

In the beginning, I was just fascinated by how a guy with a guitar looked. It really captured my imagination. It didn't really matter what I was listening to, because I enjoyed every kind of music.

It must have started with something specific, though?

It might have been the Polish band Kombi. Back then, they were on TV all the time. Actually, it's quite funny, because I'm friendly with their guitarist, Grzesiek Skawiński, today. Recently, after a few glasses of wine, I told him that I still think that the old Kombi records are perfect. He thought I was pulling his leg!

I can't help it, though: 'Słodkiego, Miłego Życia' ('Sweet, Nice

Life') and 'Black And White' really stuck in my head. I think that's how sentiment works.

Sentiment is one thing, but if somebody told you that years later you would be drinking wine with Grzesiek— not as a fan but as an equally popular musician—would you have believed it? Have you ever thought about it?

Are you kidding me? I used to pretend that I was playing on a broomstick, but I never thought for a moment that I would become a musician. It was all just a kid's fantasy. But yes, music did draw me in in a most unusual way. The sounds were like a magnet.

When we spent holidays in the countryside, our neighbours, in the house right next to ours, were a very 'musical' family—they had a wedding band. I loved going over to their place, just to sit behind the drums and hold the sticks for a while or touch the guitar. Instruments were expensive and hard to get. For me, they were like relics.

How did you get your first guitar?

It was in 1983 or 1984. I was sitting in my pyjamas, waiting for my father to get back home from work. When he came inside he was holding a guitar in his hands. An old acoustic one. It was really beaten up and it had some black stickers on it that were supposed to hide the scratches. It looked like it was about to fall apart, but it didn't matter. When I saw it, I was ecstatic.

Didn't you get bored with it, as you did your first computer?

No way! I would sit on my bed and mindlessly strum the strings with my right hand. They would give off the same sound, on and on. I sang all the songs that I knew from the TV or school. That's how it all started.

Was your brother as fascinated with music as you were?

He listened to music, but I had the impression that he was totally indifferent to what kind of music it was. He liked Polish rock music, but he also had posters of pop bands on the wall.

And what posters did you have on your wall?

My first poster was of ZZ Top. It fitted nicely into the typical Polish bedroom of the 80s: two beds, a desk, and a board with some banners above it. There was a wall unit set next to it, decorated with beer cans.

Did you often fight with your brother?

We didn't really have anything in common; the age difference didn't help either. In some ways I was afraid of him. He was older than me, and sometimes he seemed dangerous. Once, he beat me up so much that for the next few days I was bruised and in pain. Today, I remember it as a funny, tragicomic situation.

We had darts in the house. Our parents were not home, and my brother was sitting in his underwear reading TV listings, so I thought it would be funny if I threw a dart in the vicinity of his foot.

It was supposed to be a joke; I didn't want to hurt him. I thought I could put the dart in the floor, but of course I hit Paweł in the foot. He started screaming like somebody was peeling all his skin off. For a moment he was jumping on one leg, then—when he stopped—he gave me one hell of a beating.

Did he often put you in your place?

Our relations were very bad at times. He looked down on me—we practically didn't talk. Maybe it was because our parents brought me up in a different way—they were much more gentle to me. Paweł may have felt bitter. His relationship with our parents was very tense, and he cut them off quite early.

Did he move out?

He left without a word.

He worked delivering fruit. One day, our mother prepared sandwiches for him, as always. He just took the little bag and left home. He never came back. His friends told us that he went abroad. We didn't see each other again until a few years later.

Were you afraid?

I finally had the whole room to myself, so I felt a degree of relief. We all did—even my parents. Prior to that, the situation was really tense; something was in the air, and somebody had to make an extreme step. Over time, I've come to realise that he just did what he had to. Thanks to that, he matured much faster. Today, he has a really good relationship with our parents.

Were you aware of what was going on with him?

After a year, he sent us a postcard from Spain. Before that, he was in France. He had a friend who had moved there. He had sent Paweł a postcard on which he marked the location of a house he supposedly lived in. My brother found the house and started calling—all to no avail. The guy didn't live there anymore, apparently, so my brother kept going until he managed to get to the Iberian Peninsula.

How was life there for him?

For a few years he lived in Spartan conditions, often in squats. He worked illegally on construction sites, and sometimes he helped with house renovations. But he made do. He wasn't extravagant; he saved money, and in time he created a real life for himself. He rented a place, met a woman, married her, and opened up a shop. He was well built and handsome, so people respected him and called him 'The Barbarian From The North'.

In a way, I suppose I admired him. He showed me what real determination was. It might be that he has had a bigger influence on my life than I'm inclined to admit. He instilled in me much more than just the love of music ...

**Since you mention music, how long did you
have to endure playing that old guitar?**

I was killing my parents with my guitar playing. I would walk around the house, strum the strings, and sing. I think they felt there was potential there. I tried to make them sign me up to a music school, and they agreed. But by then I already wanted to play some heavier rock stuff, like what I heard on the radio. At school they made me play scout songs, and then I came back home and begged my brother to show me how to play 'Lokomotywa' by Perfect. It got to the point where my acoustic guitar wasn't enough. Luckily, my first communion was coming up.

Did you get an electric guitar?

I got money—22,000 old zlotys, to be precise. I bought the guitar myself—I spent 13,000 zloty on it. I remember it well. I still have it. It reminded me of a Fender but it was homemade. I bought it from Jacek Doniewski, my first music mentor. He had learned how to play himself, but he had an 'electric'. He asked my father to make a board and the neck, and that wasn't easy for someone who worked in a shipyard. But Jacek finished the instrument himself and taught me how to play the riff to TSA's 'Bez Podtekstów'.

Did anyone else have an influence on your musical education?

My grandfather, Klemens Iwicki. My mother's family was musically gifted. Almost everybody in the clan played an instrument of some kind: accordions, violins, guitars … my grandfather showed me how to play a waltz. It was the only time I played the bass strings with my thumb.

Thick string, thick finger …

Exactly. I don't think anyone plays like that anymore. But in order to play, you had to tune the guitar first. I couldn't do that, so I took my guitar for music lessons. My first real girlfriend, Celina, went there with me. We weren't actually an item then, but she helped me. She was learning much faster than I was because she had slender, long fingers.

I will never forget her reaction when I asked her to tune the guitar. There were no amps or radios in the room. She looked at my guitar and said, 'Let's plug it in.'

What did you want to play?

I got chills down my spine whenever I heard 'Perfect Strangers' by Deep

Purple—a timeless piece of music. That was the kind of music you would hear on the TV back then. I watched video clips on a black-and-white Neptun TV.

They played them all back during the day: Deep Purple, Iron Maiden, and so on. Even on programmes like *Wideoteka*, they always played at least one heavier song. That's how I discovered bands like WASP, Kiss, Marillion, and ZZ Top. We would hold a tape recorder against the speaker and record the songs. The whole family had to be quiet, mind you—we didn't have a cord to plug in the tape recorder. Only later did we manage to get a so-called 'piątka'. We didn't even dream of stereo gear. Stuff like that could only be found in sailors' houses and people who could go to Pewex (a Polish store that sold otherwise unobtainable Western goods).

But that didn't matter. What mattered was that I found my sounds.

What was in this music that touched you?

The energy, the adrenalin. It's as simple as that. One kid prefers playing football, some other likes ice-skating; I liked heavy music. The rest is evolution. You get in and walk into a forest, where, as it turns out, there are many more different trees.

Wasn't it difficult to get any information about this forest?

There was radio. Thanks to a schoolmate, I discovered the radio show *Music Of The Young*. It was a revelation to me. Once a week they would play entire albums. I went crazy! Every Monday at 3:15pm and every Sunday at 8:10am I would sit down with the radio on and record everything they played. I wrote the names of the bands phonetically; Krzysztof Brankowski and the guy who hosted the *Metal Tortures* show, Roman Rogowiecki, translated the song titles into Polish.

It was like light. Something you would wait a week for. I remember once, they played Kat's album *38 Minutes Of Life*. I was disappointed because I already had it on vinyl, so it was a wasted day!

It was on the radio that I heard thrash metal for the first time. At first it was unbearable; it was too extreme. I had to take things slowly. It was classic evolution. Starting with hard rock, finishing with something extreme. Music was my life.

What did your folks say?

They were very understanding. I would come back home from school, throw my backpack in the corner, and put on my coat. I asked my father to paint a skull with a 'heavy metal' inscription on it. Now I had my uniform and I had my guitar. I would play it for hours.

Doing homework didn't matter to me. I sat in my room, composing my own songs and even writing some primitive lyrics. One of my song titles was 'Kanalia' ('Skunk'). I even remember the lyrics, but I'd die of embarrassment if I had to tell you what they were.

The radio I used as an amp was in the living room. It was an Amator 2. My parents had to sit in the kitchen so I could play. The son had to play, so they gave him space. Only when I was finished could they come back into the room, sit on the couch, and watch TV.

Didn't you want to form a band?

I did form a band. I summoned a few friends, at least. The drummer played on chairs, and the only real instrument was my guitar. We didn't play covers. By then I already wanted to write my own songs. I pulled the strings. I would say to my classmates, 'You're in my band. You play this and you play that.'

Once, the drummer made a mistake. I considered this insubordination, so I beat him up. He went all red and started to cry.

Were you like that at school, too?

I was part of the group that terrorised the whole school. You become an alpha male when you're a child. But I didn't push it; I didn't cause major problems. My parents didn't come back home pissed off from parent/teacher meetings, so they didn't try to keep me on a leash.

Were your friends as enthusiastic about music as you were?

My schoolmates were not. A few guys from the neighbourhood liked heavy

31

music, but nobody was into it as deeply as I was. I was in it alone, aside from a few local insiders.

I was immersed in punk music by the time I finished comprehensive school. I even wore the appropriate clothes for each group. I had short hair, and I wore a badge with 'The Exploited' on it on my coat. I even bought some old, shabby combat boots. They were fucking awesome. I also remember a famous slogan: 'Punks from Żabianka don't drink no buttermilk.'

But you didn't stay with it?
It was a short but intense flirtation. I felt aroused by the music, and partly also by the ideology—the love for anarchy, maybe. We felt freedom. We wanted it. Then we discovered stimulants. Some of the guys took a step ahead: cheap wines weren't enough anymore, so they started sniffing glue. I used my common sense. I treated punk as a rival. Some guys went with the programme—school, college, family, kids, divorce, another wife—but we wanted to break that cycle, and metal stayed in first place.

How did you start to listen to really extreme music?
I was very influenced by my friends from the neighbourhood, Daniel Gierszanow in particular. We fed each other's interest. One summer, after the holidays, he came back totally different. Before, we were afraid of Slayer and their satanic image. I thought they couldn't play, and I considered their music to be just noise.

When Daniel came back, though, he said, 'You know what? Slayer is not that bad.' Soon I concurred.

He was constantly listening to the *Reign In Blood* album; he had it recorded on a shabby yellow Stilon tape. He was the first one to really fall in love with really heavy music, and he kept instilling it in me. After Slayer, it was Death. He loved *Leprosy* and I loved *Scream Bloody Gore*. I still listen to that record today. It's a classic. I know all the lyrics by heart.

Then it all just fell like dominos. At one of the markets in Gdańsk, some guys showed up who lined up some recliners with tapes on them for sale. I bought tons of these; I spent all my allowance. You, Krzysiek, were selling there too, if I recall. I think that's how we met: I bought Hellhammer and Sepultura from you.

I got back home, put Hellhammer on, and twenty minutes later, the music was finished. I looked at the tape—it was a 90-minute BASF cassette—and I thought to myself, 'He tricked me!' Of course, it was a mini-album. I had no idea about that, and I was really disappointed. It was only later that I came to realise that you wanted to be fair, so you recorded these albums on the best-quality tapes available. Anyway, I met both of you in similar circumstances.

It almost brings a tear to the eye.
You know how it was. You traded tapes with friends. In order to save money, everyone bought something different, so we could all have more music. That's what we did with Daniel. We also tried to play together, but with time, our relationship was fading away. Then Baal, or Adam Muraszko, showed up.

II

THERE IS NO SMOKE
WITHOUT FIRE

Did you ever want to burn a church?
Yes.

That's a pretty serious admission.
You take a lot of issues very seriously when you're a kid. I was completely drawn in by black metal music, for example—especially its radical faction, and the bands in Scandinavia. I was particularly fascinated by those who put actions before words and showed no mercy while doing so.

Between 1992 and 1996, black metal musicians and their fans burnt over fifty churches across Norway. Did any part of you want to emulate them?
Black metal showed up at exactly the right moment for me. My youthful, rebellious soul was only just coming to life but, that being said, I had already begun to notice the ubiquitous duplicity of Christian morality.

I had no intellectual backup, of course, but I could see how mendacious people were: people who said one thing but did something completely different.

That is when music came to me, and it came from the North. That fact seemed only to add to its strength and authenticity. It sounded in my soul, and in doing so it brought me something primitive. It was authentic. I didn't feel that it was posing as something else, either. It was radical, and it called things by name.

Did black metal offer you something that other genres didn't?
You played the tape, you read the lyrics, and you discovered that in some part of the world there were people just like you. It seemed like there was no distance between you and a guy from Norway whose music you listened to. He was right there in front of you. You wrote him a letter and he wrote you back. That was the essence of the metal underground.

We were all sixteen to maybe twenty years old. We grew up in one generation. That was what connected us. It was our music and nobody else's.

Black metal existed prior to that, though.
Yes, but in some other less radical form. First, I stumbled upon Venom, the fathers of the genre. They recorded an album called *Black Metal*, but with time I realised that it was really just like Motörhead enclosed in a satanic envelope. They never took themselves too seriously, but that in no way lessened my fanatical worship of them. The difference was that these bands from Norway implemented into daily life the things that Venom, Hellhammer, or Bathory were just singing about. Norwegians lived life to the fullest. Sometimes they died the same way. I don't know how the first London punks felt when Sex Pistols were onstage, but the lack of humility and rebellion against certain rules had to be similar to those present on the black metal stage at the beginning of the 90s.

Were there other people in Poland with the same tune playing in their souls?
There was a rather tight and closed-knit group, yes—and we fuelled each other's interest. When churches started to burn in Norway, we wanted to bring that to Poland.

Nothing ever happened, and it was a long time ago. I am a different man today. But I'm not embarrassed about my past. It's what shaped me.

So your thoughts about burning churches remained just that: thoughts?
It went a bit further than that. I don't remember exactly which building we targeted. It was either a temple in Nowy Port or another in Brzezno. Either way, we went as far as to scout the area. Together with the guys from Mastiphal, another band from Gdańsk, we drove past the church.

Browar took us there—the guy who played bass for us back then. He was older, and the only guy among us who had a car. When we got there we began to plan the whole thing. I think we agreed on Molotov cocktails; we wanted to throw them in through the windows.

Of course, the whole plan existed only in our minds. What was more significant was that we had created a team and that we had a common goal. In the end, I didn't become a terrorist. Common sense prevailed over youthful exuberance. I understood that this was not how things should be dealt with, and my life is evidence that I made the right choice.

Musicians from iconic black metal bands like Burzum or Emperor chose a different path. They did their time, but—ultimately—achieved a similar effect. Their music became popular, and today they are in a position similar to yours.

It's not my place to judge them. I knew—and still know—most of these people. I am friendly with of some of them to this day. Some of them have much heavier things on their conscience than burning down a church. Some of them were convicted for murder. There are some who were drawn in by criminal activities—and, of course, a few of them are now dead.

People usually associate these sorts of stories with hip-hop, not heavy metal …

Everything that is new and fresh in culture is radical to some degree. Near the end of the 70s, punk rock was radical. In the early 90s, black metal was, too. I'm sure hip-hop had a period like that also but I'd be guessing, because I don't follow that genre. Rebellion is a part of youth. Sometimes it's dangerous.

But now you're saying that this is not the path to be followed?

Instead of a sword, I hold a guitar in my hands. I'm in the same, strong mind-set, but instead of Molotov cocktails, I've got a computer. It's a much more powerful weapon.

For what purpose? To worship Satan? What do you need the devil for, anyway?

Actually there is a lot more to me than that, but sadly there are always people who see the world in just two colours. They only mention Satan. This is how they use me for their political games.

Before the 2010 Polish presidential election there were whole legions of guys like this. It's as if some of them suddenly awoke after twenty years in hibernation, just to show a lot of indignation and to mark me as their target. Others decided that they were my buddies, even though I had never met them in my life. But in the background there was always Satan.

But why him?

I suppose because he is very recognisable to Poles. People like songs they know; the same applies to metaphors.

Was he previously any less metaphoric?

He used to smile less. I showed him the way the Christians see him: as a repulsive tool for intimidation. But the Bible never really described his looks.

So the devil might actually be nice and friendly?

If I *were* to personify him, I would say he's a handsome, middle-aged gentleman. He wears great clothes, his manners are impeccable, and he speaks many different languages. Black does not necessarily mean ugly. My Satan was perfectly depicted in Bulgakov's *The Master And Margarita*, or in movies such as *Angel Heart* with Robert De Niro, or *The Devil's Advocate*. Al Pacino is just great in that. I remember his words: 'I am a fan of man. And a humanist. Maybe the last humanist.'

So you're like a Satanist-humanist?

Some people think that I painted my house black, that I sleep in a coffin, and that I don't drink milk because it's white. But I prefer sunny mornings and a big bed. My devil is colourful.

What about God?

This biblical one seems not to speak or listen, and he certainly does not respond. I can quote *The Devil's Advocate* again to illustrate. I don't remember the quote verbatim, but what it said was more or less this: 'Who is God? He likes to watch. He gives you instincts and then prohibitions. Look, but don't touch. Touch, but don't taste. Taste, but don't swallow.' So you can see that he's a bit of a sadist, this God.

And this Satan of yours seems to be a little simplistic. Don't you feel a bit like a 'nativity play' Satanist?

That's what Father Boniecki—a former confidante of Pope John Paul II— once called me. He's a nice man, considering he's a priest. Maybe that's why the church started to gag him for defending me.

Is his opinion of you accurate?

Pop culture struggles to tame every rebel, to nail his ass. Has it nailed mine? Well, I don't feel that I have a muzzle on my mouth quite yet. People still have a tendency to label me or lock me in a particular drawer, though. Some people compare me to al Qaeda; others attempt to make a clown out of me. None of that bothers me. I don't care what they say, what matters is that they call me by my name.

I read a book called *God, Cash And Rock'n'roll* by Marcin Prokop and Szymon Holownia. They talk at length about me, but despite that I get the impression that neither gentleman is too sure about how to present me. As the devil himself? As a simple atheist? A clown? That's for them to work out.

You do put yourself out there for some pop-culture stroking, though.

I don't baulk at caressing. I smile, I make jokes, but my message to the world hasn't changed. My records and my lyrics are still radical. I am nice, but I don't accept compromises.

But you don't growl at the mainstream, either. Is that a way of broadening your appeal?

I don't want to limit myself to any particular niche. I have an expansive nature. Why would I alter that? I often talk to people who are not metal fans but just simple people. Sometimes it's an elderly woman in a post office, other times a saleswoman in a shop—or a cabbie, maybe—and they often tell me, 'Mr Darski, you are right: we share the same view about a lot of things.'

Maybe they don't realise that, as a young man, you wanted to burn churches.

They will now. Maybe they will change their minds, maybe not. Regardless, I will still be nice to them. I will still smile.

Anyway, I made my choice a long time ago: the decision to become an artist, not a terrorist. I want to change the world, yes, but I don't have to burn it down to do that.

But you did burn the Bible?

My fans did. Not me.

Right—you just tore it apart. Why?

At first I did it spontaneously. We were on an American tour in the summer of 2007. We were on the road as part of the Sounds of the Underground festival that took place in quite a few cities.

One of the shows was in Louisville, Kentucky, where we played a notorious venue called the Waverly Hills Sanatorium. It was an old, long-forgotten and closed mental institution. At the beginning of the previous century, there was a tuberculosis epidemic there that caused thousands of deaths among patients. Such places draw people in; they create myths. Today it's a tourist attraction, and there are people who claim that it's haunted. This is the first place where I used the Bible as a prop. But I didn't plan it.

Did the devil make you do it?

I think it was more likely God who provoked me. The format of Sounds of the Underground was quite liberal in that there were bands playing different kinds of music, exhibiting various worldviews. On the day we played, a band called Devil Wears Prada played before us. These guys were some kind of religious freaks. You could classify their music as 'Christian metal core', I suppose.

I didn't actually see their show but I heard their singer went into spasms. At one point he took the Bible out and then started crawling around the stage, reading passages from it. So Chris, our tour manager, came up to me, gave me the Bible—the same copy that was on the stage with Devil Wears Prada—and said, 'Here, I think this is for you.'

So the Christian rockers gifted you a Bible?

I don't know. I didn't ask, but that's how I understood it. Were they trying to convert me? OK, then I will express my opinion. If they could use it, I can, too.

I took the Bible onstage. It was a completely natural reaction.

But for them it was sacred.

And for me it's an element of pop culture. Whether somebody likes it or not, religious symbols, the saints, the content of the Bible—they are all a part of it. Just like Mickey Mouse. Some may love it and some may not. But I tore the book and provoked a shit-storm.

The festival's audience was very diverse. Some people came specifically to see us and the few other extreme bands on the bill, and some others were Devil Wears Prada's fans. Half of the audience was ecstatic—they ran amok. Others left the auditorium. There were some who voiced their outrage aloud. There were riots; people fought each other.

You like to make the audience fight?

I like discussion, let's say that. Some people are able to speak their minds; some have to use fists. This particular provocation turned out to be successful. It stirred shit up. It made people think. That's what art is about.

Are you intrigued by how people rebel against norms?

It's about letting them speak their minds. About letting them say 'NO' aloud, when the world deserves such an answer.

You mean anarchy?

I didn't murder anyone; I don't abuse children or animals. I simply voiced my opinion. Some may see it as extreme, but I make no apology for that.

Did you get in any trouble after the concert, because of the riots?

After we left the stage, we were drinking cold beers by our van, and we felt everybody's eyes were upon us. Then a few police officers turned up. They stuck around because they were part of the event's security. They were standing about fifty metres away, just watching us.

I wasn't sure if their interest was our concert or merely the fact that we were drinking beer outside, but I felt for sure that we were in some kind of trouble.

So what did they want?

'Are you the band who just performed?'

I nodded. Then one of them smiled, shook my hand, and said, 'I have no idea what you were yelling; I couldn't understand a thing, but you put on a great show.'

I breathed a sigh of relief and felt much lighter—as if, suddenly, about forty kilograms worth of burden had dropped off my body. After a while, some other people started coming up to us; they complimented us, too.

Brian Slagel appeared—the guy from *Metal Blade*, the label who represents Behemoth in the States. He said, 'I think you're the only band who makes life awkward for me like this, but at the same time I love it so much when you do it.'

All that started a process in my brain: one that only developed further when a picket appeared before another show on that tour.

Where was that?

Atlanta. We played with Lamb Of God that night. I went to scout the area, and there was a group of young men at the front of the venue—all with short hair, wearing buttoned shirts and ties. All of them wore the same style of braces, too. They looked like a fascist militia group, and they all had banners inscribed with quotes from the Bible. One of them had a megaphone and was yelling some fanatical crap.

John Campbell, Lamb Of God's bassist, tried to talk to them, but to no avail—they didn't want to talk. They just came there to manifest their aversion. So I manifested mine during the concert. At that point I already knew that this would become a regular feature of our show in the coming weeks.

After that, we came back from the States and toured Europe. We were promoting the album *Apostasy*, and everything fell into place because we had also used the Bible in the photo shoot for this record.

How did you get it?

I bought it on one of those auction sites. I paid a few hundred zlotys for it. The world is a small place nowadays. People shared their feelings after the show on the internet. Others read it and showed up at later shows. Lots of them even brought their own Bibles. It often happened that, when we began the show: a few copies would land by my feet. All kinds of Bibles. The fans threw them onstage.

How did they react to what you did?

I remember a particular concert in Marseille. People ran amok there. I threw pages of the Bible at them and they ate them, burned them, or tore them apart. That was crazy. I felt that we had hit the spot. We had focused their anger. If people come to a show and explode with such madness, that happens for a reason. They saw religion and its influence on society as a form of repression, and you could say that our concert purified them.

Nobody in the audience got offended?

No. It was our audience: people who knew what to expect. We have a very specific audience, remember. They like blasphemy. We once played a show at Stodola in Warsaw. After a few songs, the lights went out. When they came back on, I made a joke that apparently God was responsible for Warsaw's electricity supply. All the people in the room started shouting 'Fuck God! Fuck God!' A few thousand throats were yelling. I just smiled.

I do realise that for many people, such demonstrations of non-faith might sound vulgar or iconoclastic, but what can I do? That's the way it is. I don't force anybody to come to our shows. It's like porn—you don't have to watch it, but you can if you want to. Our fans understand that. That's why, on the *Apostasy* tour, they were aware of what was coming, even before we struck up the first notes of 'Christgrinding Avenue' or 'Christians To The Lions'. They *wanted* it.

How should we interpret that second title? Do you really want to send Christians to the lions?

It's a metaphor and a quote—an advertisement slogan for the Coliseum, also. You can find its author among the Roman emperors if you look hard enough. That's how religion works. In Rome, Christians were considered a sect, and they were murdered for people's entertainment. A few hundred years later, it was *they* who murdered pagans, for the same entertainment of the common people.

So you're not actually encouraging people to kill believers?

Not at all. I fight with values, not with people. If I really wanted to exterminate Catholics, I would have to start with my own family, and then move on to many of my friends. That's an absurd suggestion.

If somebody recorded a song called something like 'Burn The Atheists', would that be considered just a metaphor, too?

Sure. I couldn't care less about words. They can't hurt me. If somebody feels like it, go ahead and record a song like that. Art is not politics; an artist may say more. If some party leader yelled at a rally that all non-believers should be burnt, or that all Catholics should be exterminated, that could be dangerous. But in a song? In a movie? Everything is allowed here. You can be a fanatic.

Are you one?
I don't think so.

**Maybe not in your private life, but what about
in your artistic pose?**
I prefer the word 'aesthetics' to 'pose'. It's like theatre. In Shakespeare's plays,
blood is spattered all over the place. Do you call him a murderer because of
that? No.

**If it's just like theatre, then maybe tearing a
Bible is just a moneymaking stunt?**
If I had known that it would all go down like that, I would have reconsidered
doing it, certainly in Poland. Or maybe not. I don't regret it actually. That's
not my style. In any case, the real problems came many months later. At the
beginning, nobody cared.

Besides, don't try to make us out to be pioneers of tearing up the Bible.
Blasphemy has been a part of rock music for years.

There are bands in the underground that make us look relatively
innocent. Take Wendy O. Williams from Plasmatics, for example, or G.G.
Allin, or mainstream figures like Marilyn Manson or even Madonna. In
the case of our band, everything is taking place within a niche, among a
handful of fans. We assumed that our shows would be received in a similar
way.

**Blasphemy is one thing, but what about the
books themselves? Don't you respect them?**
I do. I have quite a collection of books and I care about them. I treat the
collection as luxury—almost a fetish. I generally think that one should take
care of what he owns.

**But you did destroy a Bible. Don't you
see the contradiction there?**
No.

You buy a book for a few hundred zlotys and you draw on it with a marker. Is that your idea of respect?

If something is mine, I can do whatever I want with it. If you ask me if I punch people, I will deny it. But if you ask if I have *ever* punched somebody, my answer will be different.

When you watch a movie and you see that cars are being wrecked, you don't accuse the director of lack of respect to cars. He destroys them in front of the camera because that's what his creative vision demands. He sacrifices objects for that. Why shouldn't I be able to sacrifice a book in order to make my vision come to life?

Because, for someone else, that book is a sacred object.

So I should resign from speaking my mind because of that? Maybe let's tell people it's forbidden to say that Santa Claus does not exist, because children love him so much …

Monotheism belongs in the museum. This is what I think, and I say it out loud. But do you see me getting hit by lightning? Despite all that, I'm constantly being dragged around courthouses because I dared to say that the content of a book—a book that told stories about a guy who walked on water, calmed the storms, and turned the dead back to life—is a work of literary fiction. Christians throw accusations at me because I do something they had a monopoly on: I kill golden calves.

Ryszard Nowak of the Polish Law & Justice Party begs to differ.

I'm tired of even talking about him. People say that you always carry your own cross; well, I carry Ryszard Nowak. Literally. This man is trying to enhance his own profile by using me. Had it not been for those endless trials, nobody would have ever heard about him or his committee.

It's not like I can't sleep at night because of him; I really sleep well, and I keep doing my stuff. Maybe I even attracted some new fans thanks to him—because, let's be honest, not a lot of people promote us as efficiently as he does. What hurts me, though, is that he makes profit on it. I just hate parasites. He's not even my enemy, because I respect my enemies. I can only imagine if it was, say, the journalist Szymon Holownia on the other side of the barricade, I would have a much bigger problem. He's as zealous as Nowak is, but at the same time he is intelligent and well prepared. Of course, I'm speaking purely theoretically here, because people like him don't go to court because of a video on the internet.

But Nowak's issue was not just with the Bible. He also suggested that you are a member of a sect. Do you belong to any religious movement?
No.

Then maybe Behemoth's fans are part of a sect?
We have all kinds of fans.

We have a test for you. Here are some tips on how to recognise a sect. We downloaded them from the website of one of the archdioceses. Here they are.

1. *As little as one contact with the group causes the worldview to change.* Do you try to screw with your fans' heads?
I tell them that they have to open their hearts to Jesus Christ, because only then they will see the world as it truly is.

Surely you're being ironic?
What else am I supposed to do? Of course I screw with my fans' heads. I give them a simple message: don't believe any revealed truths, and don't trust my words, either. Think for yourself.

2. *A sect gives a simple view of the world that explains everything.*
I never told anybody that there is only good and evil, and I don't teach about

47

how the world began and how it will end. There are as many explanations of the world as there are people living on this planet.

3. In the group, the follower will find everything he's been looking for.
I can only offer a good show—a bit of rock'n'roll and some lyrics that make you think. If somebody's looking for a new family, then maybe he should turn to the Holy Ghost, not Behemoth.

4. A sect claims that the world is heading toward destruction, and that only the group knows how to save it.
Not that long ago I saw a protest march on TV. There were people who wanted to save the world from destruction with prayer. They had a banner saying 'We are the nation. They are Nergal's homies.'

5. The group rejects science, and only its own science is the source of real knowledge.
The world was created in seven days, dinosaurs are dragons, and three days after you die, you can rise from the dead. All my fans will tell you that.

More irony. 6. A sect rejects rational thinking.
How am I supposed *not* to be ironic? I'm not the one telling my fans they have to believe in order to understand.

7. Criticism and rejection by those who are not part of the group prove that the group is right.
It's all about those guys with banners again. If somebody does not agree with them, he's either Jewish, a member of the Masonic Lodge, or the devil himself. And if a Jew does not agree with them, then they're obviously right. Next you're gonna ask me if I limit the sex life of my fans in any way, and if I have made some commandments up for them to follow if they want to be saved …

That's right. That was the next question!

I'll give you a summary answer. I would love all my fans to search the internet for a tutorial on how to recognise a sect, read it carefully, and to draw their own conclusions. I'm not saying what kind of conclusions. I believe in the intelligence of people who like my music.

Do you still think that the church is 'the biggest and most maleficent sect' in the world's history?

I repeat: I believe in the intelligence of my fans.

That's what you said during one of your concerts in Gdynia, where you tore up the Bible.

I did.

What was your reaction to that first lawsuit accusing you of blasphemy for tearing up a Bible?

At first, it didn't really make any impression on me. I didn't realise how serious it was. Only later did I realise that you could indeed be punished for voicing your opinions or for an artistic performance. I still don't get it. Luckily, the court didn't get it either. There were two judgements in this trial, both of them acquittals. Maybe Poland is a country of justice after all.

Your ex-girlfriend, Doda, was convicted for saying that the Bible was written under the influence of drugs.

That shook me up a bit. It turned out that the courts view things differently. Apparently a judge is a man, too. One follows the common reason; the other doesn't even have it.

You tore up a Bible, but you won't say it was written on drugs?

I've read quite a few dissertations on drugs' role in religion's development. There are substantial authorities that claim that any belief in a supernatural world is a result of using drugs. I also read about Professor Benny Shanon, from a university in Jerusalem, who examined the Bible and its history in great detail. He also analysed the plants that used to grow in the desert where the Israelites wandered. One of these plants was *Peganum harmala*, which had strong psychedelic effects. In one of the psalms, you can also hear about Mandragora being used as a medicine for potency …

Did you tell Doda about this?
No. She read it somewhere herself, and she said it out loud at the first possible opportunity. She was actually quite direct about it. That's her style. She'll just throw it in everyone's face to see what might happen. Everybody knows that, so the biggest bullshit about all that is the fact that anyone was even bothered by it.

Should the law secure religious beliefs anyway?
No.

Not even yours?
It doesn't matter what you believe. Faith is always individual. If there are people who get easily offended by what other people say, then what is the basis of their faith? It's got to be pretty fragile if they're afraid of mere words.

You could lose your head for blasphemy in Islamic culture.
I don't know Islamic culture. I was born in Poland, which is a Catholic country, not Muslim.

You destroyed a copy of the Bible, yet you won't touch the Koran. 'Nergal's got no balls', they'll say.
I fight what I know. By similar logic, you could say that if I speak English, then I should also speak Chinese. And if I can't, then I'm a wimp?

But it *is* easier to fight a religion of love than warring with Islam.
It's a nasty stereotype to say that this is a religion of love. It's just like

saying that communism is a policy of equality. For me, both of them are totalitarian systems. It's just that Christianity is about the soul and communism was about property. What does it matter if an ideology has good intentions? It's not about the basics, but the *real* performance. Polish Catholicism is an ideology of aversion to everything that is different, not a religion of love.

Aren't you going too far by comparing the two?

The similarities between red totalitarianism and Christianity are obvious. The former changed the names of the cities: Petersburg became Leningrad; Volgograd became Stalingrad. The latter annexed gods and changed them into saints. They took pagan celebrations: Christmas instead of Sun's birth. Easter? This word comes from the name of a pagan goddess, Ishtar.

Take a look at history. When Christianity stepped on the ground of another culture, they did exactly what the Bolsheviks later did in 1939. Conquistadors were conquerors. It was not about God but about power. People were exterminated, and scorched earth was left behind.

But that was a long time ago. You don't really hear about Catholic terrorists today.

For the time being they make do with spitting venom and cursing, but for how long? I've been getting threats online for a long time. I don't get them from Muslims; I get them from Catholics. I can never be sure if one day they'll replace words with actions.

Not that long ago, there was this incident at a concert in Rzeszów. There was a girl wandering around the hotel from early in the morning. She badly wanted to meet me. I was busy; I didn't have time to talk to fans that day. I thought she just wanted to take a picture with me and maybe get an autograph.

After the show, when I was going to my car, I noticed her out of the corner of my eye. She approached me, looking very nervous; her eyes were wide open, like she was on drugs. She grabbed my hands and said, 'Adam, how lucky I am to meet you.' She had tears in her eyes. I asked her if I could help her in any way, but I felt that something was not right. Suddenly she put her hand in her pocket and took out a bottle containing hallowed water. I knocked that shit out of her hand.

She couldn't hurt you with that, though.

The problem was not what was *in* the bottle. It was that she attacked me. She invaded my private space—that really bothered me. Today, it's hallowed water, but what is it tomorrow? A knife? Hydrochloric acid?

This girl wasn't even listening. She didn't understand that I don't give a shit about her God. She just stood there and gibbered about the Holy Ghost.

But you provoke these people by, for example, comparing Christianity to communism. The Church actually *fought* communism.

Correct—just like two dogs fight for food. Of course, I do appreciate the Church's influence on how our history developed. But that is the past. Today, Christianity has lost its authority, and it has no idea what people actually need. I would say its place is in the museum, and it's happening as we speak. Churches are actually turning into museums.

In London, there are a few temples that were turned into clubs. There's no point in wrecking them; it's better to use them for something good. We played in a church like that once. Our changing room was in the old sacristy, and we performed on a stage that used to serve as altar.

Not long ago, in Pittsburgh, we played a show in an abandoned and long-forgotten temple. What perversity: we preach from the pulpit of a former temple. What's happening right now is a discreet changing of the guard.

Wouldn't you achieve more by saying all that without being so literal?

I'm not a politician. I can't lie or hide the point under a blanket of sweet words.

But nowadays you don't tear Bibles apart at your shows.

And I don't spit fire, either, even though I used to do that at every show.

Why did you give that up?

Well, not because of the people who attacked me for doing it, let's put it that way. We removed that aspect of the performance long before all the media witch-hunt.

There's just no point in repeating the same provocation over and over again. It ceases to be provocation then. You don't do the same painting twice, do you? But all of our shows still make you think.

What do you have to offer today?

Come and see for yourself. After the first show where I destroyed the Bible, our tour manager said it was *disturbing*. That's a very nice English word, but I'm not really capable of translating it into Polish. It means something that causes anxiety, but at the same time it's moving. When somebody says that about our music, I take it as a huge compliment.

It's the same with cinema. The best movies are *disturbing*. Like, for example, Lars von Trier's *Antichrist*, or Wojtek Smarzowski's *Róza*. You go to the cinema in the evening, and when you walk out of there you continue to think about the film.

You wake up the next morning and there is still a storm in your head. I would love our shows to be received like that. I hate when people say that a movie or a show was *nice*.

You don't really play 'nice' shows then?

If somebody said that our show was nice, I'd feel like I'd been slapped in the face. Cheap hookers can be nice, but not Behemoth's concerts.

I have a friend who plays jazz; he came to see our show in Bydgoszcz. He came up to me and said that we played nice. He clearly didn't get it. A girl on the street can be nice. The spring this year was nice. But surely not our concerts or—and let me indulge myself—von Trier's movies.

Disturbing art is depressing. Metal music is accused of provoking suicidal tendencies.

If somebody is prone to depression, then even a romantic comedy may trigger him or her to kill themself. Some people consider it cowardice, whereas others consider it courage. I am not going to judge these decisions; everybody determines their own life path. You choose death? Go ahead. That's how my friend Jon Nödtveidt from Dissection left this world.

Did you know him well?

Our relationship was short and intense but also very deliberate. I met Jon halfway through the last decade. Firstly, of course, I had heard his music. I was a fan as early as the 90s. In fact, I still consider *Storm Of The Light's Bane* to be one of the best black metal records ever.

I suppose it was difficult to meet him prior to that, given that he did time for being an accessory to murder.

We played a show in Denmark with them. It was one of the first concerts that Dissection played after Jon was released from prison. It was also the first time I saw him live. He was my height—a bit chunkier, maybe—and you couldn't tell he had just left prison. He was very nice, but he also inspired respect. That was my impression of him. He emanated strength and even his way of walking was epic. He came up to us after the show and said he had seen a lot of our concerts, and that the last time he ever felt something similar was at a Morbid Angel gig in 1991.

Sometimes I meet with that kind of compliment for the sake of ingratiation, but this time it was an honest opinion. We started talking. It turned out that Jon knew our records well. When he was inside, his girlfriend brought them to him. I felt that we shared a kind of understanding.

Hours passed, and we sat there, wrapped up in conversation—almost as if we done coke together or something. Thereafter, we had great contact, mostly by email or phone. We spent another few hours talking after music industry exhibitions in Germany. He was looking for a label to release

Reinkatos, Dissection's new album. He had already sent me some demos of songs from it. At first it was one song, then three, then all of them. I really supported him and I instantly knew this album was great. I got the impression that people didn't fully appreciate how great it was when it came out. Only now, after Jon's death, have people started to give it the recognition it deserves.

When was the last time you saw him?

At the end of 2005, Jon asked if we wanted to play a New Year gig with Dissection at the Kolingsborg club in Stockholm. Of course I said yes. We played on the 30th of December and, because I wanted to spend as much time with Jon as possible, I deliberately booked the tickets home for New Year's Day. I went there with my girlfriend, Shelley. She was a cute Croatian I'd met at one of our shows in Switzerland. But I wasn't a good boy in Sweden, at least not on that New Year's Eve.

We sat with Jon and talked, and the next thing we knew it was midnight. There were people everywhere, having fun, debauchery all around. And there we were, sitting for the whole day, talking about black metal, philosophy, death—deep stuff. I opened a bottle of champagne and I wanted to pour him a glass, but he declined. After a while he agreed, and we made a toast. He took a sip, smiled, and said he hadn't had any alcohol in his mouth for the last dozen years.

After midnight I went crazy—dancing my ass off to the beats of Turbonegro. Our drummer, Inferno, was with me. We were drunk, half-naked, and wonderfully unpredictable. In the meantime, Jon slipped out and went home. That was Jon.

Did you ever ask him why he killed a man?

No, I wouldn't dare. It was his personal business. He must have had his reasons.

To take his own life, too?

I don't know.

What was your reaction?

It was a major blow. I was totally bewildered. I had talked to him about the next Dissection album—he was really excited about it. Nothing indicated that he would soon shoot himself in the head and say goodbye to the world.

I started calling our common friends, people who had the chance to talk with him in the days prior to his death. This was when he played his last concert. They said he wasn't showing any signs of depression. On the contrary, he seemed to be absolutely at peace with the world and happy.

This is the decision he made; I don't want to judge it. All I can do is just try to understand.

Do you understand?

I can't even imagine a situation that could make me take my own life. I love it too much.

III

TREE OF
LIFE

When did women and sex appear in your life?

I was sixteen. She was twenty years old and already had a child. I was off my face, so it was difficult to even call what I had an erection. I then consciously lost my virginity with Celina, my first real love.

How did you meet her?

In a similar way that I met Baal: I'd known her since childhood. She lived in the same block. We went to school together, and we learned to play the guitar together. At first I wasn't interested in her as a woman. During the first years of school she was very thin, like a stick. When I went to high school, we lost touch. I had seen her sporadically, mainly through the window when she was going somewhere. I noticed how she was changing, though: she had gained more womanly shapes, and she had beautiful breasts. She grabbed my attention. Everybody in the neighbourhood had a crush on her. And she was cold and inaccessible—that kind of unconquerable virgin.

One day I met her brother, just outside the block. I wanted to know how she was doing. He told me that Celina was actually in the house, so I could go and ask her myself. It was an impulse. I just used the entry phone and entered the apartment. 'Hi, it's Adam Darski.' We weren't really in touch at that time, but she let me in nevertheless. We started talking … we quickly became a couple. She was completely out of this world, but it didn't mean anything.

When you're sixteen, sitting with a beautiful girl is enough: you can feel her close and smell her. And she had much more to offer. She knew how to speak her mind. She was intelligent, a good student, she spoke English fluently … she impressed me.

You weren't turned on by metal-heads more like yourself, then?

No. What mattered for me were the looks and the personality. You can always work on the rest.

How did you work on Celina?

I filled her world with my passion. I brought her tapes and she listened with curiosity. With time, she began to go deeper into it. She bought her own records. I think she even liked metal. She saw in it what I had seen. For a lot of people it's just mindless banging, but what I saw was a genre that could develop a kid like no other. It wasn't even about the wide range of sounds. The themes were also important: religion, love, sex, politics and social issues, history—silly and serious stuff …

Listening to music is one thing, but you also played it?

Celina got quite quickly entangled in the band's issues. She took part in the photo session for our mini-album *Bewitching The Pomerania*. Satyricon, one of the leaders of the Norwegian scene, released a record called *Nemesis Divina* at the time. The music was accompanied by a video full of eroticism and beautiful graphics. It turned out that metal bands could do some really professional stuff. A forest and a random camera was not enough anymore. We went in a new direction.

It was certainly quite a bold concept.

We were nineteen years old and we thought we were discovering a new world. Today, nudity is much more common in metal videos or imagery. It became a commodity. It used to be different back then. Celina showed her breasts and we thought it had a strong effect.

On *Grom* (*Thunder*), one can also hear her voice.

She was always a good singer, but I don't know if she ever really fitted our music. It was an experiment, and not really a successful one. What we came up with was a mix of genres. It's difficult for me to listen to these fragments now without a hint of embarrassment.

Were you proud that your girlfriend was so engaged?

Very. I have never met a woman who gave herself to me so much. Celina did everything; she would help me with a lot of things. She would go to the post office to send my letters; she would translate interviews. My English really developed thanks to her.

We lived like we were married. When I came back from school, there would be dinner waiting for me on the table. Her money was our money. During our trip to Scandinavia, I tapped her for a lot of CDs because I simply couldn't afford them myself.

Did you want to get to get to know the motherland of the music that inspired you?

Before that, I associated Norway and Sweden only with fjords, oil, and salmon. Black metal changed that. Today, even their diplomats know about the history of the genre—because, as it turns out, the whole world associates the north of Europe with this cold and brutal music. It's one of their export goods.

When I got there for the first time, black metal was totally underground; only later would it ride on a white horse into the pop-culture world. I was fascinated by the fact that such radical music flourished in the place where even sixty-year-old grocery merchants speak perfect English. It was a different world. I realised how far my country was from catching up with these standards.

Are you talking about music or general development?

Both. In Poland, communism has only just collapsed, and wild transformations were taking place. We were far behind in every respect.

Did you travel a lot at that time?

The first time I ever went abroad was on a school trip. We went to Leningrad. The city made an amazing impression. It's not called the Venice of the North for no reason. I've travelled quite a lot since. I visited people from the underground. When we were about to sign our contract with a German company, Solistitium, I thought that I should do it by meeting them in person. I also paid quite a few visits to Jürgen Bartsch from the band Bethlehem. We went to the Netherlands together. We would drink a lot of alcohol, smoke grass, and talk all night until sunrise. In Rotterdam, I visited Gorgoroth from Funeral Winds. Not far from Milan, our friends from the Entropy label lived. I went to see them with Celina, just like when we went together to Scandinavia. That's where I met Robert Mammarela, the guy who managed the Avantgarde label. We signed a contract with them a few years later.

Deep inside, I felt that the act of travelling developed me. It's not just about meeting new people and experiencing new countries. The trip itself can teach you a lot. There were no computers; we only had landlines and letters. You didn't take a plane but rather a bus, and in the best-case scenario, you might take a ferry. Today, all this sounds like an abstract idea, even though it was only about a dozen years ago.

Did you meet any musicians in person in Scandinavia?

Among other things, we went there to visit Mortiis from Emperor.

Did he receive you well?

He was really nice and modest. He had walls in his apartment plastered with CDs. I have never seen a collection like it. I even had a photo taken with it in the background.

The host himself was a guy from another planet. He would not eat for days. He just swallowed a cookie for breakfast and that was it. His equally amazing girlfriend came over in the evenings. She was from Transylvania. She used to date Euronymous from Mayhem previously, when he was still alive.

The four of us would talk for hours about the storm that was going on in the underground. Those were dangerous times. Mortiis had moved to Sweden because he had to flee Norway. He was scared for his life there.

Did he have good reason?

After Burzum's Varg Vikernes murdered Euronymous from Mayhem in 1993, as part of the feud between rival Norwegian black metal musicians, things got, shall we say, hot. The scene was divided: one faction wanted to take revenge on 'that traitor from Burzum'; the other thought that it was Mayhem's leader who was the traitor. Bluster and threats were commonplace. Anyone could get knifed. Also, the churches were still burning. No wonder the police came in. The swoops and searches didn't make life easier, either.

Who did *you* consider to be the traitor?

I was above all that. I was a little scared by the whole story, but also a little fascinated. There was no fooling around with black metal—you could actually lose your life, but that's also what drew people in. I tried not to step out of line and instead just observed the situation.

Events in Norway actually echoed quite loudly in Poland. The authorities' interest in our subculture suddenly grew. I managed to avoid them, but I had friends who were swooped upon a few times.

Black metal was talked about. People began to notice it. I remember once when I was sitting at the typewriter, writing letters, my father entered my room and without a single word placed a brochure on my desk. It said 'Black metal—growing danger.' Some jerk was handing them out in the street.

Wasn't Celina terrified by all this?

She was led by me, and she just accepted my way.

You had been together for quite a few years by then.

It was my longest relationship. It lasted because Celina was loving, devoted, and loyal. And I was rather ignorant and despotic. Everything had to go my way. My good day was her good day, and my bad one—hers, too.

Did she ever rebel?

Never. She never even gave any sign that there was something wrong. But then again I was no tyrant—nothing like that. I just created rules that I thought were normal. I had an expansive nature, and she accepted that. There was a kind of symbiosis in it, but I was definitely dominant. But the truth was that I was a jerk. After three years I felt weariness, and I started getting interested in other women. If I could turn back time, I would smack myself in the face and say, 'Man, chill the fuck out.'

Did you treat your loved ones badly?

I wasn't too nice to people. My father told me that many times. He said I didn't treat people well. I absolutely didn't understand what he was talking about—I just thought I was the one who dealt the cards. There is nothing wrong in that, but you have to know how to do it so that you don't hurt others while doing so.

I hope that I have learned how to respect people. I try to use my leadership skills without being rude and arrogant. I've been trying to reach this stage for years. I have experienced some unpleasant moments on many occasions, and it was often my fault.

Was it your fault that your relationship with Celina fell apart?

I was in college; I started meeting new people. I felt like I wanted to turn myself loose and do something new. I just dumped her. I did it without a warning, just like that. She lost the plot for a few weeks. Then she found a new boyfriend. When I found out about that, I was furious. I was the only one who could make rules, but there she was—playing her own cards. She became independent. Of course, it was a blow to my sick ego. The tables had been turned. I suffered and longed for her, but there was no going back. I had lost control. That's when I went to Scandinavia for the second time. This time I was alone. I needed to escape.

Fifteen years have passed. Have you change a lot?

There is an idiot and a wise man inside each one of us—myself included. I can be brusque and crude or hang up the phone, but an hour later I can charm somebody with compliments.

But you're still not exactly easy to deal with?

I'm working on it. I show the whole package at the very beginning, because I want to build a relationship, not an illusion. When I was younger, I used to charm girls, show them how gallant and wonderful I was. Always well-kept, in my best clothes …

Today, I never hide that I have a second face as well: when I wake up in the morning, my face looks like a pork chop, and I'm some distance from being fresh. This side is even more interesting—in women, too. I like it when there is no taboo in a relationship. I've got friends who've been stewing in their marriages for years. I ask them if their wives sometimes fart when they're nearby. They say, 'Dude! Never!'

These guys live in a terrible illusion; they idealise their spouses. Come on, are you telling me that a real women never poops? That's stupid. I had this situation recently where my female friend farted on a first date. She smiled and turned it all around. There was no embarrassment in her behaviour whatsoever. I liked that. These are the bases on which you should build a relationship. I am no naturalist, but nothing human is alien to me either.

Rollers in the hair, a facemask, cucumbers on the eyes; these things don't put you off?

On the contrary, I think it's cute. I remember one of my first dates with Dorota. I went to visit her in Warsaw, and we went to party for the whole night. I was supposed to be in Gdańsk the next day, but I promised to her that—once I had had a good night's sleep—I would come over and make us breakfast.

When I went over, it was already afternoon, but I woke her up anyway. She got up and opened the door. She didn't run to the bathroom, she didn't do makeup, and there was no boundary between us. And that was awesome!

If you love somebody, try to notice the beauty in these situations. I often talk and write about serious matters, about accepting the extreme, about the interplay between the sacred and the profane. There is no difference between a saint and a sinner—it's always the same woman.

Do you still like to impose your point of view on others?

In my life I always want to err on the inspiring side, but I like balance in relationships, too. I want to inspire and be inspired.

So girls with their eyes fixed on you, saying 'yes, yes, yes' to everything—they're not your type?

She can fix her eyes on me, but she has to make me fix my eyes on her, too.

How can a woman impress you?

In many ways. For example, by possessing knowledge in areas that I don't have. If I see that she knows about a type of art that I have no knowledge of, or when it turns out that she fluently speaks a language that sounds like aliens talking to me—these are reasons for me to admire her. She needs to have character. No taste is worse than bad taste.

I live off music and for music, so I always ask women what they listen to. There are two answers that mean instant disqualification: 'the radio' or 'everything'. It's not just about music, by the way, that's just an example. Sometimes more prosaic things touch me. When a woman cooks some exotic meal, for example.

That sounds a bit chauvinistic!

Fighting stereotypes causes more stereotypes—even bigger ones, sometimes. Just because a woman can cook it doesn't mean that her place is in the kitchen. Let's not get paranoid. There is a set of features that can make a man melt. What I am looking for is something that my mother might give me: a lot of attention and being taken care of. You need to find balance, though, so that your partner is not pampered and softened. I don't want my woman to be a housewife: I just want her to take care of things. When I hear 'Did you eat?' or 'Drive carefully', I feel much better. I need attention.

On the other hand, overprotection irritates me. A woman shouldn't be a child. But this aspect varies. What I respect in women is when they're independent, but sometimes I also like it when they behave like little girls.

And do you like to behave like a little boy, then?

I expect some space. It might seem like I'm being a spoiled kid, but she should laugh at this instead of treating it as a sign of immaturity. You just can't be the father all the time.

Maybe you should try dating older women?

When I was young, I was impressed by older and more experienced girls. But that has changed with time. I've already had a relationship with a woman who was eleven years younger than I was. She was nineteen, but she seemed sharp and mature. There was a lot of freshness in that relationship. But subconsciously, I expected the mind of a thirty-year-old from her.

But people that young can't possibly have
had any major life experiences.
This situation was even worse because the girl had grown up without a father. But I like a challenge. Perhaps it's my innate naivety—or maybe it's idealism—but I do learn how to notice things I used to ignore. Now, when I meet a girl, I check if she has younger siblings.

I was in a bar in Sopot, where I met my neighbour. I've never talked to him; we've always just exchanged pleasantries. This time he stuck to me. He was absolutely drunk and immediately started telling me how fucked up his life was. He was babbling, but suddenly he said, 'It doesn't matter if you're a star or not. Remember, Adam, you always have to know what house you come from.' That's a smart rule. When everything is OK between the parents, and the girl has younger brothers or sisters, I'm immediately calmer. Why? Because the chances of me getting into a pathological relationship with this girl are significantly reduced.

What irritates you most about women?
Pettiness.

Why?
My world is quite unusual; I fly above the ground and I get crazy. If my woman likes her life well organised, well, then there is a conflict. Suddenly it turns out that what is normal for me is a problem for her. Nothing comes out of it.

Maybe you are just too dominant for your partners?
Maybe you give them too little air?
There are contradictions in each one of us. There is no single person whose world is perfectly organised and coherent. The same applies to my life. I do

realise that it's difficult to build a relationship with me. I always say that everybody can have their own opinions, but the longer I'm with someone I'm close to, the greater my need to impose my opinions on them. Often it's about very straightforward things, too.

Do you still try to fill your girls' world with your passion?

That was the case with Zuza, the one who was eleven years younger. I remember a fight we had about a trivial matter: we were watching the movie *300*. I actually think it's a hell of a good movie. Of course, it's overblown and comic-like, but it has also become a landmark in that it began a new, digitalised trend in movie production. It's also beautiful visually.

After the first sex-scene, which for me was splendidly presented, Zuza looked at me and asked what kind of bullshit it was. There was a heated argument between us. We retreated, took out our shields, and for a few days our relations were very much cooler.

Fighting like that about a movie or music: isn't that silly?

That's what I am. I fight with my friends the same way. Rafal Szyjer—my good friend, and a great guitarist and teacher—once said that Zakk Wylde couldn't play his instrument. We were just watching a Black Label Society DVD with our friends. I love their music, and Zakk Wylde is an absolute master of guitar for me. And Rafal, just like that, started talking some bullshit, saying that the guy lacks technique, that he plays sloppy, that he misses notes … so I talked trash to him. I really went hardcore and he didn't talk to me until the end of the party. I was fucking pissed, because I couldn't stand that someone who is a musician himself couldn't see quality where it is clearly visible. You don't have to *like* Black Label Society, but you can't deny that they're a professional band.

You never negate the quality of music
you simply don't like?

I hate the Polish indie band Myslovitz. When they're on the radio, my face turns red with anger, and I feel like shooting the speaker … but I do appreciate them. In a way, I even support them, because I know that they are great within their niche. I read their biography, and I watch their interviews with pleasure.

Artur Rojek, whose singing I so despised, is not with them anymore, but I really respect the guy. He does a great job, for example by organising the *Off* Festival in Katowice. I just hate the manner in which he howled, and the way his colleagues played. Sometimes I'm even terrified by the way I can separate my taste from rational evaluation.

Is there anything that terrifies you about the opposite sex?

The hidden side of women. And I mean in terms of character, not appearance.

A 'Miss Hyde' scenario?

Exactly. You meet somebody and at first you're charmed, and then when it comes to an extreme situation, you find out what a bitch she can be. Nothing even foreshadows it. She is a true oasis of peace, she loves children and animals, and she's empathetic … and then she suddenly explodes. She becomes mean and vindictive.

I've had a few situations like that. I'm stricken by the fact that you want to build something, you even think about children, joint property, and when you find yourself in a difficult situation, it turns out you knew nothing about the person you've been seeing.

How do you cope with those situations?

I look for support and understanding from my friends. I suppose that's what everybody does. Sometimes they tell me something smart. Years ago, when one of my relationships was in the process of falling apart, I was on a tour in the States. I was sitting in a bar in Florida with David Vincent from Morbid Angel. Instead of relaxing and enjoying myself, I kept looking nervously at my phone and walking out to call the girl. She had some personal problems, and I was trying to keep her spirits up. The more I tried, the more she attacked me. Everything was heading in a very wrong direction.

Vincent, noticing I was pissed, looked at me and said, 'You're really tense. You got to chill out. If the reason is a woman, have dignity, as a man should. And remember: there are millions of them in the world.' Years later, we met in Frankfurt. He reminded me of that night and asked if I remembered his words. I just smiled.

Are your relationships usually long?

My first one lasted three years. Others: from a few months to two years. Each of them comes with a huge dose of experiences. They have helped me mature. I don't have any problem with looking back at my past for perspective. I made a lot of mistakes, but I learned my lessons, too.

Most girls I was with are still my friends, or even good friends, to this day. I've kept in touch with some of them; I sent a message to some of them after a few years. I often apologised, because sometimes it all fell apart because of me. But blame usually lies somewhere in the middle. After time, both sides see how they fucked up. But I was also with girls who will probably never learn what introspection is.

Do you like talking to women?

I'm constructed in such a way that I need to speak to someone constantly. I need to be stimulated; I need a brain boner. When I feel I can't get to the core of a person, that's not good.

Yes, but are you capable of showing *your* core?

The other person doesn't necessarily have to understand my world, but they should at least tolerate and accept it. And they have to have their own world. Only then can the two sets superimpose and create common space. Everyone has his or her own labyrinths, created by life. We can invite people there, show them around, but they don't really have to feel comfortable in there.

Let's assume that I meet a girl who is an archaeologist. I don't have to share her passion and go excavating with her. What's important, though, is to express mutual interest, support each other, and give each other space. My parents don't in any way understand what I do, but they have a sense of intuition that makes them calm. They know I'm no banker or lawyer, but they also know that I'm happy. My father doesn't get my music, but he once said that what I do is useful. My music doesn't contradict his way of life. Why shouldn't the life of two people who want to live together be like that? It's all about respect.

What do you mean by a 'brain boner'?

If it doesn't show up there, it won't show down there either. I just can't help it. When a woman is superficial and she has nothing to offer but her body, I immediately keep her at a distance. I can't make a good face to a bad game. Some guys, if they want to get a girl, can manoeuvre around and put on masks. When I think that I would do that just so that I can put my dick in a hole by the end of the evening, I feel embarrassed.

I know that because I've tried it. Sometimes I even recognise it while it's happening. Even during the 'action', I'd be thinking to myself, 'Why are you doing this, you idiot?' It's the same with food. Once or twice a month, I eat some junk food. The first bite is fine, but after a while that characteristic papery taste shows up in my mouth, along with the nasty realisation that I'm putting shit in my stomach.

Women are the same. There have been quite a few great erotic situations where my brain has screamed, 'Eject! Evacuate!' I want to get home, or talk to a friend with a beer, as fast as possible.

Are Polish girls prudish?

A friend of mine recently got dumped by his girlfriend because he hit her in the face during sex. He's no wife beater; they just went hardcore. It's obvious that you can do that in bed. I was sitting with another friend and his girlfriend in a bar. Suddenly she jumped to her feet, and he gently patted her on the butt. She screamed at him. She made a scene, because she felt like a 'servant'. Bullshit! It was simple flirtation. You can pat a strange woman on the butt, far less your girlfriend …

Strangers don't get offended?

It depends. If she does, I immediately leave.

Are there any girls who can make you blush?

In Thailand, there was this situation when we were walking from bar to bar with the guys. Of course, suddenly—and it was two in the morning—I felt like getting a massage. I got addicted to those when I was in Thailand previously. And it wasn't all about some erotic adventure, just simple relaxation. So I found a parlour on the way back to the hotel. They were just closing down, but they agreed to give me a massage.

I got into a room, undressed, and left only my underwear on. The masseuse looked at me and said, 'Pants too.' I was surprised, but she insisted. I'm not a shy guy, so I obediently undressed and lied down. She started massaging me. She stroked my penis, as if it was an accident. At first I didn't notice anything erotic in it. I felt like I was at the doctor's. A moment later, she did it again and giggled. I didn't know what to think or say. By the third time, I had no doubts: the girl took my dick in her hands and asked, with a heavy Asian accent, 'Massaaaaage?'

I was embarrassed, but for peace's sake, I asked how much. I closed my eyes, and a moment later it was over. But I felt violated.

Some people go to Thailand specifically for adventures like that.

Not me. I like spending time there because it's a beautiful country, something from a fairy tale. I've been there twice already, but that's the only time something like that happened to me—maybe because I don't visit brothels.

Let's leave Thai girls for now. If you were to compare Polish and American women, in terms of sexual attitude, are there any differences?

Polish girls are much more blocked-off when it comes to oral sex. It's changing all the time, of course, and I think that's largely due to the internet. Nevertheless, a blowjob, or eating pussy, are perfectly normal acts on the other side of the Atlantic Ocean. A lot of our women still treat these 'games' as something special, like another step of initiation, but in the USA it's like shaking hands.

Have you ever cheated on your girlfriend?

Nobody's perfect, but whenever I'm in love with somebody, I don't fuck around. When I met one of my exes, Kasia, I was about to go on a long tour, but the relationship was so inspiring and fulfilling that I didn't even think about taking part in drunken groupie parties on the road. After the shows I would just grab a beer, call her, tell her how it went, and we would plan our time together after I got back. That's what every day looked like.

I'm not a hyper rock'n'roll type who just thinks about the next way to put his dick into something and then washes it down with a bucket of booze and quickly forget about everything—at least not when I know there's someone waiting for me at home.

The house, an awaiting missus ... do you ever think about kids? Do you want to have kids one day?

I don't know if now is the right time, but someday ... I think so.

Would you send them to religious classes at school?

No. They would know everything they needed from their dad. Some time ago, my friend had his fifth baby. He has a very religious family, but not typically Polish. There's less hypocrisy there. Even so, I know that the little guy will be indoctrinated to some degree. I wrote to my friend to say that maybe he should give the choice to at least one of his children.

Don't you think it's never too late to make one's own choices?

You're christened, you receive your first communion, then it's confirmation ... how many years of indoctrination and brainwashing is that?

You don't believe in the free will of adults?

I don't if they have had a chip implanted in their brain since childhood, and then put loads of their own software onto their hard drives. If there is an answer ready for every question, it's much harder for you to think for yourself. It's like getting on a train. You get on and you don't think about it. People stare at the floor, head buried in the newspaper, and they ignore thousands of impulses. When you're in that compartment, it's difficult to get out. It's social engineering.

Aren't you afraid that other kids will point fingers at your kids?

Don't forget whose genes my kids are going to have. They will cope with any situation! Besides, there have been major changes in Poland. Secularisation is progressing. A few more years and we won't even have religion classes at schools.

Some people claim that you are the catalyst of these changes.

It's flattering, but I wouldn't place myself in that position. I'm not a megalomaniac.

You don't have influence on people?

I'm sure I have an influence on our fans, but they're usually people with a set worldview already. But maybe this group *is* indeed expanding. I had a great photo taken some time ago with Sylwia Gruchala, a fabulous foil fencer, an Olympic medallist. She's actually my neighbour, and we'd sometimes passed each other, but never had the time to talk. During the session, we finally found a moment. She told me she liked reading my interviews, because they give her strength. If this is how I am to influence people—then why not?

I feel a deep need to talk about things that are important to me, to comment on the world. I endure never-ending conversations with myself. I want to share that with people.

That's why I agreed to do this book. I want to see on paper, what I view in my head. Who knows, maybe someone will deem it worthy, or maybe I will forget about doing things like this for the rest of my life.

IV

AND THEN THE LORD
PUT THE SHEEP
TO HIS RIGHT
AND THE GOATS
TO HIS LEFT

Are you an anti-Semite?
Absolutely not.

Then maybe you're a racist?
Neither.

Did you admire Hitler when you were young?
For what?

Your first stage name, *Holocausto*, brings such associations to mind.
I was fifteen years old and I wanted to shock people. I knew what the Holocaust was, but it was empty knowledge. There were no images or emotions behind it. I didn't really care about it; I was just a kid. Besides, I stole this nickname outright. My favourite band was Beherit, from Finland. Their music was so dirty, dark, and boorish. Nobody was more radical—only perhaps Blasphemy, from Canada …

Anyway, Beherit's leader's nickname was very long, but the focal point was the word 'Holocausto', so I changed the details and took it like it was mine. He was Nuclear Holocausto Of Bloody Vengeance, and I became Holocausto Of The Seven Blasphemous Souls Of Damnations. My whole creativity was limited to adding a few words. I thought they sounded blasphemous and shocking beside each other.

That's pretty naïve!
Back then, it seemed like it made sense. My nickname was supposed to be offensive and aggressive. And it was. It was grotesque and funny, too, but I only noticed that part later.

Do you regret the sins of youth?
That's what I was. That's why I am where I am today. When I think of all the silly stuff I did, I don't feel regret. I just smile. I still like to provoke people. It's just that today I do it in a smarter way.

But you did change your nickname?
Yes, because it sounded childish. Also, I regretted having stolen it, as well as the connotations. I was Mr Holocausto for just a few months.

And then 'Nergal' showed up?
I found him in a book. We wanted our nicknames to express something, so we started looking for the right words. We would browse books: religion, mythology, occultism … we went in that direction, but I can assure you there was no deeper philosophy behind it. The name was just supposed to *sound* good.

Nergal? It sounded Nordic but it is, of course, a Sumerian deity and has nothing to do with the Nordic pantheon. What mattered was that it sounded like there was some strength behind it.

If somebody had told you then that, fifteen years down the line, the name would be more commonly associated with you than with some deity, what would you think?
I wouldn't believe it. It was an artistic name, merely a stage pseudonym. That's what the convention demanded. For years, I was Nergal only on the covers of our tapes and then CDs, but as far as my friends and teachers were concerned, I was still just Adam.

And today?
I am Adam to my parents. But for my friends I am more Nergal. The people closest to me simply call me 'Ner'.

A few years ago, my girlfriend started addressing me this way, and this was when I realised that Nergal dominated both Adam and Darski. But it's good.

I became Adam when I was christened. That's what they called me without asking for my opinion. I became Nergal because I wanted to. I chose that name knowingly and consciously. I even changed my personal data. Adam Nergal Darski is on my ID.

Kristian Vikernes from Burzum changed his name, too.
I didn't know that. But I do understand why he might have not liked his previous one.

Rumour has it that he also added a second last name, supposedly after his great grandmother: Quisling.
That's his business.

Do you even like his band?
I love their music.

It doesn't bother you that this band is and has been associated with extreme right-wing politics?
No. It's like with friends. I have friends who lean to the right and friends who lean to the left. Usually there are no conflicts. When there are, it's because someone is an idiot, not because of their political views.

Have you met Vikernes in person? What if you heard him say that you're simply left-wing scum?
Never had the chance to meet him. I think he has perspective now, and if he doesn't, that's his problem. Would I have to stop enjoying his music because of that? No—that would be absurd. You can't judge music by what someone says. If that were the case, I would have to lay off not only Burzum but also Johnny Cash and maybe the Polish punk band Armia, too.

Are you a fan of Armia?
I'm a fan of their singer, Tomek Budzynski. I love the way he sings. I think he writes great lyrics, too. Maybe he doesn't even realise it, but his words are quite … *Luciferic* …

You're joking, right?
That's how I see them—especially the older albums. Listen to the song 'Niezwyciężony' ('Invincible').

It's about God, though …

Maybe, but *which* god? 'Invincible' in Latin is 'Invictus'. One of the most important solar deities of the antiquity is *Sol Invictus*. Budzynski often refers to themes of sun and light. I know that Christianity adapted some elements of the solar cults. In the fourth age in Rome, it was decreed that from then on, every Sunday was a celebration day. And it was homage to the Invincible Sun.

With time, the gods changed, but the celebration remained. It's the same as with Christmas: on the 25th of December, people celebrated the birth of the sun.

Whether people like it or not, Christianity is deeply rooted in pagan cults. People of the cross get furious when you tell them that. It highlights the dogma in the special status of their faith. Budzynski, knowingly or not, is quite pagan in his lyrics.

So where's the Lucifer in those lyrics?

Listen to the song 'Przebnysk' ('Glimmer') from the same—genius—album, *Legendy*. 'Light, glimmer! Light, lead me! You are the way, you are the shore of day.' It's clearly about the one who brought fire. And who did that? *Lucis ferre*—the one who brings light. Lucifer.

It didn't occur to you that Budzynski could be referring to Christ?

No, and it doesn't matter. For me, it's a beautiful homage to Lucifer.

Does rock music have anything to do with Christianity anyway?

Absolutely not. Christian rock is pathology—a classic oxymoron. If somebody wants to play music like that—go ahead. But the facts are, since its very beginnings, rock music has been turned against everything that is conservative.

These are sounds of rebellion. The subjective nature of religion and rock's ethos are mutually exclusive.

Is rock music mutually exclusive with politics, too? Particularly right-wing politics.

It depends on the politics. It's just like with Christianity. I find rock Nazis funny, actually: their music comes from the blues, which wasn't really created by the Hitler Youth but by blacks. Without the immortal pentatonic scale—made by black bluesmen—they wouldn't be able to build any of their merry fascist songs.

Some people describe Behemoth as right-wing metal. You've never commented on that.

I don't have to. I was never married to Nazism; we never even flirted.

But the black metal scene did. Do people reproach you for that?

What can I do about that? I do admit it, though: there was a time when black metal turned right.

Behemoth didn't follow?

I don't think so.

At one point, you referred to the main theme of right-wing bands as being simply old, Slavic gods like Światowid or Perun.

In our case, there was no nationalism involved, but rather a form of local patriotism. It was completely detached from politics. You can browse through our lyrics. There is not a single line with a political context. Besides, as stupid as it might sound, people reproached us for *not* being political.

Who were they? Perhaps Rob Darken from Graveland—a musician associated with extremely right-wing politics?

The ones who turned right. We didn't stay in touch back then. I didn't follow what he was doing.

But he was a guest on one your previous records.
We met by writing letters to each other. Again, that was normal in those days. He released something, I released something ... we started writing. I was probably fifteen or maybe sixteen; I was too young to travel around Poland whenever I felt like it. Robert's music was based on keyboard sounds and synthesizers, and I needed sounds like these for my records, so I asked him to compose a few interludes for us.

Did he come to record them?
Actually, he mailed them. Our whole relationship never went beyond paper and pen. I saw him for the first time in 2011, when I turned up at his house in Wroclaw, unannounced.

Before that, when you *were* in touch, did he express any twisted fascination with the various 'isms'?
He has always been radical. At the beginning, though, he wasn't quite so right wing. I just remember that he signed each letter to me with the expression 'Plot the war'.

It made us laugh hard, but it also engendered fondness. We actually borrowed this expression as a kind of inside joke. Someone said it and everybody laughed.

Do you remember when he first began to lean right?
Yes, when a new drummer called Capricornus joined Graveland. He was a skinhead. Before his fascinations started influencing Robert, he visited me in Gdańsk. He came to see a football match, and he rang my doorbell at about ten in the morning and we went for a beer.

We were sitting with a group of his friends, who were football fans. Their comprehension of music was similar to my knowledge of quantum physics: zero. Capricornus himself was quite a bright guy, but his views were completely alien to me.

ABOVE Proud parents and son after a Behemoth concert in Gdansk. BELOW The family Darski, with Nergal's grandfather Klemens—who once showed his grandson how to strum a guitar—shown in the foreground. RIGHT Nergal was interested in everything as a child!

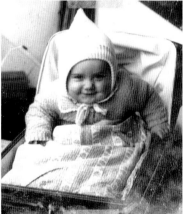

RIGHT In a Metallica T-shirt, with a Venom badge on the guitar! **BELOW** A few minutes after taking these pictures, Nergal transformed into a human torch. **OPPOSITE PAGE** With metal legend King Diamond backstage at the Masquerade, Atlanta, in 2005; Celina, Nergal, Mira, and Polish guitarist Jacek Kubiak after a Paradise Lost concert in 1996.

Akt oskarżenia

w sprawie z oskarżenia prywatnego

Wnoszę o:

I. Akt oskarżenia przeciwko Adamowi Darskiemu, liderowi muzycznego zespołu Behemoth oskarżonemu o to, że 13 września 2007 podczas koncertu w gdyńskim klubie „Ucho" porwał Biblię i rzucał jej szczątkami w widownię. Krzyczał do mikrofonu, że „Kościół Katolicki to największa organizacja zbrodnicza" i że Biblia to: „pieprzone gówno".

Uzasadnienie:

13 września 2007 roku w Klubie „Ucho" w Gdyni podczas koncertu muzycznego zespołu Behemoth, lider zespołu Adam Darski w przerwie między wykonywanymi utworami porwał Biblię i rzucał jej szczątkami w widownię, która sprowokowana agresywnymi słowami A. Darskiego je spaliła. Podczas niszczenia Biblii Adam Darski wykrzykiwał do mikrofonu, że: „Kościół Katolicki to największa „organizacja zbrodnicza" i że Biblia, to: „pieprzone gówno".

LEFT Nergal at an Egyptian pagan temple in 2009. **ABOVE** 'Do you think they'll let me on this bus?' In London for a photo shoot for *Terrorizer* magazine. **BELOW** With a young Behemoth fan in Buenos Aires.

ABOVE LEFT Great jacket! Signing for a young Behemoth fan. **ABOVE RIGHT** The event known as 'chicken party'. Those who know, know … **RIGHT** Signing for fans at Metalfest in Leipzig. **OPPOSITE PAGE** Filming the final scenes for the 'Slaves Shall Serve' video.

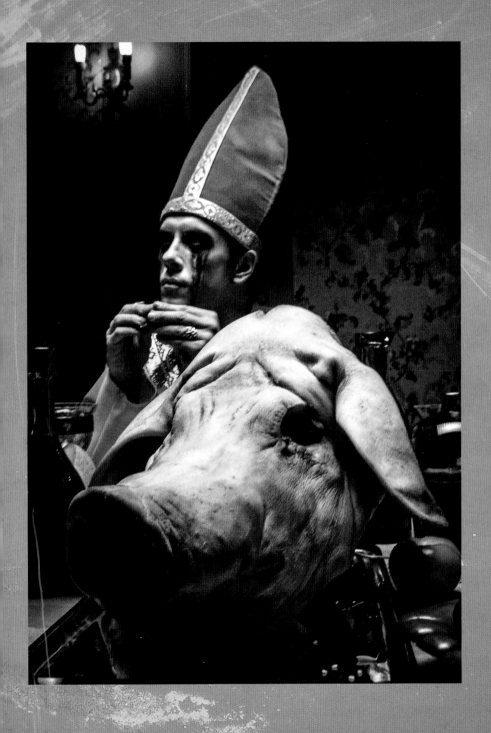

But one 'bright guy' made metal heads and skinheads come closer?

The development of the scene was a process. Black metal was not the music of nationalists—on the contrary. At first, it was created by people who would be considered 'leftist' nowadays. Suddenly, influenced by a combination of the events in Norway and what was going on in Graveland, some of the guys started changing their views.

Imagine a guy in Venom T-shirt, a pentagram on his neck and a beer in his hand. When you met him a year later, he'd be wearing a Burzum T-shirt, with a wooden figurine around his neck, and instead of a beer, he'd be drinking mead. *Now* he'd say that your views weren't sufficiently Aryan and that you were profaning the faith of your ancestors. You sing about Perun? So why is your nickname Nergal, and not Mirmił or Masław? That's the way these people thought. It was absurd. Today, it might sound sinister when you say that the black metal scene turned right. In fact, it was amusing.

We did one of our first photo sessions in the ruins of an old mill. Of course, it took place at night. We showed up in full makeup. We took a few pictures. We didn't even notice that the ruins were sprayed with graffiti, and, without further ado, we sent the pictures out to the world. One day, we got a letter from Samoth from Emperor. I opened it, and there was a litany of curses addressed to us. He almost threatened us with death because we took photographs with a peace symbol in the background.

Black metal is no walk in the park, then?

That letter unsettled me, for sure. After all, Samoth was the man—the authority of the stage. Today, I laugh really hard when I remember situations like that.

It's rumoured that somebody tried to kill you for 'profaning the faith of your ancestors'.

You guys were at my house then, so you know how the famous assassination attempt played out. There was this creepy guy with a gun hidden in his pocket. Anyway, gossip is funniest when it's just gossip. Let's leave this one there.

As you wish. How did the Slavic god Perun get into your lyrics?

History was slowly becoming my passion. It was my major in college, so it was only natural that I would try to express some broader issues by referring to history.

I remember going to Krakow with Baal earlier. We visited the Vistula Museum, and that was when I was illuminated. I saw that the raw, Slavic and Nordic heritage was a beautiful counterbalance for Christianity. It wasn't subtle but it had *power*. It personified the powers of nature, which modern religions wanted to tame and castrate.

I was also taken in by the lyricist Tomek Krajewski. He wrote two verses on our first record: 'Svantevith's children hate Christ, Svantevith's children hate the god of cross!' Everything fell into place.

Svetovid—the Slavic god of war—dethroned Satan?

Freedom has many names. Different symbols can express similar thoughts. When you want to talk about going beyond black-and-white moral divisions, then polytheism is as graceful a topic as the Bible. But that doesn't mean that my youthful fascination with paganism was shallow. I think it enabled me to turn my world upside down, and to more consciously challenge the order that I despised. All so that I could understand who I was and what I was aiming for.

With this fascination, a new stage of my life began: a more mature stage. My views ceased to be just a bundle of slogans. I began to support them with authentic knowledge. I understood that there was a range of symbols I could refer to in order to express a wider viewpoint. And it is still widening, and the wider it becomes, the more you understand that nobody has a monopoly on truth.

Nobody has the right to barge into your house with dirty boots on. I don't force anyone to adopt my views, let's put it that way. I don't mind if people insult me for them, or negate and argue them.

That is the essence of freedom. Adelbert—the patron saint of Poland—didn't subscribe to that.

**You never really liked Adelbert, did you?
You even wrote a song about him,
'Glory To Adalbert's Murderers'.**

That song was on our third record, *Pandemonic Incantations*. I was inspired to write it by Gdańsk's millennium celebrations. I was walking around the Old Town and there were slogans about him everywhere. He was a perfect product. It was irritating because I never bought that story about his martyrdom.

Didn't he die for his faith?

He died because of his own actions. And he wasn't quite the saint he is portrayed as today. He came to Prussia when he was banished from the Prague court, for various political reasons. He wanted to destroy Cyrillo-Methodianism.

As a Czech, he was far from being patriotic and he supported the emperor—maybe for money or maybe for a place in the Roman hierarchy which was set up by the Ottoman dynasty at their will. Or maybe he was just religiously psychotic, like many other saints.

In those times, people with dubious pasts leaned toward religion. It gave them an asylum and a wider range of possibilities. All his missionary activities were about barging into other people's cultures and religions, for no other reason than because they were different to his. They warned him, they banished him, but he kept coming back, like an intruder. So he died like an intruder, immediately after the mass he gave in the holy grove. It's actually kind of funny that people that feel offended by the very existence of a person with different views on TV, today enshrine him.

**Do you approve of killing someone in defence
of one's own sovereignty?**

I treat history as it should be treated—I draw my conclusions from it. Because you believe in some other god and have different values, that doesn't mean that you can fuck up people's lives and change them according to the 'one and only' interpretation.

You don't want to convert Catholics, then?

I have a sober attitude toward them. I think our relation is symbiotic. If there weren't people like me in the world, their business would have collapsed. They need me so they can scare little children with me. It works both ways. Without them, I would have had no enemy. We're in the state of permanent war, and there is no chance of a truce because our war makes the world go round.

Bulgakov described it beautifully when he wrote that everything casts its shadow. There is no day without a night. Some people see only darkness in me and only light in themselves. So be it. I like all colours, but for them I seem to be evil incarnate. That's my role.

You don't go into their holy groves?

I fight fire with fire. But I don't go into their houses. Everything takes place in the public domain. I see it as a stage—where there is a place for us both. I have also created my own space. I don't tell them how to pray and behave in churches, so why do they want to control what I do at my shows?

They sued you for the Adalbert song, too?

Some of them are hysterical; some are supportive. After releasing *Pandemonic Incantations*, I gave a copy to Professor Józef Włodarski. Today, he is the vice-rector of the University of Gdańsk, but he used to be one of the lecturers on my faculty. It turned out that his son is a fan of our music, so I wanted to give him a present. When I met the professor again, he invited me to his office. He surprised me when he said, 'Mr Darski, I am Catholic, but I can't argue with this story about Adalbert.'

That was a shock for me. These words were coming from someone whom I perceived as an authority.

But more people were offended than were supporters, true?

Yes, because in Poland we're being fed—bombarded, even—with pictures of saints who don't really have much in common with historical reality. There is Adalbert, there is Maksymilian Kolbe … just two examples.

Well, well, now Mr Holocausto is criticising Maksymilian Kolbe, the Polish friar who volunteered himself to die at Auschwitz in place of a total stranger.

I'm a historian, and I know that he also wasn't quite as he appeared. We look at him through the prism of what he did. We idealise him. But he was a guy who believed in the international plot of Jews! Some people defend him and say that Jewish issues were only marginal in his teachings. What kind of argument is that? That way, you could defend some murderer who took out a small nation, because by comparison to what Hitler did, that is just a 'marginal' case.

Kolbe's defenders claim that he left over a thousand documents, and that references to Judaism appear only in a few of them. One is enough, if you ask me. Kolbe's canonisation provoked protests in the whole world, and rightfully so. Just look at the activities of the Knights of the Immaculate, whom he founded. Extreme clericalism, looking for masons in every possible place …

Do you like looking for flaws in the saints' images?

Actually, Kolbe has been with me since high school. I wrote an essay about him back then, and the way I presented him was not exactly positive. My teacher, who was very religious, didn't even mark it. She told me that she would give me one more chance to think it through and write the essay again. Of course, I was to interpret Kolbe's history according to the convention.

This was at the time when I drew a lot of inspiration from the authors of the Young Poland modernist period: Przybyszewski and Micinski. One day, I came up to that teacher and asked if we were going to talk about this period in greater detail. She asked me directly if I was a Satanist. She also said that she couldn't let me out of school with views like that. She was on a mission.

Surely she was out of line?

She was. But, paradoxically, I was grateful. She awoke something in me. I began to read more on my own. I discovered Dostoyevsky, Witkacy … if she had just stroked my head and tried to ease my reactions, she might have tamed me. Instead, each of her attacks just made my rebellion stronger.

Did you correct your essay?

I wrote a new one. It was politically correct. I felt the lash of censorship on my ass. What could I do? Nothing.

Have you ever been to an extermination camp?

I have. I was eleven when I first saw the concentration camp in Stutthof. My young mind absorbed information. I knew who founded the camp, I knew that people died there, but I couldn't picture any of it in my head. There was no deeper thought to it than that. That only came later, when, as a seventeen-year-old, I went to Auschwitz.

What did you feel? Empathy? Sympathy? Maybe even some degree of fascination?

It's hard to define. There were a lot of emotions, and they appeared simultaneously. It was overwhelming, that's for sure. I felt death—its literal presence. Not only knowledge showed up, but also awareness that people died in this place. Not hundreds, or even thousands, but many more. I didn't fall to my knees and start crying over people's fate, but there *was* sympathy in me. But *only* sympathy.

The thought that a human did something like that to another human was terrifying. And it wasn't really that long ago—just a few dozen years. The same concept was equally fascinating. It opened my eyes. It made me realise that people are not really the way they like to picture themselves. I saw that there was something in all of us, something very strong and dangerous and able to emerge at any time.

So it's not just Nazis that were bad?

Not just them. Extermination camps are just an image of a given mechanism. As such, they represent a fresh scar, and they touch our imagination. There are still people alive who survived death camps. Cruelty, however, has been inside us since the very beginning. A hundred, two hundred, a thousand years ago … and it will still be there in the next thousand years. The only thing that changes is the actual technology of murder—the *ways* of causing death and pain. This is what history tells us about humans, and that's what Auschwitz told me.

Is there a murderer in you, too?

He's there in all of us. I have this scene from a TV programme in my head. Don't ask what programme it was, I don't remember. I may exaggerate a little, but this is how I see it in my head. An older man who survived a death camp meets a group of politicians. It was after the war. Everybody is looking splendid, young and beautiful, wearing perfect clothes. Each one of them shows a lot of respect to this man, all of them express their sympathy, and he, looking at them, asks himself a question: 'Who would you be in the camp? Whose side would *you* take?'

Whose side would you take?

I don't know. We are talking about an unimaginable situation. Here's a trivial example from real life, though. When I was in hospital, I felt that Dorota should spend more time with me—not only to be there physically but also to support me more emotionally. I kept telling her that if she had been sick, I would have spent all my time with her.

'You have no idea what you're talking about,' she said.

I didn't understand that. Today, though, I know she was right. We often squander words and speak idly. It's not even about believing in what we say. On the contrary, we're convinced that we would act in one particular way and not another. But when we face a particular event, all of that goes to shit.

Today, when I go to a hospital to visit friends—and I do have friends who are now as sick as I was—I can't endure any more than an hour. I want to be with them, I want to help them, talk to them, give them a bit of the outside world, but the reality is that hospitals are places that you have to escape as soon as possible. Of course, when I was sick, things looked different. I didn't know what I would feel later. So don't ask me what I would do if I found myself in a death camp. There is no answer to that question.

Maybe you lack a moral spine?

God leads me on that one. I love my neighbour as I love myself. I always show my faith, in every situation …

There *are* people who might say that, though.

Bertrand Russell once wrote about them: 'The whole problem with the world is that fools and fanatics are always so certain of themselves, but wiser people so full of doubts.' I'm afraid of such people. I don't trust them. I feel that, in an extreme situation, they will be the first to fail. When their confidence hits a wall, everything they try to erase from their own image is suddenly controlling them.

You don't fight your demons?

I tame them. I am aware of their existence. I talk to them. When I watch a movie—not some disposable bullshit but a serious psychological film where the protagonist has to make difficult choices—I place myself in their situation. Sometimes I terrify myself.

I wrote a song about it, 'Say Hello To My Demons'. Every one of us has our dark side. This darkness is both terrifying and fascinating, and you never know which of those feelings will prevail.

Do you ever experience patriotic feelings?

Sometimes. But I feel European more than anything else. Someone once noticed that, when I introduce the band in the States, I always say, 'Behemoth from Europe'.

There's a big Polish population in the USA. Didn't they feel offended?

Maybe, but that doesn't make much sense.

Why? Maybe they're proud to be from Poland …

… which is a part of Europe! A lot of immigrants have a strong need for identification, and this is why they close themselves off in national ghettos. Poles who live in other countries shop in Polish stores, drink in Polish bars, and work with and for other Poles. Basically they hibernate.

When you visit Jackowo in Chicago, or Green Point in New York City, you feel like time has stopped there. Everything looks exactly like it looked fifty years ago. And people have their fathers' habits too. If you live in a foreign country, you must be open to its culture and assimilate with it. That's the only way you can develop.

Don't you feel proud to be Polish?

Sometimes I do. But more often I feel embarrassed. I accept my nationality. I don't want to change it, but I can't be a slave to space, either.

You're a harsh judge.

It's not that. Poland has potential. I see it. People are hungry for success. They've got loads of energy, but they're channelling it the wrong way. They look back too often, and they take pleasure from suffering.

There are moments of glory in our history, and we idealise them: we put them on pedestals and altars instead of going onward in the here and now. We call ourselves the chosen nation, even though we're closer to being desperados.

Sometimes I get the impression that Poles feel comfortable being the world's victims. We excuse all of our failures this way. If it's not those bad Germans, then it's the bad Russians. We have always been the victims, and this is the message we send to the world. So, inevitably, they see us this way, and they treat us accordingly, and when we want to escape our national ghetto, we hit a wall that we built ourselves.

Poland is changing, though, isn't it?

For the better, that's for sure. But we're still playing catch-up with most other countries.

Is that why we have 'loads of energy'?

My peers from the USA or Great Britain haven't experienced changes as radical as Poles have. I was the guy from the People's Republic of Poland; I could eat bananas twice a year. I've experienced a clash of ages. It's a gift. It taught me determination.

As a teenager, I had to fight for a guitar, which was of lousy quality anyway, whereas a guy in France or England just walked into a used instruments shop and bought one for chump change. If I had been born somewhere else, we wouldn't be talking today. On the other hand, Poland is the land of wasted talents.

Who wasted them?

People usually fall by themselves. As a kid, I saw this downfall every day. I would come back from training or a rehearsal and I would see the same guys in front of the block, often my friends: a bench, a beer, picking their noses. This is how they created their space and defined who they were. They were lazy, bored, indifferent.

You were different?

I often sat down with them on that bench, drank a few beers, but I also knew that the world was about more than that. I didn't want to search for the meaning of life by the clotheshorse in front of the block. I felt that I wouldn't get anywhere by standing in one place. You have to move your ass to change the world.

There was always a determination and a will to act in me and it's still there. And I try to infect others with it. It's my small contribution to the development of our country.

How do you infect your friends?

I'll give you an example. Krzysztof Sadowski, a fabulous photographer who has been working with Behemoth for years now, formed a band at the age of thirty. And he said, 'If Darski can do it, I can, too.' He's chasing his dreams, even though making a band work is not a piece of cake by any means.

And what if he doesn't succeed?

He will have a clear conscience. At least he tried.

What would you do if Poland were to be invaded?

I would quickly evacuate to Argentina or some other warm country with clear, blue sea and beautiful women. Or maybe I would create some kind of diversion behind enemy lines. I'm sure I would avoid joining the army, that's for certain.

Were you ever in the army?

On my military commission papers you can read: 'Irregular personality. Adaptation conditions hindered.' I should probably get a tattoo of that. When you think about it, the army is not really that much different from the church. They both cram you in their systems and grind you. I'm not saying that the army is totally unnecessary, but I wouldn't join them anyway. It's contrary to my worldview.

Are you a pacifist?

My love for freedom is just too big. I don't get along with any institution whatsoever. Besides, war is death. It's not as romantic as it used to be; nowadays it's all business. War is just a nutrient for the media. We love watching it and reading about it. It's like today's coliseum, especially designed for TV. We feast on death. And the further away it is, the better.

You didn't support 'our boys' in Afghanistan or Iraq?

I do understand the concept of mourning soldiers who died in Afghanistan, but making it a national tragedy is overreacting. Death is inscribed on a soldier's life. He goes to fight, and he knows that he might not come back.

If anything, I am more touched by civilian deaths. Their only fault is that they were born in a particular place. They die because some abstract national business of one country was the reason to send some soldiers to another place on the planet.

I don't want to take part in games like that, particularly when I know that every human being is a victim of time and space. We have no influence over where or when we are born. When I hold a globe in my hands and move my finger a few centimetres to a new country, it will turn out that people who live there are completely different. They have their own culture and habits. A few centimetres decide whether we think of them as barbarians, even though we treat their country in the most barbaric way. Who gave us the monopoly to solve this world's problems? Earth is full of cultural and social contrasts. Why is one viewpoint supposed to be more important and better than others?

What about politicians? Do you mourn those—including then president of Poland Lech Kaczynski—who died in the Smolensk plane crash, for example?
Planes crash and people die. There is nothing extraordinary about that. Things like that just happen. I'm absolutely fed up with making a national tragedy out of the crash. When I hear about Smolensk, I see only dirty, political games. I find it all repulsive.

Is it appropriate for a Pole to say such things?
It is appropriate to pay taxes? I pay a lot. I am useful for my country.

What else do you do for Poland?
Whether I want to or not, I promote our country around the world.

Oh, really? As 'Behemoth from Europe'?
It doesn't matter. The word 'Poland' shows up in every article about us. And there are hundreds of those.

Some people claim that instead of promoting Polish culture, you bring shame to your country.
Everyone has the right to an opinion, but nobody can accuse me of not representing quality in what I do—in my niche. The rest is just a matter of

taste. True, I don't go around with a fucking loaf of bread and a jar of salt in my hands, wearing a highlander's outfit, but you can promote culture in different ways.

The situation is quite paradoxical and perverse, because a lot of people in Poland think that I am the devil himself and a not-that-necessary evil. They would love to see me behind bars, or somewhere far away, like Madagascar. And at the same time, my band and I have been working really hard for our country. If a 'national good' does not describe Behemoth, then we might as well be a 'national evil'. That sounds nice, too.

What are the effects of your hard work?

By playing on tours, you meet fans. Someone came to your show ten years ago and he comes today. People couldn't believe that we weren't from Sweden. 'Poland? How come?' Then, years later, the very same people invite me over for homemade bigos or żurek!

These are trivial examples, but they show how you can interest people with your tradition or culture. I talk to these people, and I often hear that before they met us, they had thought that Poland was a post-communist concrete jungle, and suddenly it turned out that our country has a lot to offer. They brag that they visited Poland and got to know it better.

What can Poland offer to foreigners?

We have a great history. Instead of praying to it, we should show it to tourists. Let's learn how to *sell* it, though. In spite of the major damage caused by World War II, we still have a lot of beautiful monuments. Polish nature is also very raw and beautiful.

What about your area? Gdańsk?

I can't stand the fact that such an attractive city has so much odd energy that hinders its development. The Old Town is only alive during the summer for a few weeks, when this pathetic Dominican Fair is taking place. Gdańsk has been taken over by old ladies selling their embroideries and the Chinese trying to push fake clothes on suckers. Sometimes I think that nobody has any idea what potential this town has. There's just nothing going on in the centre! After seven in the evening, the streets are empty, like there was an epidemic or something.

The best-case scenario is hordes of drunken kids. Just look at the seaports in the Netherlands. If Gdańsk had been directed in a similar way, it would have been one of the biggest attractions in Central Europe.

What about other Polish cities?

I love Krakow. I actually get the impression that our country has greatly accelerated, especially in economic terms. But sometimes I see a terrible discord between people and their surroundings.

Some time ago, I stopped at a gas station in some shithole. One of the guys who worked there recognised me and, while smirking, asked me, 'So, it didn't work out with Doda for you, huh?' There was no friendliness in it at all. It sounded like a combination of malice and frustration. By stinging someone famous, this guy could be king of the world for a moment and feel better about himself.

I just smiled and said, 'No, it didn't,' and then I thought, 'and what the fuck do *you* care, hillbilly?' And then it occurred to me that people like this guy treat other nations the same way. They show their spite just so they can heal their own complexes.

I got back into my car. That same day, I drove through the newly opened section of highway between Gdańsk and Torun and I felt genuinely proud. I do realise that we should have had this road built years ago, but I was happy like a child. I only hope that culture will follow civilisation's progress.

Have you ever considered leaving Poland, like your brother did?

I regularly leave it, but in my case it's more of an expansion. I have my own fortress and I go out to conquer new lands. Somehow, my brother inspired me. He impressed me, but I'm not sure if I could burn all the bridges behind me so radically and not get broken by all the obstacles.

What keeps you here?

The band and music have always been a priority to me. And the band is located in Poland. If I had decided to emigrate—let's say ten years ago—everything could have fallen apart.

Today, the world is smaller, of course. It's not really a problem to move between Gdańsk and New York City. If I really wanted to, I could still play with the band even if I lived in another country. But I just don't think about it. Poland is my home.

So you're not going to Madagascar?

No. But it would be nice to live in two countries. An apartment on the Costa Blanca is not such a bad idea either, but I would always be coming back to Poland, even if it were just to run in the Polish forests. They're especially beautiful in winter. The rigidity of our climate hardens the soul.

A REINDEER
TWO OWLS
AND A DEAD MAN

Have you ever done physical work?

During college I carried carpets for a week. It was a total misunderstanding. Later, in Spain, at my brother's, I worked on a fucking construction site because I wanted to earn enough money to buy a new guitar. And that was when I realised that the only physical work I can stand is banging my head onstage. During a period of two months, I changed jobs five times! I was twenty, and the gods had told me to relax. I decided that I would never do physical work again, and I would never have a boss, either. It's been fifteen years since then and I still stick to my decision.

What is your main source of income?

Concerts.

How much do you receive for one? Is it a lot?

I don't know how much constitutes 'a lot', but if you're a musician, the only way you can make your living is by playing live shows.

Not by selling records?

If you want to do something genuinely worthwhile and high quality—and that is how we always approach it—then the costs of recording, production, and promotion are so high that you don't really earn money selling records alone.

But in the beginning, Behemoth didn't really play shows.

We didn't feel the need to. The process of creation was so absorbing and energy-consuming in itself that we didn't even think of playing shows. We were kids; we were about sixteen or seventeen years old and we fell under Burzum's and Darkthrone's spell. They boycotted concerts by default. Their attitude perfectly fitted our vision of a band. We wanted to be even more radical than they were.

I still remember a conversation with Baal, during which we agreed that Behemoth would cease to exist the moment we signed a record deal. It was supposed to be our demonstration of intransigence. Of course, we were novices with only a few tapes from our rehearsals, and a real album was a totally abstract notion for us. Fortunately, my character changed.

You did record an album, but still didn't play any shows.

Our appetites grew as we ate. We were recognised in a black metal capacity, but we wanted to take a step further. These were completely different times. It was 1993 when the *Fuck Christ* tour took place and black metal emerged from the basement. The stage was shared by Blasphemy, Immortal, and Rotting Christ, and I practically wet my pants because they were my gods! They set the whole of Europe on fire, and I couldn't even afford to see any of the concerts. All I was left with was reviews in fanzines and promo leaflets. It was only thanks to VHS bootlegs of these shows that we slowly started to digest the thought of playing live.

Before that, you released the album *Grom*.

Before recording it, we felt another impulse. In the winter of 1995, I went to negotiate a deal with a label. Carsten Molitor, Solistitium's boss, took me for a long walk in the forest. He presented to me his vision of a common tour with Behemoth, Helhcim from Norway, and our buddies from Christ Agony. The idea was already there in my head. The rest was just a matter of time.

Was it difficult at first?

We began the European tour in September of 1996. Before that, just before the summer holidays, we had managed to play three shows. The first one was in Bialystok, at the Kino club. I'm not sure if the name is still the same, but I was driving past that place a few months ago. Nothing about its appearance has changed. It's certainly not an architectural diamond. But when we stood on the stage for the very first time, we didn't mind playing in a dingy cinema from the communist era. For us, it was the centre of the universe.

And the show itself?

It was just like all the others at that time: chaotic. We lacked skills and any basic knowledge of gear. It was all rather lopsided, but what we lacked in technical nous we made up for with our passion and determination. There was another show that we played in Germany, in some forest in Bavaria— middle of the night, cold as fuck, to about three hundred people. We went onstage all covered in pigs' blood. It was wild.

You said you would never hurt an animal ...

The blood? We got it from a butcher. Sometimes we ordered it from the gig promoters, too. For the first show in Bialystok, our friend Bart Krysiuk, the boss of the Witching Hour label, got some of it for us. He took us to some butcher's stand at a fair where the merchant poured blood into a vodka bottle for us. A litre of it. Of course, there were pieces of meat, eyes—all kinds of gross shit mixed in.

We poured it all over ourselves. It had a liturgical meaning for us. By covering ourselves in blood, spitting it, we challenged the Eucharist, turned it upside down. I like symbols like that.

It had an aesthetic dimension, too. Let's be honest: blood has fantastic shock value. Nowadays, after my illness, I look at blood in a very different way. It's a personal relationship, and as if to confirm it, I keep a vial of my new blood in my fridge. I actually want to use it to paint the cover of Behemoth's next album.

Have you ever killed something bigger than a bug?

Once I killed a pigeon. I love animals, but pigeons are not animals—they're not even birds. They are like rats with wings, flying cockroaches. Spreading germs, shitting everywhere, making noises that fucking piss me off.

When I was studying, I lived in one of these blocks in Gdańsk. It was a small flat, about nineteen square metres in total, but it gave me independence. Unfortunately, those flying fuckers made a hiding place out of my balcony. It was five or six in the morning, and they kept fucking cooing and waking me up. I would get on the balcony and scream. They usually got the fuck out. But they would always come back. So, once, I took my bloody revenge.

I was sleeping with my window open, and then, suddenly, one of them gets in through the window and lands next to my bed. I was furious. I grabbed a guitar strap and started lashing blindly at everything around me. I hit the bastard and I kicked him out onto the balcony, but as he was trying to escape, he caught on the guardrail with his claws. Basically, they stayed on the balcony, while the rest of his body went further. I have no pangs of conscience about that.

When did you stop using blood?

I can't remember. We used it as a prop for a few years. At that time we found ourselves in the biggest shitholes of Europe—places where we would play for a slice of pizza. None of us even asked for any remuneration. Our first tours were about 'buy-on'—our label paid the concert organisers so that we could open for bigger bands and show ourselves to a larger audience. And it worked like that for a few years.

Baal left the band before you became really big, though?

Sooner or later, our ways had to part. He was a walking metamorphosis. During the recording sessions for *Grom*, he was obsessed with Type O Negative. He even looked like Peter Steel. He started playing bass, and he was even thinking of making his own music. He also sent a few vivid signals that drumming was not as enjoyable for him as it used to be. He knew Behemoth was my child anyway. I wrote all the music and most of lyrics, and he needed something of his own. So he left and founded Hellborn.

In one interview, he said that he didn't like the direction you were going in; that there was 'too much paint on the face and too little music'.

That's a strange opinion when you consider that, after leaving Behemoth, he still attached a lot of weight to the visual side of his records and shows.

Did your friendship last?

We were friends when we were kids and today we are still cool. We greatly respect each other. It's a healthy arrangement. Baal still lives to his rules and he hasn't been drawn into the 'bug mode'. He's creative, and he keeps developing. He gets more tattoos on his body each year, too. He loves dogs and he hates church—how can one not like him?

Where did you find Zbyszek Prominski?

We shared a rehearsal room with the band Damnation, from Tricity. Their leader, Les, also played bass with us for a while. Damnation's drummer was Wawrzyn. But he left the band, and in his place they took on a young and very promising drummer. It was Inferno himself. I would stay after rehearsals just to see him play. He was amazing. First I felt jealousy, then a conviction that this guy just has to be in my band.

When Baal and I parted ways, I basically gave Zbyszek an offer he couldn't refuse. And I hit the mark. He's an outstanding drummer. If I am the brain of the band, he is the motor. I felt the difference in an instant. I wanted to play music that was more complex, and with Baal it was impossible—not because he didn't want to, but because he couldn't. I demanded more from him than he could offer.

It was different with Inferno. He gave to the band much more than I demanded.

Today, Inferno is considered to be one of the best metal drummers in the world.

And rightly so. Sometimes I think he's from another universe. His coordination and skill in putting thousands of hits together is astounding. Zbyszek is an example of a man who discovered his calling very early and developed it. I believe that there is a great potential in each of us. You just have to find it and go for it.

Was that what you did?

In my childhood I would stand in front of the mirror and imitate my idols. I would use the broom as my guitar and pretend I was singing. I wanted to be like Cronos from Venom. I couldn't even play two chords in the right tempo, but I knew it was what I had wanted: to be a musician. My brain was sending signals to the environment. My friends' five-year-old daughter wears quite nonstandard clothes and she puts two different boots on her feet and defends her rights. Maybe she's sending similar signals? 'Let her develop it,' I tell them. 'Support her.' Maybe she's the next great fashion designer or a model? That's how it works.

So Zbyszek is a born drummer?

Today's metal scene resembles extreme sports, especially when it comes to drumming. Of course, there are drummers who are faster and more precise than Inferno. But he's got something that you can't ever master by training: great feeling. When he goes out onstage and sits behind the drums, I feel confident having him behind my back. A house needs a foundation, and a band needs an appropriate drummer.

Even with Inferno on board, it took Behemoth quite a long time to get into the concert major league.

I think our potential developed the most somewhere around the *Satanica* album. We were playing more and more shows around then. But we really gained momentum when we recorded *Thelema.6*. That's when we began to play regular tours as the main act. It was a vicious circle, because the better we played, the more confident we felt; the more confident we felt about our own worth, the better we played. We were fucking rocking out onstage like there was no tomorrow. Don't hit; just kill!

I remember the *Thrash 'em All* tour, when we opened for Vader and Krisiun. Vader's position was irrefutable. They were veterans, and one of the most important bands in the history of Polish metal. In Bialystok, when I came off the stage, I passed Vader's singer, Piotr Wiwczarek, in the corridor. I said to him, 'Piotrek, burn that place down!' He just smiled and said, 'You can't burn ashes.' I felt then that we had really begun to do something meaningful.

And your line-up changed at that time, too?

It had a big impact on our form. We got wings when Havok and Novy joined us. We made for a great crew together. Everybody contributed. Havok was really young. I had to ask his parents to let him go on tours, and they made me promise that he would catch up with schoolwork. But there was fire in this guy and huge determination. It wasn't long before he was eating old and experienced musicians for breakfast.

Novy, on the other hand, brought a lot of experience into the band. He was actually a session musician, but he fitted in the band quite nicely. He had impressive hair, and it contrasted beautifully with his wicked height. It made his hair look bigger than it really was. He literally swept the stage with it. They both made Behemoth more rock'n'roll.

More revelry, more frolic?

Novy was a specialist in both of these. Sometimes he went completely hardcore. He's quite a peculiar guy, and a huge fan of Darth Vader. Whenever he got drunk, it seemed like he made a connection with the Death Star. Hell knows who or what it was.

Once, I caught him, when he was way off his face, lying on the floor, caressing a huge, paper figure of his idol. It was harmless, but it got worse when he really got into the role. It was winter, cold as fuck, and we were partying in the hotel after the show as usual. Suddenly Novy took off his headphones and got up. He opened the window, got on the windowsill, blurted out a quick *frrr*, and stepped forward.

What floor was it?

Third. We looked out of the window, and there he was, lying in the snow and moaning.

Did you take him to the hospital?

He wouldn't let us. He wasn't insured, so he was probably afraid of the costs. Nobody examined him, not even an x-ray. For a few days he wouldn't say a word, he would just sit in dark glasses and sob. I saw tears coming down his cheeks but he didn't complain. For some time we just had to put the guitar on him, because he couldn't do it himself.

Did he ever tell you why he jumped out?

Never. He probably listened to some bad music. Or maybe the Death Star told him to.

Did he often do such extreme things?

They were more, let's say, entertaining examples. Once he was even beaten by the police. He thought it was the right time to run around the 'sperm-absorber' in Adam's outfit, with only a bullet-belt on …

'Sperm-absorber'?

The youth hostel. We played in Warsaw, at the Proxima club. We couldn't afford hotels, so we rented cheaper places. We had the belts with us—they're standard equipment for every respected metal band. Guys put them on their naked bodies and went down to the reception desk. Somebody called the police, who promptly came with their batons.

Did you take part in it?

As usual, no. Somebody had to hold the camera. I've got a lot of self-control, or I am just not drunk enough or in love. I like having a good time, but with a degree of moderation.

Have you always been like that? During one of your first tours, a Norwegian band called Khold supported you. They suddenly packed their bags and fled. Rumour has it that you were 'too rock'n'roll' for them.

We were playing a show in Spain. Our promoter there was a typical Spanish woman: curly black hair and eyes like coal. She wasn't overly pretty, but she was really nice to us. She asked us if she could go to our show in Madrid with us. And I have always thought that if a girl wants to get on a bus with the band, she doesn't want to just drink tea with them.

What did you give her?

Vodka, of course. She drank quite a lot of it. We all did. Apart from the guys from Khold, that is. They were strange, drinking Pepsi all the time and saying nothing. They were as entertaining as a broomstick. So we partied without them. At one point I decided I'd had enough and went to rest on my bunk. I slept for a while and went back to the back of the bus. There was only the sad Norwegians back there, so I went downstairs ... and I couldn't believe my eyes! The girl was lying naked on the table and there was a bunch of guys around her, all of them naked. One of them was holding the camera, and the rest were arguing, all of them off their faces—trying to shoot a porn movie. I won't name any names, but I remember them arguing about who was going to put his dick in her mouth: 'Oh, come on, man, let me, you've already had it!'

Did the guys from Khold also go downstairs?

No, but the next day they saw our amateur porn movie. They were really narrow-minded, and in some strange way they deduced that there had been a rape. They wanted to go to the police. They took the tape, packed their stuff, and fled. We waited as if for a verdict, because we weren't sure what the girl would say.

Did the police show up?

We found the tape in a dumpster by the parking lot. It was in tatters. But there was some trouble looming. Our tour manager found out about everything. We tried to tell him that there was no rape. It was just a small, innocent orgy. He went to talk to the girl anyway. He wanted to know if she felt like it was rape. 'No, nooo,' she quickly responded, 'it was cool!' We played the show in Madrid a few hours later, without Khold this time, and this girl was rocking out in the front row.

She could have caused you some trouble, though, right?

I was aware of that, and I felt great relief when the situation was rectified. You often hear about situations like this one. My buddies from the band Keep Of Kalessin met a groupie in Canada once. They took her to their bus. There was no sex, just an ordinary party. The next day, the girl told the police that she had been raped. Two musicians were arrested and kept in lockdown for a few weeks. They were acquitted, but they never recovered their legal fees. All they got was a piece of paper stating they were not guilty, in case it turned out that they had some criminal record in the USA or Canada. Without it, they could have had problems entering the country.

You have to be careful about such things, especially in the States. Did you look after yourself during those first shows?

At first, the States was a very strange place for us. We had no knowledge about it whatsoever, and we felt alienated. During our first tour there we were drunk practically all the time. We drank during the day—there was no other way to do it.

One day we were at the Mexican Gulf and, drunk as we were, we decided it was a good idea to take a swim. So we let our fantasy lead the way and jumped into the water. Naked. At that time, there was a school-trip taking place on the beach. The teacher saw us and began covering the kids' eyes and running away. Our tour manager screamed like crazy: '*Get the fuck out of the water!*' I have never seen such a panic-stricken American. He went nuts.

I didn't know what his problem was, but we found out later that if somebody had called the cops, we would have never played a show in the US again. Arrest, expulsion from the country, and not the slightest chance of another visa …

It's a strange country. You can go to jail for drinking beer on the street, but yet everyone carries a weapon.

During one of your later tours, your bus was shot at. It was quite a big story, wasn't it?

It happened in Texas. As a band, we were still quite new to the States. We didn't really earn any money, so we spent most nights in our van. We could afford a hotel two or maybe three times a month. And it was one of these times. We got to the motel just before sunrise. I went to bed. It was a real blessing. I was exhausted; there was complete silence. Suddenly I felt like there was someone sitting next to me, pushing the mattress between my legs. I jumped to my feet.

A ghost? Do you believe in such things?

I'm sceptical. I don't know if there's anything more than the material reality. I don't care either. Whether it was a ghost or a hallucination, it doesn't matter. Anyway, I looked around the room and didn't see anyone, so I went back to bed. I was woken up by a knock to the door. I opened the door and saw a black police officer. He said that somebody had shot at our van. I went out to the porch, and sure enough, our van had bullet holes at seat level.

Did anyone hear the gunshots during the night?

No. I suppose they used a silencer. To this day, I have no idea why anybody would do it.

How did the guys react?

We were all bothered by it. In the car there were a few CDs that I had bought during the tour. Some of them were shattered. I still have them as mementos. But that was not the only time we experienced guns in the States. On another occasion, we drove up to a gas station that looked like it was taken from a Robert Rodriguez movie: a desert, two gas pumps, a small stinky shop, and a cowboy thrown in for good measure.

An old man appeared by our van and started talking to our tour manager. He must have asked what band we were, because there was the standard answer that we always gave to such questions—as a joke—for people who don't get metal. We told him that the band's name was *Antichrist*. The old man went to his truck, took out a shotgun, aimed at us, and said, 'So you boys worship Satan, huh?' I have never heard tyres screech so loud in my life.

By comparison to Mexico, the USA is an oasis of peace—agreed?

In Mexico, we literally brushed against dead bodies. Well, one dead body. It was in Juàrez. It's a very unusual and notorious city. Since 1993, a lot of young girls have been disappearing there. I was told that by the winter of 2005, more than four hundred girls had been kidnapped. People would smile and say that according to unofficial data, the number might be actually ten times bigger.

Did you play a show there?

Yes. The city lies just next to the American border. You could say that we were smuggled across to the Mexican side. It's a place that's visited by a lot of Americans who want to have cheap fun. The borders are practically open there. The show organiser told us that we are not to leave the venue under *any* circumstances.

As usual, before the show I had to go to the shitter. I just have to sit on the toilet for a moment to loosen up—it's my ritual before every concert. The toilet in the club was so hideous, even a dog would have run away from it.

Even in the USA, toilets are usually in pitiful condition, I've noticed. Sometimes, toilets are only separated from each other by small partitions, so you can see what your neighbour is doing. It's really astounding that such a well-developed country can offer you so many extremes. But in Mexico, it's even more brutal.

I asked a bodyguard from the club to walk with me. A few blocks down the road there was a bar. I went inside and went to the toilet. The partitions reached the ceiling, but there was no door. I sat on the throne and waited for a miracle. It didn't come. So we're going back to the club, and there's this guy lying on the ground in front of it. He was dead. And that, apparently, was completely normal …

People die …

It is accepted in a lot of places in the world. People just get over it.

I've seen similar things in the Himalayas. I went there for a holiday. I was alone and I was completely unprepared. I didn't have the right trekking boots so after a few days my feet hurt. On the way from Kathmandu to Pokhara, I realised how different people were in that part of the world.

They are unusually reconciled with the rhythm of life and death. We were driving on a road by a huge precipice. The very sight of it made my blood run cold. You could look out of the window and see a few hundred metres of emptiness, and car wrecks at the bottom—one next to another.

'Look how high it is here,' I said to the guide. 'Do buses fall off the road sometimes?'

'Yes,' he said, 'a few every year.' He was absolutely at peace with that possibility. He was aware that his life was in the hands of the driver, and he still enjoyed his trip. He just shrugged, and I was reminded of a quote by Aleister Crowley: 'God gives, God takes. Praise the Lord.'

Do you find it hard to put your life into someone else's hands?

I feel that if I lose control over certain things, everything will fall apart. I do realise that it's irrational, because a lot of people have influence on how my life is going. Nevertheless, I want to take responsibility for everything.

You don't like chaos in life then?

It depends. Sometimes I clean everything up obsessively, and sometimes I just go with the flow.

And at home?

Sometimes.

You don't like washing the dishes?

Since I bought a dishwasher, I've become a real god of dishwashing.

Do you do your own laundry?

I do have a washing machine. But I never do the ironing. It's overrated. If you hang the clothes properly, you don't need ironing anyway.

Some people even iron their socks.

There are people who have lost their minds.

You like to be a perfectionist in certain areas.

A *professional*. That sounds better.

Your friends say that you can spend weeks mixing one song. That you go to people's houses and play them five versions that are basically the same.

I think this is changing. I used to be more fanatical about it. I couldn't sleep at night because I didn't like how the snare sounded. Nowadays I give more opportunity to luck and chance. I let the music and lyrics live their own lives. There's more air in all that. A few years ago, I had the chance to speak to a real legend of metal music—Tom Gabriel Fisher of Celtic Frost. It was right after the promo concert for their brilliant album *Monotheist*. We had the honour of opening for them. Their music isn't really too complicated when you examine it. It's actually quite primitive. But it does have some kind of undeniable magic. You just stand there in the pit with your mouth open and you pray to the stage.

I asked Tom what the secret of this sound was. He said that you have to let the music breathe—that you can't overwhelm it with too many sounds. He also commented on our show by saying that we play more sounds in each song than they do on an entire album.

Did you take that to heart?

I think you can hear that on *Evangelion*. With time, I began to listen more to what the guys in the band have to say. I don't impose everything on them. At least I'm trying not to. I fight my dictatorial tendencies.

We've talked about some of the former members of Behemoth. What about the current lineup? It seems stable, and you've been playing together for years. Do you often fight?

A band is like marriage. Sometimes it's perfect. If the show goes great, then we transfer all the ecstatic energy to having fun until morning, with no inhibitions, but then there are moments when you can literally hang an axe in the air because the atmosphere is so dense. We know each other very well—maybe even better than our wives, girlfriends, and lovers know us.

Let me give you an example. We were at a gas station in some desert in the middle of Texas once. We stopped for a while and wanted to use the toilet. There were ten cubicles. I chose one and sat on the throne. After a while I heard footsteps: sloppy, like a bear walking in. There were also grunts and coughs …

'And I saw a beast rise up, having seven heads and ten horns …'

Nope. It was just Zbyszek. Another moment passed, and then I heard more footsteps: the pitter-patter of tiny but chubby feet. The pitch of these was much higher, like that of a large mouse. I didn't even have to think who it was because I knew already that it was our sound engineer, Malta.

And your point is?

The point is that we spend so much time together, that we can even recognise each other by the way we walk, snore, or even fart. I often say that a band is not a group of friends; it's a family. I treat them all like brothers.

You threw darts at your real brother.

I throw insults at these ones. That's what it's all about. A friend is someone who you can always count on, for better or worse. You can have different relations with your brothers. Sometimes you can be friends, but sometimes they're like a splinter in your ass. That's the same way with a band.

Do fights also happen?

No, but it got close a few times, in various configurations. They can sometimes fight each other, too.

And then Nergal gives them a spank, pats them on the head, and punishes them?

Sometimes you have to say who is right and who is not. I always try to be objective. And I speak openly if one or the other goes over the line. But that doesn't mean I am always the father. Sometimes I get fucked up and do stupid shit like a spoiled kid. Then somebody else straightens *me* out.

For example, during the promo tour of *Apostasy*, I had a toxic combination of excessive arrogance and dangerous ignorance. All the guys gave me some signals that I wasn't all there in the head, and I was beginning to lose connection with the planet that is Earth. It took a while, but I finally stopped, looked at myself, and saw that something was not right indeed. I had to let off some steam.

So your band family is just you and the three other musicians?

It used to be like that. But with time it all expanded to a huge size, and I slowly lost control over it all. There are people who go on tours with us, there are people on the other side of the planet who run our shop, our website, people who help me set up interviews … Behemoth is a complex mechanism today. A lot of these people are members of our family. For example, Maciej Gruszka, our irreplaceable webmaster, and the guy who runs Behemoth's internet shop. And, also, the guy I mentioned above—Malta.

Do you treat him like a brother?

Once, we were playing a show in Costa Rica and it was his birthday. He can't swim, so we thought the best present would obviously be to throw him into the water. We knew he had had his passport in his pocket, so we had to trick him. We started looking at our passports, and I said, 'Arek, show us your passport. How do you look on the photo?'

He gave me the document, and then he was immediately in the pool. He almost drowned. We took him out like a wet rag. To appease him, we offered him a shot of coke. You can buy things like that on every corner there, like apples at the market. We had a whole bag. But I had secretly replaced it with powdered vitamin C. I told him, 'I'll show you how it's done.' And I snorted loads of that shit, and I literally licked the rest of it from a windowsill.

He looked at me in admiration, nodded his head, and said, 'That's exactly why I like you!' He rolled a dollar bill and took his turn. Someone asked, 'Arek, how's the stuff?' and he said, 'Fuuuuucking awesome!'

True brotherly love, eh? Do you support each other on tour? Do you guys often need each other's advice?

It happens. I remember that, right after the *Demigod* premiere, we started a huge tour of Canada and the States—fifty concerts in all. We played the last show of the American leg with Danzig. It was the grand finale, the most important concert of the whole tour. Los Angeles, Gibson Amphitheatre, over fifty thousand people …

The next day we were due to go to Canada by ourselves. We had only a few hours before the show was to begin, so we started preparing, and then our bassist, Orion, suddenly started changing colours and sweating like a pig. He was pale one minute, and then he was purple the next. We thought it was food poisoning, but visiting the toilet did not help. It was getting worse by the minute. He fainted, and we called an ambulance, but a fire-truck showed up instead. These guys saw the state Orion was in and they took him to the hospital.

Did you cancel the show?

We were worried, because we didn't know what was wrong with him, and it was the most important show of the tour! But we decided we would wait for him. In the meantime, we began preparing to play without him if we had to. We tried calling him every five minutes, but he didn't answer. We had about an hour to spare. We started painting our faces and biting our nails.

Fifteen minutes before the show, Orion walked into the dressing room. He didn't say a word; he just sat down and started applying his makeup. We looked at him quizzically, and all he said was, 'What's going on? When do we go onstage?'

It turned out that he had kidney stones. They wanted to keep him in the hospital, but he said that was out of the question; he had to play the show. There was this huge responsibility for the band in him, too. The doctors gave him a shitload of painkillers. He later told us that they had given him an injection, and a few minutes later he just stood up, like Lazarus, and took a cab to the club.

We looked at him every now and then during the show, as we weren't sure if he would make it. It was tough, and he did almost faint a few times.

We went on to Canada. Orion was popping pills for about two weeks. He was lying down practically all the time, and parties were out of the question. Finally he peed those stones out, and by the time we got back to Poland, he was fine.

You had been touring Canada for two weeks?

Longer. We broke all records during the *Demigod* tour. We played over a hundred and fifty shows in North America—twenty-six of them in Canada. Who would play so much in one country? In *December*, no less! But we did it. People who came to see us play were astounded, because even Canadian bands didn't undertake tours like this.

How did it go?

Everything was upside down. Orion was suffering, and we were playing shows in places that weren't even on the map. Sometimes we had to set up the stage ourselves, because there was nobody else in the bar. We even played one show for eight people. There were a few dozen others—mostly local, random people. All we needed was a reindeer, an owl, and a crippled dog. We played in a city that had two streets. Literally. The show took place in an old cinema. We felt that there were no Behemoth fans in front of the stage, and we were seen as a mobile circus.

Was it similar in the bigger cities?

It was better. In Montreal, there were over four hundred people. In Toronto, we sold quite a lot of tickets. But bear in mind that in the States we would play for a few thousand people on the same tour, so these numbers seemed rather humble to us. But it was all worth it.

On the next American tour we played only two shows in Canada as a headliner. Both of them were sold out. There were eight hundred people at one of them and nine hundred at the other. These are rather astronomical figures for Canada. They were also the first shows of this magnitude where we didn't open for somebody else but were the main act. These people came to see *us*. Just *US*. We harvested the crops. That's how we built our position in the world.

What does your average concert day look like?

We've talked quite a lot about the good fun, but primarily a tour is a really tough job. Our time onstage is something between forty-five and ninety minutes, but the concert itself, not including the transport, takes a few hours for us. We get onstage about nine in the evening, but we start preparation at about six. I don't eat after that time, because a heavy meal could turn out to be a redundant dead weight. We try to relax. I like to exercise a bit, stretch out, read a book. I want to feel that I go out onstage prepared.

A beer before the show, perhaps?

Almost never. Sometimes, of course, I drink until morning, go to sleep, then take a shower and play the show, but that hardly ever happens. I don't like to do that because I consider it a lack of respect for the people who pay to see our show. I want them to get a high-quality product, not a drunken parody. Instead of drinking beer, I stretch and warm up my fingers. That's especially important when we play a show outdoors. The older I get, the more I have to exercise.

Interviews?

It's worst when we go on tour right after releasing an album. I remember when we played the Mayhem Festival in the States. I didn't know what was going on. We were to sign the CDs at noon and play the show about four in the afternoon. After the show I just took a quick shower and went for another autograph session. Then I would go to the interviews. I finished these practically at night. I would do twenty-five a day. When I couldn't make it alone, Orion and Inferno helped me.

And you said that the gods told you to relax ...

Being a musician is no easy ride. But my life motto is as follows: 'Find what you love and you will never have to work.' Playing music is like having a baby. The first years for parents are hard work: you don't sleep much; you're constantly tired, but would your father tell you how hard it was? No. Every one of his baby's moments makes him happy.

So you make your life your work?

That's how I have always approached my life. Now, after the illness, I am even more convinced that that is what our existence is all about. One day, when we were shooting an episode of *The Voice Of Poland*, one of the contestants came up to me. He wanted to understand how I was functioning after leaving hospital, how the sickness had changed me. I told him that I treated every creative situation I found myself in as fulfilment. Tomorrow I may not be here, but I know I will leave something behind. I sow and observe my crops. My departure will not change anything, because anything I sowed will continue to grow.

That sounds a bit pompous.

My albums will continue to exist when my body dies. I can see in my mind this video recording, with Malta as the main actor. Seth, our guitarist, recorded him at one of the parties when I was asleep at that time in another room. But the guys kept drinking. Malta is completely different when he's drunk. Sometimes I'm even a bit afraid of him. In the movie, he is standing in the middle of the room; he looks like a crazy man. 'We're creating hiiiistoooryyyyy!' he yells.

It was indeed a bit pompous, but there is undoubtedly something to it. Our crusade, this everlasting journey with the band; it's not just more money in our pockets, it's also about creating something bigger than ourselves, something that will outlive us. We're changing the world a little bit.

VI

A DREAM ABOUT
WARSAW

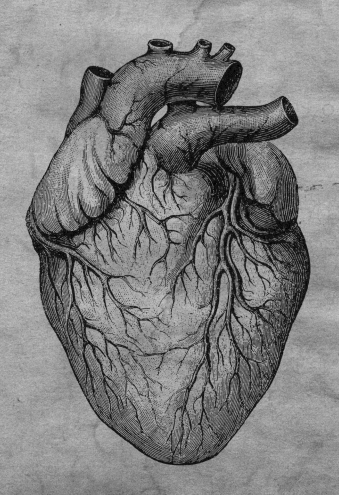

Let's talk about Dorota.
That's a difficult subject. And a complicated one.

**How did you two meet? Did you pick her up
or did she pick you up?**
It's not that simple. Polish show business is a small world. Everybody knows each other. Suddenly I started hearing that Doda keeps asking: who is this Nergal guy?

How did she know there even *was* a Nergal?
She seemingly saw me on Kuba Wojewódzki's talk show. She told me about that later. Supposedly she was impressed by what I said, and she remembered me.

Did you even know who she was?
For me, she was just a girl from those colourful magazines, but without any negative associations. Maybe I was a little intrigued by her. I can't say I followed her career, but I did watch how it developed from a distance.

Didn't you laugh at her a bit?
Maybe a little. But even if I did, it was all in good fun.

**'Poland seen from afar has the face of Doda
and the Kaczynski brothers.'**
These are my words. I did say that in an interview. Years ago.

Yes, while you were criticising Polish music.
That's right. But remember, I'd been talking to journalists long before I ever met Dorota. Her stage image and songs were a bit … *unleavened* at that time. She underwent a huge metamorphosis, and she herself was aware of that.

Let's be honest, when I look at pictures of me from years ago, I can't help but smile, too.

What did you think when you found out that this girl from magazines wanted to contact you?

I had two feelings: surprise, but also curiosity. A few days earlier, I read a long interview with Dorota for *Pani* magazine. This interview, as well as having a beautiful and sensual photo shoot to accompany it, boosted my curiosity. But it didn't occupy my head entirely.

And later?

She just wouldn't let go. We were at the Musikmesse in Frankfurt with the band. It's the biggest music fair in Europe. There was some nasty party going on when someone called me—a journalist friend from MTV. He started telling me that he had met Doda and that she kept asking him for my number. 'If you care about it so much, I will call you first,' I thought. So I got her number and sent her a text. She wrote me back and the rest is history.

We met for the first time in Gdańsk. Behemoth was finishing *Evangelion* at that time. Dorota was from a different world to me, but it only made me want to meet her more. It made the whole situation even spicier. We met in the evening, somewhere around ten, and I drove her back to her hotel around six in the morning. We agreed to meet the next day for dinner in the Przystal bar in Sopot. I slept for maybe six hours. I woke up when my telephone rang. I picked up and heard Dorota say, 'So, how about that fish?' She was really disarming.

So the chemistry was always there?

Chemistry, and more dates—in London, where we mixed our record, and in Warsaw. And I think that's when it all started. For the first time in my life, I saw these strange creatures running around with cameras. Paparazzi. Prior to that, I lived in a cocoon. I existed in a metal niche, and I was completely unaware of such people. I knew that the tabloid press existed, of course, but I never dared peek inside that world. I didn't feel the need to do so, either. But I had no idea there was this whole other world of gutter internet journalism.

It was a shock: I'm on a date with a girl, and now there are people with cameras, secretly taking pictures of us. I never suspected Dorota of selling us out to the paparazzi. But there are always doubts. Now, from experience, I know that if you really want to, it can be done. But why would I speculate now? It doesn't matter anymore.

How did you feel as a new inhabitant of this world of gossip?

I certainly didn't know it would all end in such a storm. I did realise that if they took pictures of us, they would publish them *somewhere*, but I never assumed that the whole country would make such a big deal out of it. What actually happened later was way too much for me. I called a few friends and the guys from the band and I warned them that some things that could potentially appear in the press and other media might surprise them.

Did they already know about your dates with Doda? How did they react?

I don't normally feel the need to ask my friends for permission when I want to meet a girl. But it was funny. The shortest conversation I had was with Paldzioch, our second guitarist. He just said, 'Bullshit, I don't believe you,' and hung up the phone. I shrugged and kept calling people. Orion was speechless for a moment, then he just uttered an old and beautiful Polish word, 'kurwa'.

Finally, I called Zbyszek. He listened to me—didn't interrupt—and when I had finished, he said, 'Fucking awesome, man, such positive stuff!' I really didn't feel any negative emotions from them. It wasn't shocking for them that pictures of me might show up in glossy magazines. The fact that I was dating Doda was, though.

Did you have the impression that everyone was looking at you the next day?

No. I was used to people recognising me in the street because I am a performing artist. The context was different but the rules were the same.

Your pictures were everywhere.
That's life.

How many photo shoots were set up?
None. I never got so low as to set up photo shoots. I've heard that it's a quite popular thing to do among various stars and starlets, but I find it repulsive. I'm not looking for fame at all costs. Paparazzi, stalkers, impudent fans, tabloids—these are the tax that you pay because you're famous. And I could afford it.

Weren't there any staged shoots at parties?
That's a different story. Self-promotion and taking pictures is a part of those events. In that situation—if they have to, you let them shoot. In other situations, we always ran away. I actually get the impression that this environment is evolving, and not necessarily in a good way. At the very beginning, when I had no clue how it all worked, I met a few paparazzi. They were ordinary guys and sometimes we even exchanged a few words. But I never felt quite right in their presence. After all, if you decide to take on a job that involves stalking other people, there has to be something pathological in you. A normal person doesn't become a paparazzo, just like they don't become a dogcatcher.

Or a black metal musician.
True.

**So how did this pathological black metal guy
interact with pathological paparazzi?**
One of them seemed quite normal. He would say hi and ask about my health when I left the house to buy toilet paper and cucumbers. He wasn't too rude, either. He was just trying to observe a basic level of decency.
   One day, I was leaving a bar with Dorota, and he was there, waiting. We were walking, without a car; there was no way to run. He took our pictures, but he was kind enough to offer us a ride. He drove us all the way home, and

it turned out that he was an old metal fan. Suddenly he pointed at me and said to Dorota, 'Woman, do you know that this guy has toured with Slayer?' And she said, 'What's Slayer?'

It wasn't staged, then?
No. It was just a one-off situation. These people were changing—for the worst. The more we tried to avoid them, the more they tried to take pictures of us. At first the escapes were quite easy, because most of them drove old, shabby cars. When one couldn't catch us, there was another in his place—in a black BMW, for example. They looked like mafia. They always attacked as a group, never alone. There were always three or four of them. One got out of the car with the camera while another waited nearby. They'd expect me to attack the first one or wait for me and Dorota to go the other way. Two more would wait in the car, in case we tried to escape.

Were these people from any news organisations in particular?
Maybe. But I get the impression that most of them functioned independently, and according to different rules. They had one boss in common, however: money. You take a picture and sell it to whoever pays the most.

You had your calm life, you were respected in your niche all over the world, and you could afford to buy food; what did you need all this for?
I didn't ask for this. I just wanted to date a girl. That's all. I had no idea that I was heading straight into a wasp's nest.

And if you *had* known, would you have still taken that step?
Cronos from Venom, one of my childhood idols, when asked if he would change anything in his life, answered with his innate subtlety: 'No fucking way.' Taking bricks out of a standing building is risky, because you have no guarantee that it won't fall apart. And, equally, you can never be sure

that a little change or a different decision made in a given situation won't make you sit with your old, fat wife, babysitting spoilt brats instead of giving an interview.

Of course, Cronos put it slightly differently, but that was the essence. And I think in a similar manner. That's my nature. I appreciate the nasty situations in life that I sometimes get embroiled in. My illness, for example. At one point, some of my friends and colleagues said that my sickness was a result of actions taken in the previous year of my life. My quite stormy relationship, all that media witch-hunt, moving to Warsaw, new people … all these things generated quite a lot of stress. My body just couldn't handle it, and this manifested itself with a cancer.

I didn't comment on that then. And I will not do it now.

Why did you move to Warsaw?
I wanted to be close to the person I loved.

One of your previous girlfriends, Zuza, lived in Warsaw too, didn't she?
The situation and circumstances were different. I wasn't ready for such a step then. Besides, Zuza liked coming to Gdańsk. I treated Warsaw more like a place from which I could go to other places in the world and where I could party from time to time. One day in Warsaw has more to offer than a month in Gdańsk. But at that time I really liked the somewhat provincial character of Gdańsk. It allowed me to rest and regenerate. Living by the beach, everyday exercise by the seashore—it was difficult to say goodbye to these things.

A year and a half passes, you meet a new girl, and just like that you run away from this idyll. Why?
Dorota showed up at the moment of my life when my routine and discipline had started to wear me down. I felt a bit like a robot in Gdańsk. I am an inherently restless soul. I can't choose one road and drive on it for my whole life. My life needs its own dynamics. Sometimes I need stabilisation, other times to run wild. This is my natural cycle. A new relationship was

an impulse for change. I packed my most important stuff—some clothes, a few records, a guitar—then I got in the car and drove to Warsaw. I left my friends, my family, my house behind me. Practically everything.

Did you suggest the move to Dorota?

I declared my feelings and said I'd like to live with her. Of course we had spoken about that before, but with no particular plan in mind, so I just waited for a clear sign from her. It didn't come, so I went all in on my own volition. And she said yes.

How did the band react?

Inferno—with his typical brand of fatalism—prophesied an apocalypse. I tried to calm him down—told him it was not the other side of the world, and that I could always get in the car and be in Gdańsk in four hours. I also reminded him that there were bands where the lead vocalist lived in the States and the guitarist in England and they managed to work it out. And it turned out that I was right. After I moved, we functioned like we did before—maybe even better.

Wasn't it frustrating for the guys that you became a household name in Poland almost overnight?

I was always on the front line and they were always more in the background. You know, it's like how Malcolm Young of AC/DC was always jealous of his brother, Angus, because the latter is always in the spotlight. I don't think there is as much rivalry between us as that. Besides, we all know where our place is. That's what our characters are like. Zbyszek pushing forward to the cameras is the last thing I can imagine.

And what did they think of Dorota?

I think they just saw an attractive girl that I was dating. Even if they didn't like something about her, they certainly never told me. But I do feel stupid to this day because of one thing. Right after I started dating Dorota, Behemoth set off on an eight week US tour. Our relationship was fresh; I was still working on it, so I spent a lot of time on the phone. We still didn't know each other too well, so we often fought. There was quite a lot of stress and frustration involved. I was tense and nervous. I would get onstage in such a state and let off steam on the guys. The whole band had to keep away from me. It wasn't nice—for the guys or for me.

What about your fans? Did they mind their idol dating a pop starlet?

Watch what you're saying! Dorota was a star, not a starlet. I live according to an old maxim I heard a long time ago: 'If you want to steal, steal millions; if you want to love, love the queens!'

My friends' reactions varied, but I didn't encounter any open hostility. Just jokes. There was one particular email from a guy who said that when he saw me on the cover of a magazine with Dorota, he burned all our albums. The metal world is quite rigid and conservative in some ways, but if they could accept that the metal god, Rob Halford, is gay, why would they be concerned about me?

There were various comments on the internet, too, correct?

Right—various. Some people criticised, others wrote that if Lemmy of Motörhead screwed Britney Spears, they'd be ecstatic for a month. Let's be serious: I'm not going to lose sleep over that kind of criticism. Most Behemoth fans are smart people. They don't care who I am dating, or what magazines my pictures are published in.

But there are people who claim that tabloid covers are not the right place for a serious musician.

I am not going to be anyone's hostage. And it's not just about my life but also about music. When I create, I'm not wondering about what people are expecting. If I did, I would feel like a whore, not a musician, for sure.

You're not the first guy to leave the black metal cave.

I'm glad you noticed.

Satyricon opens the skiing world championships; former Gorgoroth leader Gaahl patronises fashion shows ...

Yes, because black metal, first and foremost, means individualism. It also promotes freedom from limitations.

Financial limitations, too? Surely that's placing high social status ahead of your basic ideals?

I flush all that bullshit about ideals down the shitter. Just look at human evolution. We lived in caves, and then we left them. We passed through the forest to get to the sea. We wanted to explore what was beyond the water, so we built ships. Everything was subordinate to expansion, because expansion, motored by curiosity, is rooted deep inside our nature. We've always wanted to go further and further, and my life is a reflection of this evolution. And so is my music. It's based on crossing, transgression, and constant development. Why would conquest translate to whoring out?

Maybe the *direction* of the conquest is wrong?

Behemoth is an extreme band and it always will be, but why can't we have photo shoots with the best photographers—people who normally deal with fashion? Why can't we have a video made by Patric Ullaeu, who makes clips for Madonna or Lady Gaga? Why should this book not be available in every mainstream shop?

Do you get pissed when people pick on you for these things?

A little. But it pushes me even farther. I keep quoting Russell: 'Every great idea starts out as blasphemy.' If there is resistance, it means that the direction is right. I want to share what I do, so I share. I am curious about the world and I want to absorb it. I have no fear of it. I look at everything like a little boy, with my eyes wide open. Sometimes I wonder, sometimes I scratch my head. But I do get into awkward situations. Sometimes I act first and *then* I think. Sometimes I get burned and sometimes I have an amazing experience. As Lemmy says, 'Pleasure is to play, it makes no difference what you say.' What's important is the very process of experiencing the world.

You can experience many things.

It doesn't matter, because experiencing is neither good nor bad. Sometimes it brings laughter, sometimes tears; sometimes sickness, sometimes money.

Right, money …

My life is not about the next deposit in my bank account, but about the everyday load of experiences. *They* make me rich. I am thirty-six years old and I think I've experienced quite a lot. But the world always has something to offer. It's endless.

Of course, everything is relative. Money is energy. I like money, and I like having money. I know how to get it, but I never treat it as the sole aim. In the context of all this media confusion about my meeting with Dorota, the question of money is unsupported. Back then, as now, the main source of my income was the band. Even when I was in Rome, I didn't have to do as Romans did, and I didn't have to brag. If I really cared about these things, I wouldn't be driving a Honda.

Didn't Dorota sneer at you for that?

She did, she did! She thought it was embarrassing to drive a Honda.

But it's a real Lucifer's chariot! It shines with blackness.

I didn't get what she was on about. Having a car that was worth more than $50,000? I do understand that something may fit or not fit someone, but I don't think it's got anything to do with the amount of money you paid for it. I was fucking pissed by that opinion.

Did you run from the paparazzi in the Honda?

One day we were driving through Sopot. The traffic was quite heavy. Suddenly, we noticed that there was a sporty BMW behind us. It was these guys from Warsaw who looked like mafia again. They had come to Sopot to take our pictures. I remember that the driver was some ugly, fat guy with an especially nasty face. In theory, their car was a cheetah and mine a donkey. And that was when Dorota started deriding me: 'You want to lose them in this piece of junk? Look what they're driving!'

I kept my cool, even though anger was boiling inside me. If you could draw up this scenario in a comic book, you would see a little cloud over my head with skulls, grenades, bombs, and rifles in it. So I made a few breakneck manoeuvres, accompanied by Dorota's yells of, 'Kurwa! What the fuck are you doing?'

I managed to overtake a few cars and turn into a small alley, then I ran a red light and went the wrong way. It all happened in about a minute, but, importantly, the BMW was gone. It turned out that you could run away from a bunch of jerks even if you were in a Skoda. If you've got balls, you can travel around the world on a donkey.

And it was on this donkey that you entered Warsaw?
It was a zoo—a strange world. But I liked that jungle. Warsaw had a lot to offer. You can feel that it's a real metropolis—one that can unabashedly shake hands with Berlin, Moscow, or Prague. I am a city guy, so it kept me flowing, at least at the beginning.

Didn't you miss the sea breeze?
I had to start a lot of things from scratch. I had no beaten tracks. I started exercising in Mokotów Field. I tried to create a substitute for the closed world that I had built in Gdańsk.

I understood how important the rhythm of life was for me. I had to rebuild it, maybe even create it all over again.

Did you miss your friends?
Very much so. At the beginning, my social life was rather limited. I lived on planet Doda. Around me there was Doda's entourage, which consisted of various people. I found common language with most of them, though. I met a lot of valuable people. It was fresh, but …

She was always in the centre?

Yes, *everything* revolved around her. I didn't stake my position in our relationship and today I think that was a mistake.

Dorota, just like me, is very expansive. Sometimes, in her expansiveness, she could be very aggressive and possessive. Let's just say that she defends her world. I lived a year and a half at her place and not even once—I repeat: not even once—did I play an album from my collection in her company. I listened to my music in my car and on my headphones and when I exercised. And that was when I was back on planet Satan.

I guess, somewhere deep inside, I felt that Dorota would never understand my world. I don't think she even tried too hard.

Was she at least interested in it?

She hardly ever asked about my life. I was the one who asked questions. I wanted to understand her reality.

And what is she like in her everyday life?

I think she's quite pragmatic. She likes to take and have fun. She doesn't analyse too much. But listen, I wouldn't like to publicly vivisect her personality. Let's just say that I just hoped that some things would sink in eventually.

Love is one thing, but the consequences of your relationship were also visible elsewhere. You became a celebrity.

That world was strange for me. Sure, I did show up at a few parties, but I always kept my distance. I wasn't drawn to people from glossy magazines. I didn't act, I didn't change the clothes I wore; I didn't *try* to fit in. I didn't grin at everybody, and I didn't have a gleaming smile fixed on my face.

And how did other celebrities react to you?

I didn't feel excluded or pushed into the margins, if that's what you mean. These people, in general, turned out to be nice and friendly. I don't know how sincere it was, but I just think they found me interesting. But there's no doubting that I was like a meteorite that had fallen into the middle of their little village.

Or like a savage at the royal court?

No, I wasn't looked down upon at all. Rinke Rooyens, the head of the Rochstar production company, came up to me during one of the parties. He introduced himself and we started talking. He was the kind of guy who had no prejudice whatsoever; he was very empathic and communicative. After a few years we managed not only to make a TV programme together, but we also became true friends. The other day, the TV presenter Krzysztof Ibisz came up to me and introduced himself, too. There were also others. It was all very positive.

And you didn't want to wipe their fake smiles from their faces?

I don't treat people that way. If someone is kind to me, I try to respond in the same way. In my head, this whole world of celebrities honestly wasn't a big factor. We were doing our best with my band; we played tour after tour. That's where my people and my environment were. I came back to Warsaw not for the parties but for my woman.

And did you feel more like 'Doda's boyfriend' or the leader of the most famous metal band in Poland?

It's a stereotype that metal music is a niche, and that only the chosen ones hear about it. These people knew me before I started dating Dorota. I met Kuba Wojewódzki, Czeslaw Mozil, and Maciej Malelczuk long before my face started appearing in tabloids. They knew me as Nergal, not as Doda's boyfriend.

Behemoth is not on the radio, but it was difficult to ignore the numbers of records we were selling. After all, Behemoth is the first and only Polish band to have appeared twice on the American *Billboard* chart. We won awards, and *Evangelion* ruled the Polish charts for three weeks! Even the officials of Gdańsk awarded me a prize for being a Young Culture Creator.

**So, people like the renowned vocal coach Ela
Zapendowska came to you and said, 'Mr Darski,
your latest record is fantastic, but in the fourth song,
around the fortieth second, you seem to struggle
with the high F-sharp.' Is that how it went?**

I don't know if these people liked our music, and to be honest, I didn't really care. I didn't have any complexes. They knew who I was, and it was hard for them to undermine the musical status of my band.

**Everybody's nice, smiling, friendly—are you trying
to tell us that this is what this world looks like?**

It had its dark sides, too. It was very showy and plastic from the outside.

What was underneath?

Nothing. That's the point. Some time ago, I read a great essay by the sociologist Zygmunt Bauman. It was about today's forms of communication, which he called 'tweeting', leaving no place for real relations. And that's what this world looked like. It was shallow. It lived under the dictum of media that described it. Gossip, slander, little wars, secret photos—all of that was in the foreground.

The media has its targets, however.

Yes, because the tempo of our lives is getting faster. Colour and flash is what matters now, and there is less and less actual content. On the cover of a magazine, the word 'BETRAYAL' has to scream out with capital letters, because, usually, a photo takes up the whole page. Then, at the very end, in fine print, there are just a few words. We buy this because tricks like that grab our attention, but it's just like fast food. We devour it, but there's no value in it whatsoever.

You didn't enjoy this glitz?

I was including myself in that analysis to some extent, too. Sometimes I do swallow news without a blink; I get excited like a kid, but shortly afterward,

I realise how superficial all of this is. But I do learn with each day. I recognise the concept of 'tweeting' more every day. This amazing desire that some people have to accentuate their presence for the sake of it: 'Attention! I'm here! Look! I shaved my legs! Wow! My breast fell out of my bra! That's my ride! My dog smokes marijuana!'

Big fucking deal! It's all bullshit. And by that, I don't mean that the *only* valuable thing in the world is watching Bergman or Fellini movies or reading the encyclopaedia. We'd go crazy on that path, too. Small things are also important; we can't escape from the prose of life. But it's all about balance.

You're not exactly being innovative in saying there's no balance in the glossy media.

Balance in the whole world is quite shaky nowadays. We focus on trivial things, and they become the determinants of quality. There were moments when I bought into this illusion, too.

Don't get me wrong: the time that I spent with Dorota, that year and a half in Warsaw, is a nice memory. I had fun, and I learned a lot—maybe the most I've learned in my life. I was made a celebrity, yes, but I had no power over that. I found myself in the eye of a camera; it caught me. Sometimes it was embarrassing; sometimes it was just plain funny. If they still want me to be a character in this fairy tale, that's also OK with me. But in one moment I realised that I could be a ticking bomb—or a foreign body that spoils the apparent harmony of this gigantic reality show.

But you still attend the 'business' parties, and you smile to the cameras.

As Roman Kostrzewski from Kat once sang, 'I'm a funny devil, so I laugh.'

VII

THIS IS MY
BODY
AND THIS IS MY
BONE MARROW

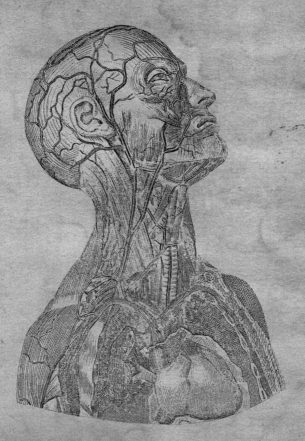

Is your body important to you?
Very important, yes.

Do you take care of it?
I do.

Why?
I've instinctively always felt that way, but it certainly isn't a family trait.

But didn't your brother exercise a lot?
When he was eighteen, he was pumped. That's what I'd call it. He took some chemical shit and gained some mighty impressive musculature in no time at all. But I don't really think that's where I got the motivation, nor do I think that's what it should be about.

So where did you get the example to follow?
From the movies, I think—Bruce Lee. I remember in the 80s, when everybody in the neighbourhood wanted to be like him.

I became a man of two passions: music showed up, and martial arts did, too. First judo, then other martial arts. I was totally absorbed by training.

Was it driven by vanity, or simply a desire to keep fit?
It was and still is the golden mean. My attitude toward my body and appearance might seem a bit skewed, but I'm not a fanatic.

There are people who spend their lives conforming to the ideal of looking good and having a perfect body: special diets, defined exercise cycles, sacrifices …

That's not me. I know moderation. But that doesn't mean I don't like to feel healthy and strong and look good at the same time. I do like it. I like it very much. But I don't go over the line. I can break my diet whenever I feel like it. I can grab a beer or any other alcoholic drink every now and then and I can go party.

And when you sin against your body, do you have any pangs of conscience?

That's far too strong a way of putting it. It's more of a natural cycle. If I pass up on exercising, or party a little bit, I tighten the screw again afterwards. I don't even need anybody to force me. I just look in the mirror and see that I have gained a little weight. Then there is no mercy.

Your eyes are so sharp that you can notice even a little bit of excess fat?

It's a matter for your consciousness, not your vision. The fat may not even be there, but if it's there in my head, that's enough.

I look at man holistically anyway. You can't separate body from mind. When you feel like shit, you look like shit. That's why I describe my exercising as a golden mean.

But admit it: you like looking at yourself, don't you?

I like myself. I am of the opinion that if you want to love at all, you must begin with yourself. I often meet people who talk a lot about love and want to pour it on everything, dead or alive, but yet they can't accept their body and their appearance. Something is wrong there, don't you think?

Do you love your body unconditionally?

I am aware of its imperfections. But then again, maybe 'imperfection' is not the right word, because that would assume that there *is* some form of perfection in the first place, and that concept exists only in our imagination. What I'm alluding to are the limits of our bodies. I know them. But I'm also determined to overcome them.

Maybe you should have become a sportsman?

I could be a sportsman. In a way, I am. It's not just that I run and exercise. Our music is extreme not only in name. Behemoth concerts are a huge effort, like a marathon.

143

People associate rock'n'roll with something else.
Just like sport is supposedly not associated with drinking. Just take a look at the lifestyles of a few soccer players to disprove that theory.

Playing in Behemoth is very physical, then?
I would compare our gigs to a hurdles race with a guitar on your back, but one that lasts for over an hour. You can really lose a few pounds. It's quite a challenge, and every time that challenge is getting bigger. And that is why I have to exercise, too. There's a tendency people have where, the older they get and the more they feel the frailty of their body, the more they indulge themselves. They let themselves go. It's exactly the reverse with me.

Is health itself important for you?
Very. But as I said before, human is a whole concept. Health, psyche, appearance, these are all elements of the same puzzle. Healthy mind equals healthy body. It may be a cliché, but it's the truth.

Did you see the doctor a lot when you were a kid?
Quite a lot, but never for anything serious. I used to have chronic tonsillitis and throat problems, though, and I am still haunted by these.

Do you worry whenever you don't feel well?
I used to worry less. With time, a little hypochondriac started to grow in me. It's maturing all the time.

Do you try to make yourself believe you're sick?
I think I tend to focus on specific health problems, even if it's nothing major. A little infection, a cold, some allergy; it all affects my frame of mind. Some people react to stuff like that by loosening the screw even more. They go drinking, get wasted, and they don't give a crap about their sickness. In my case, every problem with health drives me mad. But maybe that's a good thing. If it wasn't for this little internal hypochondriac inside me, maybe I wouldn't be sitting here today with you, answering your questions.

**You genuinely believe that you were saved by
your fixation on health?**

Sometimes I think it saved me from death, and sometimes I feel that by
being aware of it, I missed the first symptoms of my sickness. I'm also sure
that the fact that I don't fool with my health too much didn't do me any
harm.

**There are people who do fool with their health
and have still achieved a quite impressive age.**

Everybody has his or her own way. I don't want to judge that. It's obvious
that there are people living on the edge who, even when they're old, are still
doing great. Just look at Keith Richards from The Rolling Stones. If you
believe what he says in his autobiography, then an ordinary human should
have at least twenty lives to be able to survive what he has. Big respect. He's
a wonderful guy. But I know myself, and I know that if I lived the way he
did, I'd have been dead a long time ago.

It's a question of awareness. I'm aware of my body and mind, and I
know how to treat them. Guys from the band have ridiculed me for years.
They're always asking, 'What the fuck do you need those yoghurts and
exercises for?'

**Right. And then you got leukaemia. 'What did
you need those yoghurts and exercises for?'**

Well, here's an example. When it got me and I ended up in the hospital, at
least the doctors had a piece of healthy and functional meat to work with
and not some kind of worn-down carrion. I don't know if that saved my life,
but surely it was a factor?

If I could turn back the clock, I wouldn't change a thing. But I do realise
that health is a lottery. When I was in hospital, there were sportsmen and
alcoholics, a twelve-year-old and a seventy-year-old—as broad a demographic
of sufferers as you could think of. How did all those people get leukaemia? No
idea. The doctors could only shrug. I only heard that there is some kind of
epidemic among thirty-year-olds. Maybe we're the Chernobyl generation.

Doesn't that lack of awareness hurt you?

I always rationalise; I just assume my life as a whole led me to the hospital. But it also led me to my winning over the sickness. The air I breathed, the stress, moving to Warsaw, the media witch-hunt, and on the other hand there was my character, determination, and persistence—all of these things mattered. It's like the butterfly effect. An insect on a tropical island flaps its wings and causes a tornado on the other end of the planet. Analysing this stuff is a waste of time. It all just happened.

And how did it start?

First there was a feeling, a kind of inner conviction that something was wrong.

You knew from the beginning that it was something serious?

Yes and no. If for a week—and that's how it was—something is wrong with you and you feel progressively worse each day, then an alarm goes off in your mind. You know that it's not flu, let's put it that way. On the other hand, I tried to fight my intuition and so did my environment.

I remember one particular situation: it was right after a concert in Poznan, somewhere around July or August of 2010. Dorota and I went for lunch with Orion, our bassist, and his girlfriend Kasja. I told them about my symptoms, and, out of kindness, I'm sure, they tried to convince me that I was overreacting and that I was just imagining things.

By way of illustration, Kasja told me about the situation she'd had a few years previously. She was in the hospital and she felt like she was dying. The doctors examined her and told her to go home and stop pretending, because there were people who really need help. As it turned out, it was all stress-related. When she heard that, she immediately felt better. So everybody suggested that it was the same case with me.

Did they convince you?

I *wanted* to believe them.

What were your symptoms? What was going on with your body?

It all started with a small bump. Today it might sound silly, but I grew a horn on my head—some strange callus under my skin. I don't even know exactly how it looked because it was mostly covered by hair. I know that it was hard and protruding though—like somebody had put a button or an implant under my skin.

At first I thought it was some kind of cyst or atheroma, something of that kind. I was hoping it would just go away. But it didn't. What's worse was that, on the other side of my head, another horn started to grow. I still thought it was funny, but then it all started to gain momentum. Soon, there were more calluses on my skin, one after another. They weren't visible, so I didn't tell anyone about them. I thought it was some skin disease. I didn't worry too much, because I still generally felt good. So I decided to not give a shit about these bumps and I went on the European tour. We played with Decapitated. But then, more symptoms showed up: stomach problems, constant diarrhoea … a steaming cesspit of shit in all colours of the rainbow.

Stuff like that happens on the road, though, right?

And that's another reason why I ignored it—at least at the beginning. I still hadn't connected the dots by then.

When did the alarm go off for real?

After three weeks I grew restless. Right after the tour, Dorota and I had planned a holiday in Greece, so I was conscious not to spoil that. Before we left, there was one more festival to play in the Czech Republic—Masters Of Rock. I went to the dermatologist before the trip and I was hoping he would look at my head, smile, and give me some pills that would patch me up in a week. He gave me antibiotics, but he also told me he had never seen anything like it.

Did you take the antibiotics?

I did. We went to the Czech Republic, and there, new symptoms appeared.

I got on the bus we were travelling in and I immediately felt weak. I had problems breathing. Again, I thought it was just because of stress and high temperatures. I'd felt like that before and I was used to such situations. Once, I even ran away from a hospital to play a tour.

That's just beautiful!

It was a few years back. I think it was 2001. We had managed to book two large tours, one after another. We were a much smaller band than we are now, and we really thought it was a great challenge for us. Earlier, about a week before all the main fun started, we were supposed to play two additional concerts: in Portugal and Spain. It was a crazy trip; we spent thirty-five hours in the bus, practically without stopping. We got there; played one show, then another one, and then we went back to Poland. And that's when it all began.

Problems with breathing, you mean?

That too, but mostly issues with my heart. It started living its own life and beating irregularly. I ignored that, but a day passed, then another, and another.

I was already back in Poland, and in a couple of days I was due to start a huge tour but the damn thing just wouldn't get any better. On Saturday, we were to begin conquering Europe, but on Friday I broke down and ended up in hospital. They put me on drip—gave me magnesium …

So it was stress?

It's hard to say. Only a preliminary diagnosis was possible. The doctors said that I had an irregular heartbeat. It was overwhelming. But this was more than a matter of my health—this was about responsibility, too. There was a storm in my head because I knew that I was irreplaceable in the band. The guys just couldn't tour without me.

Meanwhile, the doctors made themselves clear: at least three days of observation. Then, depending on my results, either I could tour or I would remain in hospital. Well, I started panicking and calling off the shows. An hour later, I changed my mind, so I called everybody back again. Basically, I was fighting with myself.

And what did the band say?

Most of them did what I would do. They supported me, asked about my health, tried to convince me that calling off the tour was not such a big deal. They understood and supported me.

But you said *most* of them …

Novy, our then bassist, really surprised me. He asked me what I was thinking, and he made reference to the certain amount of Euros he would earn from the tour. It wasn't nice.

He wasn't with you long.

No, but that wasn't the reason behind my decision. I did however draw certain conclusions, and I remembered what I had to remember.

You chose his option in the end, though. And, as you said, you ran away from the hospital.

But it was *my* decision. And I made it because the rest of the band understood the situation and didn't push it. That's why I stepped into their shoes, and ultimately my stupidity won over reason. I told the doctors that I was going home to get my stuff and that I would be back that evening. Of course, I didn't show up again at the hospital. I left and never came back.

Would you do the same today?

I don't know. Later, there were more situations when I didn't feel quite right. At one time there was something wrong with my spine, then other issues with my throat; another time it was flu. But I never called off the shows. *The show must go on.* There are doctors in every city, after all. Whether we played in Krakow or Berlin, or maybe on the other side of the globe, I was always aware that if I didn't feel OK, I could find a specialist, pay him, and he'd patch me up.

Did someone have to patch you up after your escape?

No. At first I took it easy. I didn't drink at all; I went to bed after the shows. There was still something amiss, but gradually I was getting better. With time I diagnosed myself, and I began to take it for granted that it was anxiety. I got used to it and I ignored the symptoms. Halfway through the tour, I'd forgotten anything was even wrong.

You felt that similar things might be going on in the summer of 2010?

Yes. We went to the Czech Republic for a festival. I felt better for a while. Probably adrenalin did its thing. But immediately after we finished the show, I went down with a fever. I think that is when I realised that something was *really* wrong with me. Now I started connecting the dots. Fever, strange bumps, diarrhoea, and enlarged lymph nodes on my neck. There was a surgeon friend of mine at the show. He examined me and told me to do a morphology test as soon as possible.

Did you listen to his advice?

There was no time to. After the show we had to sign CDs. When Orion saw what shape I was in, he told me to let it go, but I resisted and went to the meet and greet with the fans anyway. It took about ninety minutes. I was so exhausted that the only thing I was able to do later was to get to the bus and try to sleep.

Did you manage to sleep?

Not right away because I was sweating like all hell. That same night we were headed to Poland. I got some aspirin at the first gas station. I took two pills, went to sleep, and woke up in Warsaw. There was no time to go and see a doctor because Doda and I had a flight to Greece in a few hours.

Did you go to Greece after all?

Yes. It was awful. The prescribed antibiotic didn't work. I stopped taking it after a few days. And I was sweating like a pig.

And the Greek summer is warm as it is.
That's what I was thinking. Furthermore, because Dorota hated air conditioning, we didn't use anything like that. But I've visited the tropics often enough to know that, if you wake up in a pool of sweat, it's not only because of the high temperature. The alarm was wailing from all directions.

I also had problems breathing all the time. I tried swimming in the pool. I can normally do a few dozen laps and still breathe normally but that time I could barely manage any. After a few rapid movements I'd be coughing uncontrollably. When I went to bed, my lungs would give out a strange whooshing sound, almost like there was something blocking the air. Dorota laughed at me, she mocked me even … I think she tried to cheer me up by playing down the symptoms and joking about them. Partially she succeeded, but I was growing more and more restless each day.

Did the word 'cancer' go through your mind?
Maybe. I think once I even said it out loud. I asked Dorota what would happen if I had a tumour.

And?
'What are you talking about? Don't be crazy'—that's what I heard.

**Didn't you think about going back to Poland
and getting examined?**
No. I didn't completely ignore the symptoms, but I disregarded them somewhat. I just started calling a few doctors that I knew, more often. I had a hotline to them.

Did it change anything?
Well, we jointly acknowledged that in the absence of morphology tests, there was nothing we could do.

That's not very helpful.
Maybe, but what else *could* I do? We'd finally gone on holiday together, and

I was really putting a brave face on things. I didn't want to spoil the trip for Dorota, and I needed a break myself.

As far as I can remember, I think that was when I started thinking that all these skin problems, the fever and diarrhoeas, were nothing but symptoms of some kind of tropical sickness. It didn't sound like a death sentence but it did explain my general state of health. I analysed the previous months, too. I had been in Japan, Australia, Thailand—plenty of opportunity to contract something, and Thailand seemed most probable.

It was still in my mind also that—a year previously—my ex-girlfriend got sick after returning from Thailand. Strange patterns formed on her hands; it turned out that she had some kind of parasite, so I thought my case was maybe similar. And I stuck to this belief until I came back. I had a plan. I wanted to get examined at the Institute of Maritime and Tropical Medicine in Gdynia.

Immediately after landing?

No. I had my duties to attend to: I had two shows to play. The first one was with Smolik, where I was supposed to present a show as part of the Meskie Granie festival, which is sponsored by a Polish beer company. Later, we played at Castle Party with Behemoth. But I had a bed booked in hospital, because I knew that I would be spending at least a few days there. I felt much more at ease knowing that.

Were those concerts that important to you?

Let's put it this way: if I had known I had leukaemia, I would have cancelled them. But I didn't know, and both of them seemed important enough to me at the time. Smolik prepared a really nice, avant-garde version of 'Lucifer'. It was more of a theatrical performance than a concert. Besides, let's be honest, if somebody wants to give you five thousand dollars for an eight-minute show, you just don't say no.

What about Castle Party?

We played there the following day; Behemoth was headlining. I really wanted to play because I love stirring shit up, and a Behemoth concert at a gothic festival was a kind of demonstration of strength.

You don't like gothic stuff?

I do, I actually love bands like Fields Of The Nephilim or Sisters Of Mercy, but this was something completely different. Castle Party is about flounces and ruffles. I hate that kind of thing; it's terribly pretentious. We were about to fucking rock that place down, and to offset that there was confetti to be blown out from the stage and girls dancing with fire. It was supposed to be heavy …

Was it?

I have never played a show in such a state and I hope I never will again. I was going through the motions the whole time. I choked on words; I didn't finish the verses. I was taking steps back from the microphone and not singing all the lines. I was terrified. I couldn't breathe; I was counting the minutes until the end of the show. Besides, the audience didn't buy into us at all. I think we were too brutal for them. It was a terribly surreal experience.

Why did you even go onstage in the first place?

I felt OK, that's true, but before the concert I took some pseudoephedrine, which gave me a solid kick for a little while. Basically, I thought I could make it. Before that, I actually took half of our promoter's first-aid kit, too. He was suffering from asthma and had a whole set of medicines for breathing. I used all his inhalers.

So you couldn't catch your breath before the show?

Castle Party, as the very name suggests, takes place in a castle. In order to play there, you have to climb. It's not really a big distance, but on that day it was a real challenge for me. I lost my breath every few minutes. I had to make a few stops to get there. Each time I stopped for a couple of minutes to recover. Maybe this is what deceived me, because, as I said before, I had

had problems with breathing previously, but that was always stress-induced. I was sure for the whole time that I was simply making up some of the symptoms. I knew I was sick—maybe I even knew it was serious—but I was convinced that my psyche was really adding to it. All of us joked about it, really. It was the day after the lunch with Dorota, Orion, and his girlfriend, where they all suggested that I was being a little hysterical. They didn't take it seriously at all, despite the fact that, on the way to the festival, my lymph nodes already resembled two ping-pong balls. Dorota even sucked on them to cheer me up! I think it was only after the show that everybody knew it was not only my psyche that was showing distress signs, but my body, too.

What happened then?

Nothing in particular, but I think I must have looked like a piece of shit. Orion and Inferno dragged me out of the room and informed me that we are not playing any more shows or doing anything else before I got thoroughly examined and treated. They made it sound very firm, and this time they were really worried.

In the morning we were supposed to go to Tricity, and the next day I had the hospital booked. Dorota's brother arranged it all. That night I slept no more than four hours. I was really suffering. I was terrified by the thought that I would have to drive across the whole country. I'm still not sure how I did it. Today, I can barely remember any of it. Actually I have just one funny image from the trip …

We were just about to get in the car when somebody comes up to us, you know, a typical Polish guy with a moustache. He was maybe forty-five. He was yelling as he saw us: 'Miss Dorotka! Miss Dorotka! Could you please give me an autograph?'

He got the autograph, then his eyes suddenly got bigger and he asked if this was, perhaps, Mr Nergal. Dorota looked at me and then said to the guy, 'No, it's fucking Krzysztof Ibisz.'

Did you give the man the autograph, Mr Ibisz?

It was too late; he went away disappointed.

**It's strange that when we ask you about that day,
you remember something relatively trivial.**

That's how I am. I can focus on some silly stuff and worry about trifling matters, but when I'm really sick I look at the bright side of life. Somewhere in my head I always find optimistic scenarios.

**And it was with this optimism that you went to
the hospital?**

We were in Gdańsk by evening. I remember that my brother had sent me a text message because he was in Poland for a few days. He wanted to meet me, even for just a moment. I think he was due to return to Spain on exactly the same day as I was going in to hospital.

I evaded the meeting—or at least I tried to. I was just about to leave my apartment when I heard the doorbell. Paweł never gave up, and he paid me a surprise visit. He was there with his kids. I took him to the other room, briefly described the situation, and asked him not to tell our parents.

They didn't know anything?

I didn't want to upset them. Paweł promised not to say a word—he said he would keep his fingers crossed for me, and with that we said goodbye. Later, I finally got to the hospital.

What did the doctor say when he saw you?

'Please undress, take the blood test, and then we'll X-ray your lungs.' Standard procedures. But he obviously noticed that I had problems breathing, because he offered me additional oxygen.

Did he tell you to stay?

Yes, for three days I had various tests and examinations.

Did the doctors indicate what the problem might be?

No. They didn't want to upset me, I suppose. But I learned about their suspicions by accident.

I saw the message that was sent to Dorota. It touched upon three possible options. I have to admit that this message gave me chills, even though the first option it mentioned didn't seem too bad.

Tuberculosis was first on the list. Two or three months in the hospital, and then I could go home. I thought that wasn't the worst possible scenario. But then it got worse, because the doctors said it could also be lymphangioma or HIV. When I saw these last three letters I felt weak. Suddenly, flashing before my eyes like a twisted highlight reel, were all the sexual encounters of the last few years. There were quite a few, too, but as far as I could remember, I was always careful. I don't think I had ever had a random sexual encounter without protection. Anyway, there was only one thought in my head: 'Be *anything* but not HIV.'

When did you hear the final diagnosis?

After three days I was moved to another hospital, to the haematology ward of the Medical Academy in Gdańsk. They didn't tell me directly that it was a tumour, but there was evidence enough for me to draw a few conclusions of my own. They did a few more tests, and finally a doctor showed up at my bedside.

'You have leukaemia.'

That's exactly what he said. Nothing more. He just gave me my results. I waited until he left and then I burst into tears. Dorota was with me, and she also cried. It lasted a while—maybe two or three minutes. There was this huge, overwhelming feeling of debility.

Did you even know what leukaemia was?

I had no idea. I mean, I knew vaguely that it existed, and I knew that it was serious, maybe even terminal, but that was all I knew. So I wiped away the tears, picked up the phone, and started calling all the doctors I knew. The question was short and to the point: 'What is leukaemia, and how do I fight it?'

I quickly realised that I was in for a few months of serious battle.

How did you start it?

I'm sure it sounds strange, but I asked Dorota's brother to bring me an electric shaving machine. I decided that if I was to go into a battle, I needed a battle haircut. I shaved my hair; I only left a stripe in the middle. I was ready. I could begin to study my enemy.

What exactly did you find out?

That it was *lymphoblastic* leukaemia: very aggressive, but easier to defeat than *myeloid* leukaemia. It didn't attack me from a position of hiding; it showed itself right away.

Did you beat yourself up about not having gone to the hospital earlier?

It was only a matter of a few weeks. Besides, I asked the doctors if an earlier visit would have changed anything and they said no, even though my condition was relatively serious. I'm guessing that without immediate medical intervention, I would have lived maybe another month or two. There was about half a litre of water in my lungs. That's what was causing all the breathing problems.

How did it get there?

Sometimes water gathers in the lungs. Of course, not usually in such volume, but it does get there. And from there it's filtered away. In my lungs, there was something—as it later turned out, a bloated tumour—that was stopping it. So they put a drain in me.

I now had a hole in the side of my body. Like Jesus. The difference was that they didn't do it to me with a spear but with a special tube. For two days, gross red-yellowish liquid drained through it into a glass jar beside my bed.

Today when I look in the mirror, I see that scar—and two others from the central venous-line insertion—and I smile to myself. I give thanks to these wounds. They're my stigmata. The scar from the drain reminds me of my first victorious battle. When the water was drained out of my lungs,

I could breathe easily for the first time in many days. I felt stronger, and I could keep fighting.

Did you finally tell your parents about everything?
I called my dad first. I told him the story in great detail and I asked him to prepare my mother. Irena is a very sensitive person—sometimes I think her psyche is like that of a little girl.

What was her reaction?
It was wonderful. When my parents showed up at my bedside, they really surprised me. There was no drama in their behaviour. After all, I didn't need their crying; I just needed their support. And that's exactly what they gave me. They were very mature in their reaction.

When we talked about the time prior to your diagnosis, you were very tense. Now, when we talk about being in hospital, you seem relaxed. That's surprising.
It mirrors the state of my mind at that time. When I got to know my enemy, I stopped panicking and cooled down. Diagnosis was a blow, but the numbness and doubt didn't last long. I knew that I had a challenge. When you go through a dark forest and you know that there is something hiding in the dark, you start panicking. But when you see your enemy in the light, you focus on strategy, on how you will play it. I like fighting and playing, so I treated my sickness as a challenge, like a game of chess.

But ultimately you were playing with death. Didn't you have any moments of doubt?
Of course I did. There was this older guy on my ward—he might have been sixty-five or so. I called him Jankowski, because he reminded me of a famous priest from Gdańsk. He was the most positive guy in the whole hospital. He always told jokes; he kept everyone's spirits up. He had cancer, but he never showed that he was sick.

One day, they closed him down on the isolation ward. I was returning from a walk when he knocked on the glass and asked me to come to the window. He asked me how I was and wanted to know how I felt after my first chemo. He wished me all the best and … that's the last time I ever saw him. He died two days later.

That was one of the first moments when I thought that things might end in many different ways. There would be more of these moments in the weeks to come. I met a lot of people who are not here anymore.

Didn't that affect your optimism?

They say that your attitude toward sickness is vitally important. I didn't know if that was true, but I assumed that's just the way it was. So, with that in mind, even if I had moments of doubt, I tried very hard to ward off all negative thoughts.

I didn't want to die. That was my creed. I refused to accept the fact that my life would be aborted. I still had too much to do.

How did the treatment map out?

I tenderly called it 'throwing down the napalm'. It was a 'total' therapy, you could say. But a few days passed before any decision was made about how the treatment was going to proceed.

The most important decisions regarding the nature of my treatment were to be made by Professor Andrzej Hellmann, the head of the clinic. It was he who, at the very beginning, presented two distinct options to me. He spoke at length about them, but I had no idea what he meant on a medical level. All that I managed to deduce was that either we went with moderately strong chemo … or we went hardcore.

You had to decide on one of these options?

As you can imagine, I didn't have to think for long. I don't really like half-solutions in my life, so I chose the radical way.

Leukaemia attacked me fast and brutally, so I deemed it necessary to retaliate in the same way.

Weren't you afraid that you wouldn't be able to handle it?

I don't think so. I already felt better than before my admittance to hospital—much better, in fact. The strategy of total war with cancer actually seemed quite exciting to me. Everything was filled with this kind of military terminology and metaphors. It was not a hospital, but more a front line, and I was already in the trenches from where there was no retreat. I acted according to the famous quote from *Art of War* by Sun Tzu: 'If you know the enemy and know yourself, you need not fear the result of a hundred battles.'

How many rounds of chemo did you receive?

Before the light therapy I took two full cycles: that equates to four chemo sessions in total. Then, as a precaution, I had to take one more before the transplant.

How did you feel after the chemo treatments?

At the beginning it was really bad. It literally brought me to my knees. I remember that for a few days I was so weak, I couldn't even stretch. I felt completely powerless; I was lying in bed for most of the time. The biggest problem, however, was vomiting, or, more specifically, trying to prevent it.

A few years earlier, I had almost choked to death on my own vomit.

A very rock'n'roll death that would have been.

Bon Scott died that way. Jimi Hendrix did too. In my case it was a really close-run thing. It was after the last concert of the *Demigod* promotional tour. We played in Gdynia at the Ucho club. After the gig, of course, there was a small party. I didn't drink much, but I had a few vodkas with Red Bull. I was home by about two in the morning, and I immediately went to bed.

I woke up before five, nauseated. I lived alone at the time. I crawled to the shitter and I put two fingers down my throat, as I always did in such situations. The problem was that whatever left my stomach didn't make it to my mouth but instead blocked my gullet.

Suddenly, my nose got clogged, I couldn't breathe, my eyes bulged from their sockets, and I fell to the floor. For about a minute I was saying my goodbyes to the world. Finally, something down there moved and I started coming back to life, slowly catching my breath. Since then I have just never vomited. I couldn't. It was too much of a trauma.

So you didn't vomit even once after chemo?
Not even once. I made it through. Of course, that was mostly thanks to the humongous amounts of anti-nausea medicines that I begged the doctors for. I was really lucky that they worked for me, because they don't for a lot of people. They were vomiting like crazy.

Did you avoid all the other common side effects?
It varied. There were nights when I was delirious, and I had some strange visions, probably due to the medicines I was taking. There were also some moments of unusual illumination, so much so that I wanted to take a notebook and write down everything that came to me via this stream of consciousness. But I was too weak. And I constantly felt terrible.

Chemo was the worst. It seriously damaged the mucous membrane of my oral cavity. A lot of patients ended up with bleeding, wounded gums, and they couldn't eat normally. They were fed intravenously. Before my chemo, I talked to people who had already been through it. Somebody gave me a great piece of advice: they told me to suck on ice cubes.

Did it work?
I think so, because I found it all reasonably tolerable. I had a thermos by my bed filled with ice cubes, and I always had at least one cube in my mouth. When it melted, I spat it out and took another one.

Were there any tricks to keeping your hair?
Oh, no. Every hair on my whole body was gone. I felt quite strange. All pale, no hair, like a huge toddler. I overheard two nurses talking once. They were going through my papers when one of them looked at the other and, pointing at my bed, she asked, 'This boy right there is thirty-four years old?'

No point in pretending that you didn't look a bit odd.
I was surprised at my appearance myself, but I was also curious. There was something fascinating about the metamorphosis that I went through. It was my body, but at the same time it wasn't entirely mine. I tried to look at myself as a participant in some strange experiment—as a guinea pig. I didn't feel any repulsion when I looked in the mirror though. I was, after all, watching myself.

From a distance, though?
You could say that. In fact, I always try to look at myself from a distance; it makes life easier. It made the fight with sickness a lot easier, too.

Pictures from that time didn't make it into glossy magazines. Did the paparazzi let you off the hook?
Hyenas are attracted to a carcass. They took a few photos of me but they weren't published anywhere. I have no idea why. It's hard to imagine the tabloid bosses having any conscience.

How did the paparazzi manage to photograph you?
That's a longer story. When I got to the hospital, there was total insanity. When the media found out about me being sick, there was a whole queue of shady types with cameras, camped out in front of the building. For a few days they limited themselves to hunting down Dorota. They took pictures of her when she was walking into the hospital and they did likewise when she was leaving. With time, that was not enough, and it was then that they started hunting me.

Did they try to get on the ward you were on?
They barged in there by force. They insulted the nurses, a few of whom stood in their way, so they started struggling with them. I was so fucking pissed that I really wanted to get out of my room and just fucking beat the shit out of them. I was on steroid therapy at the time so my emotions were definitely heightened. Something broke in me that day, so I talked to

Dorota and we decided to hire bodyguards. Actually, she said that it was our only available option. She organised and financed everything. Besides, I wasn't strong enough, and I didn't have enough money.

Were they by your side all the time?
Yes, there were a few of them there. They took shifts: one of them worked days, the other one did nights. We still keep in touch to this day. They were very helpful and turned out to be really wholehearted people. Not only did they guard me from intruders from the outside but they also helped me in everyday situations.

Did they scare the paparazzi away?
If an asshole like that senses blood, there's no stopping him. One day, two of these vultures dressed as doctors. They visited the rooms, as if they were doing a round. Fortunately, they were quickly exposed.

On another occasion, one of the bodyguards ran into my room with a huge green sheet and started covering the windows. I had no idea what was going on. It turned out that the ward I was on was being renovated, and there was scaffolding in front of it. Some of those guys were so desperate, they climbed up the scaffolding to take a picture of me. As I later found out, one of them managed to shoot Nergal half-naked on a hospital bed, and I'm still waiting for these photos to be published in some tabloid magazine.

Maybe these editors have some inhibitions after all?
I doubt that.

Didn't you ever consider treatment abroad? You could have avoided all this, and the conditions might have been better.
I heard this a lot. 'You have the money. You can go and get treated somewhere quiet.' That's what they said to me. From a financial standpoint it wasn't that easy, but such a thought did cross my mind.

The problem, however, was time. Sickness kept attacking, and we had to act immediately. Looking for another hospital could have been risky. I would be probably still paying back my debts now, too. Besides, there is no place for a doctor's creativity when treating leukaemia. It's a standard therapy, the same everywhere in the whole world. The medicines are the same, too.

Of course, I did my research quickly. I asked people who knew about the issue, and I found out that it was not easy to find a specialist who is as good as doctor Hellmann. But I had other doubts.

The Medical Academy buildings are not really very modern; they're notoriously sad, dark, and daunting. I wondered—at least at the beginning—if such conditions would hinder my struggle. Ultimately, some other factors affected my decision, too. Staying in Gdańsk kept me close to my home, my family, my friends—the people whose presence and support I cared about. I have no idea how I would have managed without their help. My mother and father were with me the whole time. That was so damn important to me. I could also afford long phone conversations; that was really vital for me, too. Besides, if I had a break from the hospital—a day-pass—it only took me ten-to-fifteen minutes to get home.

Did they let you go home often?
I did leave a few times—in the breaks between particular chemo cycles. But those were short passes. Most of the time I was sitting in the hospital room.

How did you cope with all that on a normal day?
I worked. Or at least I tried to work. I had my own system. I called it 'ramming the harpoon'. In short, it was about doing everything I could to get mobilised. I didn't think about the present; I made plans for the future. And whenever I planned something, I always tried to do it, step by step, as if there was no other way. Every toehold was of vital significance. I felt better with each one. Work made everything make sense and I fought for the band as well as for myself.

But how is it possible to work as a man with leukaemia, tied to a hospital bed?
I had lots to do, actually. I had a computer; I had a phone, so I could make

moves. Working on our *Evangelia Heretica* DVD took me a few weeks, for example. I designed the cover—the whole layout. I took care of all the details. Every day I would just sit with the phone in my hand and talk to the graphic designer, the publisher, and the guys from the band.

When I was so weak that I could not even move my hand, then—for a while—Orion would take over and continue with the work. Whenever I felt better again, I was right back in the game. When the DVD was finally out, I sat on my bed and signed a thousand copies for the fans. It took me two days.

**Did it ever occur to you that these autographs
might have been your last ones?**
It did cross my mind. But I fought thoughts like these. On some deeper level, I really just wanted to feel wanted. What if I don't make it? What if I lose the battle with this sickness? Even if that turned out to be the case, at least a thousand of my fans would be happy. I assumed a motto that I cling to until this day: I treat everything as if it's the last thing I will ever do in my life. I put all my heart into it. *That* gives me a kick.

What else kept you fighting?
Do you remember that cartoon, 'Once Upon A Time … Life'? I viewed a similar movie in my head, every night before I fell sleep. I imagined an army of red blood cells marching on the ultimate battle to defeat the sickness. It was like a ritual. It helped me to program my psyche—to direct it toward fighting. I wanted to be focused and ready for action at all times. I avoided numbness or apparent calmness. I did everything not to give up. *Peace is only for the dead and the dying*, as the New Model Army song goes. And I was still alive …

How did you manage to maintain that discipline?
Despite everything, it wasn't so hard. Being in hospital is a bit like being in the army. Or like in prison. Each day looks the same.

You get up at six. The nurse would come into my room. I normally get up much later, so I was usually half-conscious when she showed up. I just gave her my hand; she took my blood and set up the drip. When she left, I tried to fall asleep again. I woke up again for breakfast at around eight o' clock. Then I checked my mail and started working.

There was no time to relax?

There was a lot of time for everything. I decided to change the appearance of my room, for example. I started with the cross. I took it off the wall, and in its place I hung a rosary with Mahomet's figurine. Next to it there were portraits of Bruce Lee, Crowley, and Nietzsche—characters who inspired and turned me on in different periods of my life.

Later, I hung a golden medal next to them—one that was brought to me by a friend. It turned out that some anonymous man ran a marathon in Gdańsk for me. He won the medal and decided to give it to me as a token of his support. It really meant a lot to me.

When my isolation room looked a bit cosier, I got addicted to watching movie serialisations. I fell in love with *Spartacus*—the one where Andy Whitfield played the main part. I learned by accident that he was diagnosed with lymphangioma during the shoot. Then they said that he had overcome it and they were shooting another season. My story corresponded beautifully with the theme of the series, and the hero became twice as heroic in my eyes for me. Just like him, I wanted to come back, because what I feared most was that I would never go onstage again. The stage shaped me, hardened me; it was my element. Can you even imagine how much strength it gave me?

But in the end, Andy lost his fight with cancer.

I found that out a few weeks later. That news daunted me a little. Fortunately there were other heroes who had won their fights. I'm a huge fan of *Dexter*, for example. It's one of my absolute favourite shows. The actor who played the main part, Michael C. Hall, also had a type of lymph-node cancer. He underwent chemo between seasons. He beat cancer and came back and shot two more. That was a strong kick for me.

Did you read in hospital?
Habitually. I made up for the last few years.

What did you read?
I was under the spell of Robert A. Heinlein's *Stranger In A Strange Land*. And Cormac McCarthy's *Blood Meridian*.

The latter isn't really the most optimistic read though?
But it's perfect! I actually read various books. I had the Bible with me and, for contrast, Richard Dawkins's books. In one of them I found something that really turned me on. He described an experiment conducted on two groups of seriously sick people. There were masses conducted in church for the people in one group. People prayed for its members. The other group was left to fend for itself. Of course, both were treated normally. It turned out that differences in these people's states and self-feeling were negligible— so much so that that the numbers could in fact be a statistical error.

Nothing particularly revelatory there, then.
But that's not the whole story. There's another more interesting element. The most surprising conclusions came from the second phase of the experiment. That's when the first group was actually told that they were being prayed for, and that they had this spiritual support.

Did they recover?
On the contrary! Those patients' results suddenly got worse.

Did Dawkins interpret it in any particular way?
I think he left it with no comment. But just think. You're sick, and you know that somebody prays for you. *If they're praying for me, I must be in a really bad shape.* That's surely your first thought. Besides, when you're a religious person and you know that somebody is praying for you, when you believe that it can help you, then you give yourself to God and relax. You let go, because you think it's not you who influences the results of the battle.

People prayed for you, too.

I even got a special certificate from one of the Polish religious communities in Berlin. It was official confirmation that the members of a particular community had got together and prayed for me. My friend Kikut from Pneuma also came to the hospital. He's a real practicing Catholic. He also tried to pray for me. I kept telling him, 'Fuck, man, give me a break, or, at least don't do it when you're here.'

Did he listen to you?

I don't know, but I can't imagine that he would give up very easily.

But your results didn't get worse as a result?

They couldn't, because I don't believe in that bullshit. I think it had a reverse effect. Kikut really cheered me up.

There were also people who interpreted the commandment of love in a little different way. They said that your sickness was a punishment for sins; that Nergal now had one last chance to convert.

I read about that. I even got emails, often full of hatred and contempt. Sometimes I wanted to write back in a really harsh way. But I let it go. What do I need that for? The only effect these people achieved was that I became even more firm in my convictions.

VIII

THE COLD
WAR

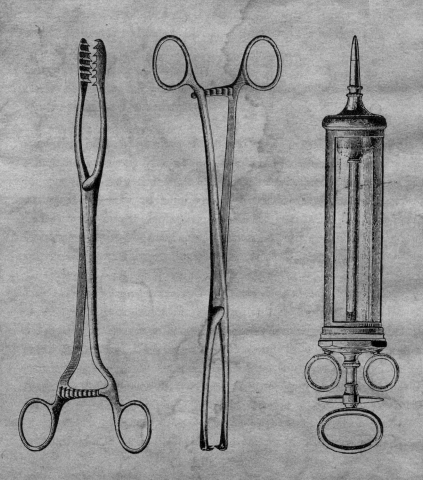

Why did you dump Dorota?
What kind of question is that?

The papers said you behaved badly and insensitively.
And you actually believe that bullshit?

People are presented with simple facts: he picked her up, used her, and dumped her. That fits your image, because you keep saying you're the alpha male.
But I'm not like that 24/7. And that's what Dorota had a problem with. She expected that I would always be like that, no matter whether I was sick or healthy and if it was sunny or rainy—like a comic-book character.

You couldn't show your weaknesses?
I took Dorota for a date abroad; we went to Prague. I got a cold. It happens. No big deal, just a fever and a runny nose. But there was no mercy shown. She was fucking pissed that we had three days off and I was indisposed.

Maybe you complained too much?
I like to complain. Everyone likes to complain when they're sick. I value people who, in that situation, don't press you and just take care of you. And I pay back the same way.

Maybe Dorota was afraid that if she gave you too much space, you would complain in every situation?
In my normal disposition I fly high, never low. Maybe she just didn't know that ...

But later, when you were fighting leukaemia, you didn't complain.
That was a war for my life, not just a runny nose. You react differently when mosquitoes bite you than when you stand in front of a lion. Of course, I

170

had moments of weakness. When I was in the hospital I complained, too, but it took a while.

Did your illness destroy your relationship?

It certainly sped up the process of decay. It was a catalyst for all the doubts. But I tried to turn a blind eye to many things. When you're in love, you ignore certain signals or push them down into your subconscious. In hospital, all these thoughts crawled out of my head and I started wondering what really connected me with my partner. And, unfortunately, I saw more discords than harmonic notes.

On the outside, though, you both kept your cool. A very simple message was sent to the outside world: you were fighting cancer and she supported your every step.

That was true to some extent. I can't say a bad word about her involvement. She did what she could and she did it because she wanted to. There was no strategy in it or playing for the crowd, as some people suggested. If something started to rot, it was not because of bad intentions, but more because of a huge difference between our characters and priorities. We were from different worlds, and a critical condition brought that to light.

Did any cracks show up earlier?

Much earlier. I started to suffocate terribly, even though I had a lot of genuine feelings for her. I really cared about her—maybe even too much. I got so involved that I gave up too much ground at the very beginning. After all, every relationship is a compromise. In this case, however, it was different. Never before in a relationship with a woman had I been so tolerant, elastic, and conciliatory. But even saying that, I really felt that our compatibility was flawed.

Do you mean chemistry, fascination … ?

It was an enchantment, sure. Everything blossomed beautifully at the beginning. We wanted to be together despite all the obstacles. We turned a blind eye to what divided us, but the rose-coloured glasses started falling off my nose after a while. Even before my illness, we had a few serious arguments. For six months we lived like a married couple. During that time I packed my bags twice and moved out of her place.

What divided you?

I moved to Warsaw for Dorota. I left my friends and family in Gdańsk. I needed contact with them, so I would often spend hours on the phone with them. For her, that was a sign of weakness in that, in critical situations, I sought help or support by calling a friend. In Warsaw I had no one to talk to. Rational dialogue with Dorota was almost always impossible.

You agreed to it, though.

Yes, because at first I saw a sweet and fantastic woman. Only with time did I realise that there was an intellectual gap between us—that there was no bridge to connect us intellectually. This relationship was a misalliance. It doesn't have to mean that it was wrong; my whole life is based on extremes after all. So I believed in that misalliance deeply and sincerely. I pushed all the doubts somewhere deep.

And what did your friends tell you?

They kept their distance. I take pride in the fact that my friends are very mature people. They never judged me or, for that matter, Dorota. They always tried to give me good advice, even when I was sad and bitter. It would have been easy to say, 'You know what? Just dump her, or she's going to wreck your life.' Instead, I would often hear, 'If you're happy in this relationship, it's OK. We're happy for you.'

But you were not happy.

Remember, I had been independent my whole life. I had my own apartment, my own car, my own job and passion … I valued the liberty and space I had. Suddenly everything changed. I was suddenly a guest in somebody's house.

I had a designated wardrobe and toothbrush, but that's where my space ended. I was overwhelmed. From every wall there was Dorota looking at me. Doda's figurines, Doda's photos, a painting of Doda … I felt like I was in a museum. It was constraining me second by second.

Was she a bad woman?

It was more a question of her nature, not any bad intentions, per se. Dorota is just very dominating. She openly admits that she has a lot of manly features. And there is something to that. She's a testosterone-woman, no doubt. She used to play sports and she still loves rivalry. One day we had an idea: *let's do paintball!* We were supposed to go with our friends. *Let's make teams, it'll be fun!* She agreed, but under the sole condition that we are in *opposite* teams.

'Why?' I asked.

'Cos I want to kick your ass!'

It was a joke, of course, but the whole situation illustrates her attitude toward men rather accurately.

She was much younger than you. Age has its issues.

I was aware of that. You suggested previously that maybe I should have gone for an older woman. I actually do lack that kind of woman in my life, but not necessarily from a love perspective. I'm thinking more of an older sister influence. I have a brother, as you know, but he lives in Spain and our characters differ. A female version of that, maybe? Yes, I feel quite a gap there. I would need a kind of female/educator/acquaintance—somebody who would explain everything to me, comfort me when I needed it, take my hand and walk me through life. Like in The Doors' song: 'Girl you gotta love your man, take him by the hand, and make him understand …'

You're saying that as if you never had a mother.

With parents, the situation is that they take care of you until you reach a certain age, then the roles are reversed: you become independent, you cut off the umbilical cord … and then they start to need *you*. Parents become naïve like children in this very sweet way. I'm beginning to be that kind of a guide for Irena and Zenek in today's world. Of course they're still functional and self-reliant and they still help me, but the relationship is different from how it was a few years ago. Nowadays I take over quite often.

But you couldn't take over with Dorota?

Normally I'm more than capable of pounding a table with my fist; I was like that in most of my relationships. In this case, however, it was different. As I said, I gave up way too much ground at the very beginning. At one point, I had the impression that I was standing against a wall, banging my head against it. It was unbreakable. I didn't know what to do. But I was stuck with it because I was deeply in love, and I was honest. I wanted to keep that relationship at all costs.

Maybe it didn't work out simply because one egocentric met another?

Artists, people of the stage, often have tendencies like that. I am an egocentric; I don't deny that, and that's probably why I became a musician. But in this situation I let go. I didn't press. But Dorota? Maybe we were two magnetic poles pushing away from each other—such an artistic combination.

Here's a typical evening: she comes back from performing at the theatre, and he says, 'Hey, I'll play you a great song!'

'Maybe later,' she replies, 'I'm tired now. *I* played a great role tonight, though.'

You know how it is: 'Me, me, me! Mine is more important! I, me, mine!'

When did you realise that this building would soon collapse?

In the hospital. Medicine, chemo, proximity of death—all that made me look at the world differently. I began to ask myself questions: What do I need? What do I care about? What do I expect from life?

I wanted to talk about it with Dorota. When someone close to you is sick—terminally sick, even—maybe one should retreat into the background. It's not the time or place for power struggles, but Dorota saw it differently.

She wouldn't let go, and I began noticing that more and more vividly. I needed closeness and understanding, not a chessboard and head games.

And other people?

My close friends came to visit. My parents could take everything I threw at them. I could pour all my frustrations out on them and they wouldn't even blink. Every other day my friend Krzysiek Sadowski was at my bedside; he would bring soup from his mother, Lidia. He would come for half an hour, but what mattered was that I could talk to him; he spent this time with me.

Kikut also visited. He prayed; it pissed me off but I knew that he did it because he really wanted to help. Another friend once brought a whole bag of sushi. I couldn't eat raw stuff so I called my parents. It was the first time that they had ever eaten stuff like that and they fell in love with it.

My friend Patrycja also visited me; she would cook broth for me. Poles believe it's a life-giving soup; personally I don't, but it was nice. I got lots of food—also some types I, theoretically, couldn't eat—smuggled in by Maciej Gruszka and his wife, Agnieszka.

You guys were also there for me. *Everyone* supported me as much as they could. I remember once that Rafal Szyjer came to visit; he wanted to play the guitar with me. I couldn't even sit at the time, far less play guitar. I just laid there in some kind of lethargy, but he grabbed the instrument and started playing anyway. He didn't say a word for two hours. There was no need to. I was lying down, listening to his music. I even thought it would be a nice soundtrack to my death, because I felt like I was dying. Fortunately, a few months later, we could play together.

Dorota also visited regularly?

She could sit with me for twelve hours. But she was there only physically. I felt quite a shortage of empathy and understanding.

Maybe she was tired of the situation?

I'm sure she was. I told her frequently, 'Honey, you don't have to be here for twelve hours. An hour is enough, but only if you actually spend that time with me. *Talk* to me.' And she just sat there, looking for new shoes for an upcoming event …

I think that was when I made the decision. I felt it was ready to collapse.

But you didn't break up in hospital?

In spite of all that I tried to keep it going. Less than a month after leaving hospital I got in the car and drove to Warsaw for Valentine's Day. I felt enormous stress; I was torn apart. One part of me wanted to spend time with Dorota; the other part screamed 'No!'

The party itself was great. We made sushi together. On the outside we shined with our smiles, but inside everything was going down. We painted the grass green without noticing that it was rotting under the paint.

That night I didn't sleep in the bedroom; I slept on the sofa. I woke up before morning and just started to cry. I couldn't hold back the tears. I stared at the ceiling and had no idea what to do with myself. I knew that Dorota would wake up in the afternoon, and I had nowhere to go.

I called Pablo from Piaty Element. He was kind of my Warsaw soulmate. He came to get me and took me for coffee. We talked for a long time. When I got back, it was much better; I had a grip on my emotions. When I was driving back to Gdańsk, I felt relief. Five more hours and I'd be home. No fighting, struggling … but I cared all the same. Dorota did too. But it was rotten. I started sending signals. I became more and more assertive. Before, I treated her like a baby. I was always the 'smart' one, but I couldn't take it any longer.

After the illness, I started exercising. I was becoming stronger, and not just physically. And she, in turn, was taking care of her new album. Everything was falling apart—until it finally collapsed for good. Another argument on the phone, another misunderstanding … this was the last time. I hung up and immediately felt like my wings were back on.

Did she burn your stuff?

I received a picture of my stuff burning, yes. Her reaction was, as always, very emotional. I wasn't surprised.

Then what happened?

We met once more in Warsaw. I knew it was over, but … it was agony. There was just no point in talking about it and scratching old wounds—either hers or mine. I came back to my own reality and Dorota returned to her own world.

What do you mean?

There was this paparazzo. He would follow me nonstop; he spied on me for weeks. I lived in her apartment in the Mokotów district at the time. One day, I drove to the Stodola Club in town to take care of some formalities. He was on my tail the whole time. I weaved my way around, tried various tricks, but I just couldn't lose him. My irritation reached its peak and I stopped in the middle of the street and started honking. I just wanted to force a reaction from him. He didn't do anything.

A moment passed and I drove further. I was pumped beyond belief. I stopped my car on the parking lot in front of Stodola; he did too. I wanted to punch him in the face. He made a scene: 'What the fuck are you doing? Why are you trying to make this hard for us?' He pointed at his car and the bumps on it and told me that by taking Dorota, I had taken away his means of earning a living. He yelled at me that he'd been chasing her since the beginning, but now he had no money for food, far less to renovate his car. She was like a tree for them, and they were like tree-huggers.

You broke up, but the paparazzi didn't let you go.

It got even worse. In Gdańsk they surrounded the Musicollective music school. Rafal Szyjer—the guy who played the guitar so beautifully for me in hospital—was the manager there. I liked going there to jam with other musicians, and those maggots with cameras noticed that. I was inside, I looked out the window, and I saw two of them …

A lot of bullshit had appeared in the popular press about my romances. It all began when I was still in hospital. Supposedly, when I had leukaemia, I cheated on Dorota. I didn't deny or acknowledge anything. I don't talk to such media. But it did irritate me a little. My image wasn't the issue;

beautiful women don't spoil it. To really piss me off, they would probably have to write that I fuck goats. I was more irritated by the fact that they were peeking into my pants. So I said to Rafal, 'Man, let's do it this way: we walk out of here holding hands, we approach my car, you give me a tender kiss, and I go away. We're going to absolutely fuck up the system.'

We burst out laughing, but after a while Rafal spread his arms and said, 'I can't, I teach kids here! Parents already look at the school in a strange way because they know you come here. If there's a gossip that I'm gay, I'll go broke.' That's Poland for you.

Would they have bought that anyway?

It would have at least been funny.

I met Radek Majdan some time ago. We'd been trying to get in touch for some time. I'd met a lot of his friends and I often heard that he was simply a cool guy. 'You have to meet, you'll like each other'—our mutual friends told me that often. Well, truth be told, we had similar experiences. We were being compared; in a way, you could say we also shared a bed. I simply wanted to meet him.

It actually happened at a party, among a horde of photographers. We bear-hugged each other and talked for about thirty minutes. We had a few drinks and exchanged phone numbers. It was nice—as if like I'd already known him for five years, not just five minutes.

After the party, a guy from *Fakt* came up to me. 'What did you talk about with Radek? Is it a secret? Tell us!' He fawned like a dog, but he was slimy like a reptile.

I made a surprised face and said, 'Oh, you don't know? We're a couple!'

I looked at him with pity and went the other way. I didn't even turn around.

But you've said that sometimes you exploded when you saw the paparazzi on the horizon?

They're like cockroaches. Sometimes you ignore them; sometimes you chase them. When I was a student I lived in one of these university buildings, and

I sometimes hunted these bugs. I would come back to the apartment a little drunk and on my tiptoes, very quietly, and I'd approach a kitchen cupboard with a can of deodorant and a lighter in my hands and open one of the doors quickly. There would be dozens of them, and I'd kill them with fire. They sizzled beautifully. And, equally, I occasionally chased a few paparazzi.

Did you ever hit any of them?
No.

They wrote that you beat one of them up.
He fell down himself. It was a few months after I left hospital. I planned a morning Nordic walking session. I instantly felt that there was someone lurking nearby. A moment later I recognised the guy. I'd seen him hanging around my house before. He was one of the worst hyenas and a total pussy at the same time. I usually lost him with my car in a matter of seconds.

He didn't see me this time, so I thought I'd scare him a bit. I ran to my garage and got in my car. I started the car and with tires screeching I stopped in front of him. When I got out, this fucker started to run. I tried to chase him, but I was still rather weak after the sickness, so my legs were like jelly and I hit the concrete with my face.

In the corner of my eye I saw my fitness coach running on the other side of the street. He must have seen everything from afar. 'Get him!' I shouted. He tried to catch him, but the paparazzo fell down. He fell on his own camera. We had him. He started wailing: 'Police! Poliiiice!'

I didn't even touch him; I just looked at his face with disgust and hissed. 'Get the fuck out of my life, you pussy!'

**But the guy went to the police and reported
that you beat him up?**
And he waited in front of the police station with his buddies. They had their cameras and camcorders ready. It was all beautifully directed. He sued me and then continued to lurk to take more pictures. Fucking opportunist! I didn't want him to make any profit on them, so my attorney drove me into

the station in the trunk of his car. The police officers turned out to be cool. They absolutely understood the shit I was dealing with everyday. I gave my deposition and went back home. I was never called upon again about the issue, so I can only assume that the investigation was discontinued. But it still doesn't change the fact that this guy deserves to get a solid whooping.

Why?

A few months earlier, I was out of the hospital for a few days between chemo sessions. I went to get my girlfriend from the airport. The very same paparazzo had been lurking around with his buddies since morning. There was a similar situation: they tried my patience and I tried to chase them. I was extremely exhausted, so I literally fell on my face. I scratched my hands and knees and drew blood. I lifted my head up and saw this cunt standing fifteen metres away, cackling.

Do you regret getting involved at moments like that?

I actually live in two worlds. One of them is mine. I was raised in it; everything there goes slowly, according to its own rhythm. That part is my actual life. In the second world, on the other hand, I always play some kind of a role. I don't know who or why I was made to play it, and I end up in the tabloid newspapers as a consequence. It just happened. I don't care about this world. I don't belong there; I'm just a guest.

I actually think a lot of people exist on the vague boundaries of these two worlds. I once talked to the journalist and TV presenter Tomasz Lis about the paparazzi. He was in a similar situation to me. Once he caught one of these people. And because he's quite big and formidable, he held the guy so that he was literally suspended above the ground. Lis really wanted to punch the guy in the face but he managed to contain himself. He didn't cross the line. And neither did I.

Doesn't that piss you off that you can't meet a girl, because the tabloids will be all over it?

Who said I can't?

**There are occasionally stories about Nergal's
new girlfriends …**
In Gdańsk I have no problems meeting anyone. It's my turf, and it's more
difficult to catch me here. I have a lot of female acquaintances and friends
that I sometimes meet for lunch or dinner. I'm not anonymous, but there
are places where I can show up with a girl and I can be sure that nobody's
going to take our pictures or call the tabloids. It's much worse in Warsaw. A
simple meeting for a coffee with a friend, and the next day it turns out we
have a brewing romance.

Were you in any relationship after Dorota?
No.

So all the media hearsay was bullshit?
I'd been seeing a couple of girls, but it was nothing serious. I was in a moment
in my life where I just didn't want to get involved. I'd got a grip. I'd got on the
right track and I was focused on realising all my professional plans.

At the moment there is no place for another person in my life. I'm very
clear about that. If I meet someone, I explain the situation immediately:
'Honey, you can have me, but only until four o'clock, then I'm unavailable;
I'm going on tour. I will be back in a month; we can meet again but don't
count on it.' I think that's honest, isn't it?

**Aren't you afraid that some 'honey' will try to get
recognition because of you?**
Maybe it's naïve but I don't think so. I don't think I've ever met a girl like
that. Maybe once. She loved disco music but I quickly cut contact with her.

Is Warsaw out of your system completely?
Not entirely. I like Warsaw, I like it very much, but I live in Gdańsk.

Do you have a place in the capital?
No, but I'm thinking about it. Czeslaw Mozil has given me a spare key to

his apartment. I complained to him that whenever I show up with some girl in the city, they immediately make her my new girlfriend.

He smiled and said, 'Where are you taking them? Go to some dingy pub in Praga district, they won't catch you there. Or, better still, take her to my place!'

And so he gave me the key. When he's not home, I take advantage of it, sometimes …

Are you close?
He's a great guy and we have a lot in common.

Some people claim that you even copy him a little.
We've been through similar trouble, and we think similarly. He is also a guy from nowhere. He wasn't born in the spotlight; he got there by accident, and he did it with a bang. I met him when he lived in Denmark. He came to see our concert; we had a lot of fun and it stayed that way. A strong feeling of autonomy and independence connects us. One day we're on TV, and the next day we drink beer in some joint on Zabkowska Street. He's authentic and honest in what he does, and I treat him like he's my little brother in some ways. We call each other, I support this guy in everything he does, and I know I can count on the same in return. He's a real expert when it comes to women. He often gives me valuable tips and tells me what mistakes I am making.

Was your relationship with Dorota a mistake?
No other relationship taught me so much about life. It's difficult to call something like that a mistake. It gave me knowledge and made me richer inside. I have never known so much about human beings as I did when I lived in Warsaw. For this experience, and not only for it, I am very grateful to Dorota. Besides, she showed me a lot of amazing things. Sometimes very small things, but our life consists of small details as well. Maybe it sounds stupid, but thanks to her I discovered Indian cuisine, and I've become a huge fan of it.

NERGAL   †   Confessions of a Heretic

You're rather careful when speaking about Dorota.
Are you afraid of airing dirty laundry in public?
It's a question of manners. I speak openly about my feelings; that's why
we talk after all. But I don't want to play dirty. Some time ago I denied an
interview to a journalist, who often played dirty games with Dorota in some
sick and twisted way. I told him directly that he was a piece of shit in my
eyes. His face looked like I had killed his mother.

You're friends with Kuba Wojewódzki, the Polish
comedian and talk show host. He sneered at Dorota
a bit, too; were there any problems there?
He's a very smart guy with a great sense of humour, which I like. Even if he
sometimes crosses the line, I think he's very useful. He says what he thinks.
He bashes *everything*; that's his job. He bashed me, too, but I've always felt
a sense of warmth behind these insults.

Dorota and I did have an argument about him once, though. We were
channel-hopping one evening and she stopped on his channel for a second.
'Wait! Wait! Let's watch it!' I shouted. And there it started. She accused me
of being disloyal. For her, loyalty must have meant that I should feel the
same thing as she does about every person. Dorota had a very peculiar view
on these issues. Sometimes I even got the impression that she wanted me to
log on to random internet forums to defend her from attacks by anonymous
people. It was the same with Kuba: she thought I should get in my car and
drive to punch him in the face because he dared make a joke about her on TV.

What if somebody had really insulted her?
Would you have punched him in the face?
Of course. I didn't have any situations like that with Dorota, but I remember,
some years ago, that some tramp attacked Celina in a very unrefined way.
We were at a train station, going to Torun. Suddenly, a bum came up to
us. He was boorish and impudent. I didn't say anything; I just waited. But
when he started grabbing Celina, I couldn't hold it much longer. I kicked
him in the head. Literally.

Do you like fighting?

There are moments in life when you just have to fucking punch someone in the face. I used to be a volcano of emotions. As a twenty-something I did things that only make me laugh today. I had a girlfriend; her name was Kasia. We are actually good friends to this day. I was deeply in love then, but the situation was much more complex, because there was this 'other guy' on the scene. Things like that undermine the foundations. Nothing strikes a man as much as when there is a rival in the picture. No way is everyone getting out alive.

Did you beat him up?

He got battered physically. I was battered emotionally after that skirmish. In such a situation, even in a medium-sized dude like me, there's a titan who can destroy the whole world.

That was a long time ago. What about today?

It's not easy to change your character. Still, if something is not right for me, my negative emotions are sent out to the whole world. On the other hand, when I'm really happy, everybody feels my love. With time, though, there's more and more harmony in me. When I'm pissed off, I'm not as furious as I used to be, but it's also more difficult for me to be uncontrollably and childishly happy.

I must have come to terms with that fact that the strength of a man lies in his ability to pass some things over in silence and not get into emotional scrambles. It's good when a man has this kind of stoic calmness in him. He can't just be a mutt who jumps at someone's legs. A big strong dog ignores smaller ones.

IX

THE VISION
AND THE VOICE

A nice juror on a TV show or a radical black-metal musician. Which Nergal is real?

Both. Or neither. Depends on the who's looking.

They're just masks?

The real Nergal is in constant movement. He constantly searches. Like in Witold Gombrowicz's books. I escape from one form and I fall into another. I don't stay there too long because I'm always changing.

First and foremost, I'm a musician, but I don't limit myself. I don't want to close myself in any ghetto. I take up new challenges, I will try to write, and I may try to find my place on the TV screen if possible—who knows what's next.

Do you have a problem with your identity?

It's more of a comfort than a problem. I don't have to stick to any given canons, and even if I do, it's simply because I like them.

Which one of you likes it?

All of 'me'. Nergal is a process. I'm still becoming. *Panta rei*. It's the same with the music I play. Behemoth still escapes the schemata.

These escapes are not too radical, though.

It's relative. Of course, we are not as radical as, for instance, Ulver. We don't meander between primitive black metal, acoustic folk, and modern electronics like they do. They're great, and I admire their attitude, but we're Behemoth, not Ulver. We're also not like AC/DC, who have nurtured their fans in such a fashion that any deviation from their style is perceived as sacrilege. We nurture our fans differently.

There are constant elements in our music. There is also a similar dose of extremity and, there is always—I hope—consistently comparable quality. What's also unwavering is our honesty. The rest is fluid. I like that combination, and the fact that we can play what you might call 'technical twisters' but also simultaneously evoke simplicity.

But you don't go beyond metal?

No, because we love it! It may be my biggest musical love and I want to embrace it. It's our niche. But believe me: if ever a moment comes that I don't feel these sounds, I will leave that arena and start playing something else. Behemoth will never pretend.

What about the other guys' opinion? Could you imagine Inferno drumming to alternative music, say?

You'd be surprised! He recently convinced me to listen to Jane's Addiction, whom I absolutely couldn't take. The 'idiot drummer' is just a myth functioning among musicians. Inferno has a really unique taste in music. He plays the guitar better than I play the drums, and he can also make do on a keyboard. He might look like a metal radical, but I know him and I know his sensitivity runs in various directions. He loves Killing Joke, he adores Polish protest songs from the 40s; he also turns to new-wave stuff from time to time.

Isn't it trendy to do so, these days?

I don't know much about trends.

Is Behemoth trendy?

I hope so.

Some artists might consider that to be an insult.

Some people go with the flow; some fight it. I just don't give a shit—at least when I act according to my own code. The rest is not that important. They are just categories. And it's not just about music. I get the impression that we became trendy as a result of our attitude, anyway.

Are you sometimes a fan of attitude, too?

Morbid Angel, one of my favourite bands, recorded an album recently. They combined death metal with underground techno and industrial sounds.

After giving it some time and attention, I would assess this experiment as mediocre when it comes to actual results. In the context of everything they have done, I would say the album is pretty poor. But, nevertheless, I am a fan of it, and I bow before its intransigence. These guys wanted to turn the system upside down. It didn't work out? Too bad. But they showed huge balls.

Is Behemoth a commercial band?

I ate dinner with the guys from Anthrax, the guys from Ozzy Osbourne's band, and the guys from a nu-metal band Ektomorf. We all talked about commerce. I said that the topic did not apply to me because Behemoth is an inherently underground band. The guy from Ektomorf almost spat his food out. He looked at me like I was crazy: 'You think you are underground?! You have no idea what you're talking about; look at your videos!'

I said that it didn't matter how much money you spend on a clip, or that it's viewed by a few million people. That only says something about your popularity. You can be famous and still stay out of the mainstream. 'Underground', first and foremost, is a message brought to people via music, and our message is undeniably extreme.

Danzig, at the beginning of the 90s, were both recognisable and radical. They sold out shows at stadiums, but that didn't matter; it didn't humble them. Another example: Laibach, another one of my favourite bands. These guys are extreme *all the time*. They provoke their listeners and live on the edge, but at the same time they've been flirting with the mainstream for thirty years.

Laibach ridicules pop culture, though.
That's a part of their ethos.

That's right, but we're called Behemoth, not Laibach. Our ethos is different.

More commercial?

If Behemoth plays music for the masses, then how would you describe the music of Red Hot Chili Peppers or Lenny Kravitz?

**Maybe in your case we're just referring to
the metal mainstream?**

I was at a Rammstein concert. There were ten thousand people in front of the stage. About a thousand people show up at our shows. Rammstein have about three hundred staff; we've got three people. Each evening they spend thirty thousand euros whereas our pyrotechnics don't even cost three thousand zlotys.

I think Rammstein is a representation of the metal mainstream. Even my mother could conceivably like them. She actually hummed 'Reise, Reise' when I played it in the car.

What about Slayer?

They're not commercial.

Every child knows Slayer, though.

Everyone knows who the devil is, too, but does that mean he's a mainstream character? The devil is underground. God is from the mainstream.

**And TV shows, like *The Voice Of Poland*?
Are they commercial or underground?**

They're an adventure, let's say that.

A good one or a bad one?

A good one, for sure.

What made you take part in that project?

Two factors: fun and money. I'd been fighting with sickness for a few months. I hadn't played shows, so I hadn't earned money. My savings began to melt. Whether I was healthy or not, I still had to pay taxes, and my treatment wasn't cheap. Of course, a part of the costs were covered by the Polish national health fund, but not by any means everything. I went into the hospital as a wealthy man, and I left it with debts. We were due to play shows in the autumn. The devil himself gave me the TV programme on a platter.

So it was for money after all?
Maybe it was the deciding factor, but not the only one.

**A lot of artists would rather eat their own shit
than admit they did something for the money.**
I'm honest. I can look at my own face in the mirror and I don't lose my credibility. I don't want to cheat the whole world and tell anybody that I did it for free. I did it also for the money, and I don't see any problem there. I didn't whore out; I dictated my conditions and they were met. So why would I say no? I signed the contract a few hours before shooting, when everything was agreed upon. And I'm not talking only about financial issues.

Did you earn a lot?
Enough to prepare for the autumn tour in relative calmness, yes.

How many zeroes exactly?
Six point sixty-six zlotys. Plus what was upfront. And I'm talking about each instalment.

Didn't you hesitate?
I fought with myself for a long time.

How did the opportunity come about, anyway?
A nice lady from Rochstar called me and invited me for a conversation. I was at my friend's house in Krakow, resting after my first stage appearance since leaving hospital …

**You're talking about the show with
Fields Of The Nephilim?**
Yes, it's an amazing story. Back in the 90s, I was focused mainly on extreme music. There were only a handful of non-metal artists that really conquered my heart. I mean artists like Dead Can Dance, Diamanda Galas, or the

aforementioned Fields Of The Nephilim. I got to know their music when I was sixteen, and they had a huge influence on the development of my music taste.

Did you meet them in person before the show in Katowice?

Yes, we actually recorded our own version of their song 'Penetration'. And that was the song I sang on the Mega Club stage. Carl McCoy accompanied me; I had met him a few years earlier. I sent him an email and he wrote me back. It turned out that his daughter, Scarlet, was a fan of ours. He asked me for a CD with a dedication for her and that's how it all started.

Some time later, my friend Ilona, who worked at Stodola in Warsaw, called me and said that Fields Of The Nephilim were playing a show there, and that they wanted all of Behemoth to come along. That's when I met Carl for the first time. A few months after that we shared a stage because we played the Tuska Festival in Finland. Then there was an offer made for me to sing 'Penetration' with them at their next Polish concert.

I had to decline, though. We were touring with Behemoth in a different part of the world at that time. Then I just forgot about it, and I got sick, but as luck had it, Fields Of The Nephilim played in Poland again, a few months after I left the hospital. They offered me the same thing again, and I thought it was worth trying.

Did you feel up to it?

I was weak but I *had* to take part in that show. I felt that it would really be a magical moment. I remember the whole journey from Gdańsk to Katowice. When I entered the club, I could barely stand up. Not only was I debilitated physically, but I was also moved emotionally. I immediately smelled the characteristic scent. Every club in the world smells like that. It's a bizarre mix of dirt, wood, spilled beer, cigarettes, and sweat. I love it. I immediately realised that I was in a place where I belong. That stage is my life.

Right before the show we divided the lyrics between Carl and me. I was on my knees when he introduced me. Normally, between songs, he says nothing and he gives just a quick 'thank you' at the end of the show. This time he introduced me as his friend. It was really damn emotional.

I got carried away onstage, and my throat was immediately dry because, in hospital, I had had enormous problems with the mucous membrane in my mouth. The problems kept coming back months after I left. The stress was paralysing, and I couldn't even lift a bottle of water standing next to me.

In spite of all that discomfort, though, I suddenly felt, at that very moment, that I was experiencing the very essence of life. When I started singing, I got shivers. I have never analysed the lyrics to this song. Only then, on the stage of Mega Club, did I realise what they really meant:

Shining like gods, new body, new blood.

Just a few months previously, I had had a transfusion, the effect of which was a complete change of my blood type! I saw the people in front of me. They pointed their fingers at me; their eyes were burning.

So you managed it?

I felt terrible the next day. The trouble began during the night, and I had all the symptoms of a rotavirus. I went to the hospital, and that's when the doubts came. I was wondering if I would ever go back onstage, or whether it was time to just retire. My friend and surgeon, Piotr Guzik, examined me. He let me stay in a room in his apartment. I was lying there under a drip that was put on a piece of bandage stuck to the chandelier by a nurse, Beata, who was also Piotr's girlfriend. They took great care of me.

I was surrounded by thousands of vinyl LPs, almost all of them heavy metal. Piotr's mother would come there every day and say, 'It's because you eat too little. Come, I fried some pork chops for you.'

I would always say, 'But miss, I can't—I have diarrhoea. I have to stick to my diet.'

'No! You have to eat or you will be too weak!'

She would fry more pork chops, which she gave me with potatoes. They took care of me for three days. And that's when I got a phone call from Rochstar.

'Mr Darski, would you like to appear in the Polish edition of *The Voice* as a coach?'

Not quite. It was: 'Mr Darski, we're working on a project that you might find interesting. Would you come visit us in Warsaw for a noncommittal conversation?'

Did you know what it was about?

I figured that it was about some TV production. To be honest, my first thought was 'over my dead body', but I did agree to the meeting. I just stopped in Warsaw on my way back to Gdańsk. The people in the company were all very friendly. They welcomed me wholeheartedly, sat me in front of a screen in a comfy armchair, and played back a western version of *The Voice*. At that moment I already knew what direction the conversation was going to head in. I looked at the screen, watched the show, and thought to myself, 'There's no chance that I'm going to take part in that.' I can't sing, so how could I teach somebody how to use his or her voice?

Did you share these doubts with the people from Rochstar?

They tried to convince me that my role in *The Voice* would be different from that of a vocal coach—that would be the task for professionals. I would be there to unearth real talent. They counted on my intuition, and the fact that if I had gone all the way from a basement to the top of my niche. They made good points, but I still had doubts. I kindly thanked them for their hospitability, promised I would call them back, and headed to Gdańsk.

Was there any talk about your remuneration?

No. Besides, I didn't even want to hear any figures. Later, I called the musician and one-time talent-show judge Kuba Wojewódzki and asked him a few questions. He told me what to expect and gave me a few good tips. He basically encouraged me to accept the offer. But I still battled with my thoughts. I felt good in my niche. Because of the relationship with Dorota, I had become recognisable. I'd been at a few media parties and, yes, I'd let some people photograph my face. But I still wasn't exactly drawn to this world. Something about the idea was growing on me, however …

Were you weakening?

Rochstar sent me a recording of the show. I would turn it on from time to time and watch it. At first I thought that it wasn't too bad, but despite that, I didn't seriously think that I would take up the challenge.

Why did you change your mind?

I told my friend about everything; I really value his opinion. I bombarded him with questions: 'Should I get involved? What will my fans say? How will it affect the band? How will I cope with the stress and responsibility?' He told me that I shouldn't even give it another thought, and that the name of sin is limitation. I felt more confident. I came up with a list of pros and cons. I was still too weak to go back onstage, and I still had a few months until the tour.

In my mind, I viewed my going on *The Voice* a bit like stepping out on a lake that's just become frozen. When you realise that the ice is quite thin, you don't just run to the centre of the lake and jump around. But you *can* slide one foot on the ice, when your other leg stands on firm ground. Stars dance on ice; I don't. I barely touch it, and I decided to treat the programme like that.

One leg on the ground, one on the ice.

A lot of people manage it. Musicians, too. Just look at the guy from 30 Seconds To Mars, Jared Leto. He's good at being both the actor and the lead singer. He had a great role in *Lord Of War*; he was in *Fight Club*, *Requiem For A Dream* … these titles speak for themselves. He's doing well with music, too. I don't really like his band—their music is rather shallow—but they did succeed, so there has to be something in it.

There are quite a few similar examples: Tom Waits, Iggy Pop, Keith Richards. The last one is a living legend, the absolute giant of the guitar riff. He somehow acted in a movie and his halo didn't come off. He actually didn't have to play anybody; he just went on the set and played himself. He has charisma x 1,000!

Well, yes, but there are many more people from heavy metal who haven't appeared in front of the cameras than have.

There is *one* guy who came there from a dark cave. His name is Jonas Åkerlund, and he debuted as a drummer on the first album by Swedish legends Bathory—the unquestionable pioneers of black metal. He began his adventure with the camera by shooting videos for other black metal musicians like Dimmu Borgir. Today, he is one of the most desired video producers anywhere. Now he makes videos for artists like Duran Duran, Lady Gaga, Madonna. In Poland, the very concept of someone like this guy being in the mainstream is something completely new. But in the West, a lot of people from the musical margins have managed to infect popular culture.

But Åkerlund abandoned his niche and focused on something totally different …

… and I didn't. The show, the big screen, challenging myself in other music genres—all this is good, but I know my ground, and I stick to it. There are people who claim I crossed the line a long time ago, but that's not what I think. I don't visit discount stores and I don't play shows at shopping malls. In all that I do, I find happiness. I think that if there's adrenalin in your stomach, then everything is OK. The programme gave me that feeling, and I don't think I whored out in any way, shape, or form.

How did you view yourself in the role of a TV juror?

Good, I think. But that doesn't mean I didn't have any fears at the very beginning. On the first day of shooting, I went for coffee with singer-songwriter Ania Dabrowska. It just so happened that I made friends with her at the very beginning of the whole process. I started telling her about my doubts and she just smiled and said, 'Adam, now you can do anything.'

Isn't life about being able to say these words to yourself? I had entered into an absolutely alien world. But I wasn't intimidated; that's not my nature. I don't really have any difficulties with meeting new people, so I quickly found myself on the right track. In a way, the show actually liberated me. My tolerance level for the world was quite high prior to the show, and it became even higher thereafter. I met a lot of wonderful people: at Rochstar, in the crew, on the show; they approached me with no apprehension, very wholeheartedly and friendly. And I paid them back by being the same way.

What about the other jurors? You made friends with Ania quickly, what about Piasek?

Artists such as Andrzej are people who are normally laughed at by people like us—rebellious and defiant: 'Oh, here he comes, the guy from the radio with his tear-jerkers.' Stylistically, we were light years apart; we were brought up in totally different environments, but it turned out that these two different worlds are actually similar.

With the same groupies?

No, in Andrzej's case they were definitely not the same. Anyway, it quickly became apparent that he's just a cool guy with a lot of self-distance. He also had this huge curiosity about the world and also for my world—although I didn't know how to perceive him at the beginning.

I went up to Andrzej before the show when he was getting his makeup done. I introduced myself, said I was happy to work with him. He responded in a serious tone. 'I heard you're all right. I hope it's true.'

I wasn't sure what he meant, but the distance quickly shortened. A few days of shooting and it turned out we were on the same wavelength. There was this verbal ping-pong between us all the time. I subtly tried to abuse him verbally, but it was impossible to knock him out. On the contrary: he always paid back, even if he did it very subtly and discretely. I felt that we were on the same level, and with each day our mutual fondness grew. We respected each other. We are still in touch to this day, actually. We meet when we can, and sometimes we even eat dinner together.

What about the other judge, Kayah?

At the beginning, Kayah was distant—not just from me. There was some friction between her and Piasek, and especially between her and Ania, like there usually is between women … sometimes Andrej and me would just look at each other when we didn't know what to say. Kayah responded very emotionally to normal conversations about age, appearance, or motherhood, but I got used to it, and later it was all much easier. I found common language with her, too.

Of course, sometimes there were frictions between all of us; sometimes it got really rough, but I think we complemented each other perfectly. Ania: always distant, sometimes maybe even blasé, because that's the way she is. Kayah: very emotional, sometimes choleric, sometimes even hysterical. Andrzej, with his quotations of classic Russian writers. And me … I'm not going to judge myself. I was unpredictable, that's for sure, a bit of a jester, a bit of a wise guy.

Did you get along with the hosts, Magda Mielcarz and Hubert Urbanski, too?

These relations were purely professional. They're pros. I'd even take that a stage further and say they are cold pros, and that's in no way negative.

Did you ever feel that maybe you didn't belong there?

There were certain situations that irritated me. During the initial days, when we chose people to be on our teams based only on their voices and performances, I felt insecure. I second-guessed my selections.

I had the impression that I didn't have anyone really good—that is until Monika Urlik showed up. The other teams seemed strong. I was getting frustrated, even though I reminded myself that the show was just about having fun.

Besides, I did make a few mistakes. I don't want to name any names, but some things sounded good in the studio, I was delighted, and then when I watched back on the TV, I just couldn't listen.

Maybe your own technical limitations were being shown up?

Maybe. The other jurors sometimes let me feel that I was not a vocalist; that I didn't really know much about the art of singing. Like when I chose Ares, the Crazy Greek. He was damn effective, even though technically he wasn't too good and, stylistically, he was rather one-dimensional—just like me—but he had his niche and he could sell himself in it. He certainly wasn't a dud. I knew he wouldn't win the show, because he wasn't an outstanding singer, but he showed this and that to some people. Just like the metal representative of my team—Filip Salapa. I hope they both succeed and conquer their musical backyards.

You're not a distinguished singer either, but you did sing on the show, or at least you tried …

I'm a screaming vocalist, not a singing one. There's a huge difference. My art requires the scream—something primitive and wild. It's atavistic. I do understand that for some people, seeing a growling guy on the stage might seem weird, but for me it's as natural as breathing. I don't think I can sing—I just pretend that I can.

But it wasn't a *voice* that turned out to be the biggest sensation on *The Voice*.

As my friend Lipa sings, 'Everyone has his own thorn.' My presence on the show turned out to be a thorn for a lot of people; it was like stirring up a hornet's nest. What happened after the broadcast of the first few episodes was like *The Matrix*. By that time, we had already begun the first rehearsals with the band, and we were preparing for the tour.

The show became sidelined a little and, suddenly, my being on the show became the main topic of a nationwide discussion. I felt like a comic-book character, like somebody was drawing my history on the spot, only I was standing on the sideline watching. Bishops, politicians—people whom I have never even heard—suddenly made it a point of honour to say something about me and describe me as either a blasphemous Satanist or their buddy. I knew it would pass; I tried not to get involved emotionally. Usually, it just made me smile.

Weren't you afraid they would remove you from the show?

That was not a possibility. Both the producer and the TV network wouldn't have stomached that, from a financial perspective. They would have had to pay me compensation. I've got a great lawyer, and he took care of all that before I signed the contract. Also, there were a lot of people who supported and defended me. People from Rochstar had my back, too. All in all, the producers risked the most.

Wasn't there any pressure from them? Didn't they want you to sign a get-out clause?

We got along with the producer, Rinke Rooyens, from the very beginning. But he did, in fact, worry that I would do something stupid during the live shows. But I didn't go to *The Voice* to insult people. They mentioned some clauses, but I didn't sign anything. That's what my lawyer advised me.

Were there any other suggestions from the producers?

There were some from the TV people. Before the show was broadcast, some people already started imagining potential problems in their heads. They knew what they were signing up for, but as soon as I actually put my signature on the papers, somebody thought it might not be a good idea to put me in front of the cameras.

Rinke called me, desperate, and said, 'Nergal, go on some other talk show, maybe Szymon Majewski's, and show people that you're a cool guy and you don't bite.' I declined. That was not an option, because Majewski—as much as he is nice and intelligent—cracks really poor jokes. Or maybe I'm just an idiot and don't get his sense of humour.

A few million Poles like his shows, though.

And to this day I have no idea why. There is no content in the discussions;

it's all just a cabaret of poor quality: a lot of confetti, glitter, and noise. It's definitely not Monty Python, let's put it that way. Somebody likes it, so what? There's this saying, 'People—eat shit! Millions of flies can't be wrong!' It fits perfectly. Going on Majewski's show would insult my intelligence, and Rinke respected my decision.

But the media storm was not going away.

It calmed down a bit when Zbyszek Holdys—the musician, poet, and journalist—appeared on the show. He's a real authority—a guy who always has his opinion. I respect him and I always have. When he became my aide in the show it was a message to the world that Nergal is not as bad as they paint him. However, some people with intelligence issues still criticised me, and Rochstar did all they could to warm my image up. They wanted me to go to a hospital and take pictures with sick kids.

Did you do it?

I did visit hospitals. I did visit people, but I didn't do it for the spotlight. That would be pure opportunism, and I despise such things. I considered it enough for me to focus on being a good judge.

But you did put Baphomet's figurine on your neck.

So what? Some people wear a cross; some people wear a devil. Whatever works for you. I'm not the kind of man who is bothered by religious symbols on people's chests. Such things don't necessarily have to divide people.

I was at dinner with Frank Bello of Anthrax recently. He was born and raised in a very religious Italian family. He doesn't hide his beliefs—there's always a cross hanging from his neck. You think I ripped it off him? That's absurd. I respect his views and he respects mine. We've talked for hours, and it was never an obstacle for us. Of course, there are people who shouldn't necessarily show off their faith in such a way. I mean teachers, politicians, police officers … but let other people put what they want on their necks.

TOP With Gus G. of Ozzy Osbourne's band at the Frankfurt Music Fair. **ABOVE** Behemoth receiving a platinum award for the *Evangelica Heretika* DVD, released in November 2010.

TOP 'Yes, it's my face!' Reading in hospital. **ABOVE** Agnieszka Piekarska taking care of Nergal during one of her hospital visits. **RIGHT** Enjoying three types of kebab at a restaurant in Gliwice after months of a diet of liver.

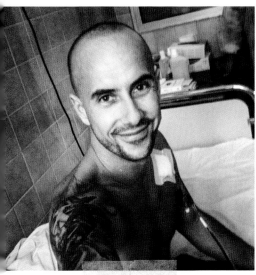

ABOVE With Kinga Dubicka from the DKMS foundation. A good friend during tough times. **LEFT** 'This is my stigmata.' Inserting the stent during chemotherapy. **BELOW** Shining like gods. New body. New Blood.

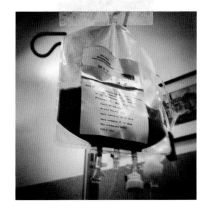

LEFT 'I'm looking for a healer.' The fan who approached me after the concert in Torun. **BELOW** Behemoth backstage. **OPPOSITE PAGE** Playing at the MusicCollective. A return to old form under the guidance of Rafael Szyjer.

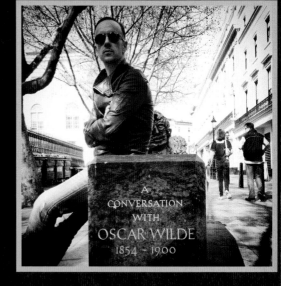

THIS PAGE Travelling the world; visiting a memorial for Oscar Wilde in London. **OPPOSITE PAGE** 'Artists don't like admitting they did something for the money.' Nergal as a judge on *The Voice*.

You were a good boy on TV but it wasn't so great off air. There was an issue with the disabled …

I think that was the crowning moment of that litany of bullshit about me. The level of absurdity reached its peak.

At a Times New Roman concert, you were wearing a stole and pretending you were healing people in wheelchairs.

Everybody who knows this band also knows it's pure cabaret. These guys have been playing for years and they organised a concert for their fiftieth anniversary. The idea was that they would dress as themselves, but from the future. It was supposed to be funny, and my performance was absolutely spontaneous. It had nothing do with any provocation whatsoever. Roman and Patryk are my good friends, and when they asked me to go onstage, I just did it. Sometimes I get the impression that I can't even smile in public, because people will find some new meaning to it and look for a hidden agenda.

But there have been accusations that you were ridiculing the disabled?

And who formulated those? The media and politicians, or the disabled themselves? I've never heard a word of criticism from the disadvantaged people. But, indeed, a lot of people didn't really understand what happened at the concert. People accused me of ridiculing the sick after I myself had managed to overcome leukaemia. That's not the case. I showed something completely different: I keep a distance between myself, from death and the world around me.

Sickness is not a taboo for me. You can't treat people in wheelchairs as any worse or better than others—this is what's twisted. I know their situation is fucked up.

Some time ago, I was signing albums in a bookstore in Szczecin. The first thing I said to people who came there was, 'So, you've come here to see a dead man?' It's not about putting myself in some kind of elevated position and showing people that I'm better. You just have to prepare the world for certain subjects. Besides, what has more healing power than laughter?

A few weeks after the Times New Roman show we played a concert with Behemoth in Torun. Right after we finished, my friend, the singer Agnieszka Krysiuk, came up to me. She said, 'There's this guy in a wheelchair, he'd like to have a picture with you.'

I went to talk to him. The very moment I posed for the picture, he took out a piece of paper that read, 'I'm looking for a healer.' It's just beautiful that a guy in such a difficult situation has such a great attitude to the world. Besides, I have a few seriously sick friends—do you really think I would make fun of them?

We know you, though. People who read these glossy magazines may not.

Take Adrian Kowanek of Decapitated, for example. When I met him, he was an extremely vigorous twenty-year-old with his whole life ahead of him. In 2007, he went on tour and he had a tragic accident. One of his fellow musicians, Witek Kieltyka, died.

Adrian is in a wheelchair; there's practically no way of communicating with him, although the doctors say that he's aware of everything that's going on around him. I met him during one of our concerts in Kraków. I smiled at him, took his hand, but inside I was screaming in pain. I felt terrible pity and debility. He was a great singer in a great band. And it's amazing how much love he experiences from his family and friends. They treat him like a normal and healthy guy. They talk to him, take him to concerts …

Let's go back to *The Voice.* Were you a good judge?

I'm not in the position to judge that.

Try.

We were in a producers' meeting, just before the final episode of the show, where each of the contestants was supposed to present their single—a song they had written themselves. I hadn't discussed this with the producer previously, so I was thinking hard about how and where to get a song for Damian. I knew that I wouldn't come up with anything myself on the spot. My brain boiled, and my stress levels grew. They were enhanced further because the rest of the coaches had already managed to get things done with their contestants, long before the finals. But next to Damian's name they had written, 'We have nothing.'

All of them talked about their songs, and then it was my turn. I was trying to talk my way out of it, so I told them that we hadn't had enough time. I panicked a little and I asked one of the producers, 'What are we going to do?'

They stared at me like I was crazy and told me that Damian already had his single. I showed them the piece of paper in front of me and told them that, unfortunately, he didn't. They all burst out laughing. It turned out that 'We Have Nothing' was the title of the song that Damian did with Michal Grymuza. So that's the kind of coach I was.

But you did win the show.
Damian did. I only chose songs for him.

Didn't you favour him a little?
Since the very beginning I said that I came to *The Voice* to find a strong rock voice—a vocalist that Poland lacks. But that doesn't mean I favoured Damian. For a long time I was sure that Monika would win the show. Ukeje won with her in a fair fight; he developed incredibly throughout the whole show. I'm really proud of him, like I'm proud of all my team who managed to get to the live shows.

Did they make a solid team?
I still see them walking happily off the stage. I cried with laughter. The cameras didn't get that but it was beautiful: a crazy blonde with ADHD in the front; a long-haired, fire-breathing Salapa right behind her; then we had pregnant Monika; then we see Ukeje looking like the guy from *The A-Team*; and at the very end of the line there was Ares, looking like an Orthodox

priest. All we needed was a parrot, a midget, and a wooden leg! Each of them had a lot to offer as individuals, but I saw a team that would perfectly fit in a movie, for example.

Is Damian going to make it? Will anyone even remember him in five years?

I absolutely believe so. I will try to help him. We got to know each other; we even started working on some music together. I've got my career and he's got his but we have serious plans for a music project. At the moment we are recording some demo tapes. They sound genuinely rock, very classic: a bit of AC/DC, a bit of blues, some elements of Alice In Chains. We let the music flow and develop, not necessarily in the direction we planned at the beginning.

Do you think a TV show like this can produce a real artist?

What do you mean by a 'real artist'?

OK: let's take David Bowie and DJ Bobo. One of them is an artist—the other is not.

From this kind of show you can get plastic dolls that give the common people some cheap entertainment. That's obvious. But nobody said that a TV show couldn't create someone who can beat the circus and have a strong personality that dictates its own terms.

Do you know any such artists?

I don't have to search that far. Polish *Idol* gave us Ania Dabrowska. Her debut album showed us that she is not going to bow before anyone. She did some ambitious—and I stress that—*ambitious* pop. She was appreciated by critics and by the people. The second album was even better, and Ania showed to everybody that she is an aware and independent artist.

Another example is Monika Brodka—very nice girl. I went to her concert and we met. She's very young and very mature as an artist. It's a beautiful combination. She literally shined on her single, 'Granda', even though a lot of prophets said she would burn out.

Doesn't taking shortcuts, like going through a TV talent show, kill determination?

A lot of talented people can't take such a leap. They quickly flare up and burn out. Fame, just like fear, has short legs. I've been climbing my mountain for years.

In most cases that's how it looks. But you can't generalise. Ania and Monika made it, but there are people who had some quality in the programme, but when they left it, they became blank and featureless. Szymon Wydra, for example.

Do you know him?

No. I have nothing against him, either, but his music is as blank as a piece of paper. People who buy records like this should go to jail.

There's one more type, represented by people like Gienek Loska. This guy has spent his whole life in music. He played, and he still plays, on the street. The programme gave him a boost, he released an album, but nothing changed: he still plays on the street for money, and he's still the same guy. The only difference is that now he plays for three hundred people, not thirty, as before.

Apart from Damian, who else from *The Voice* is going to make it?

I'm counting on Filip Salapa. He's a talented guy, very ambitious, and a nice growler, too. He didn't have to win the show because he's got his band, and he's invested in grassroots work. He fights for success, and I believe he will go far.

Do you know any young and talented people who didn't take the shortcut?

You mean Polish metal bands?

For example, yes …

Blindead is great, but can I describe them as young and talented? They're a recognised band, and they've created their own brand. But I think they deserve more. I follow the underground all the time. I'll tell you more: bands of my youth, all these metal gods, don't really give me as much excitement as they used to. That's why I'm looking down: I'm searching for exciting things deeper, where music is accompanied by freshness and a lack of compromise. I can openly admit that I'm still inspired by absolute stylistic caves and sonic rubble, bands that release a thousand copies of their record. I meet these people and help them. I keep one foot in the underground at all times. And I go on air in a Watain T-shirt …

Some people would consider Watain to be mainstream!

And some people like onion ice cream. We're going back to what we discussed before: there are people who don't see the difference between being popular and being a sell-out.

What position do you see Behemoth occupying nowadays?

For years, I didn't realise how the band was growing. Only after time did I notice that we've climbed pretty high. It's an eight-thousand-metre climb—like the fourteen highest mountains in the world. In our league, of course—because Behemoth was, is, and always will be an extreme band—we can go only so high. But we can always rise another few hundred metres.

Can you see other climbers ahead of you?

No, because we're almost at the top. Of course, there are a few eight-thousand-metre peaks to climb, and there are climbers on them, too. On ours, though, I can feel the breath of the young and talented on my back. There are also bands that are neck and neck with us.

Like who?

I think there are quite a few. I can name a few names, but I'm sure I'll omit a lot of them: we are in the same league as Nile, Gojira, Electric Wizard, or the aforementioned Watain.

Of course, I'm not talking about the pioneers and bands that are already on top, although I'm not really sure if it's the same top as ours. That's the problem I have with Mastodon—is that still extreme metal? But they certainly are perfect.

Your participation in *The Voice* didn't weaken the band's position, then?

No way.

You became recognisable outside of your niche. Aren't you inclined to tone down the sound of Behemoth and start playing music that's more digestible?

No, because I don't want to entertain people with my records. I want to entertain myself; I'm an artistic egoist.

So how about another TV show?

I never say never, but I don't think so. The experiment went well. Why would I go back and do the same thing? I would probably win again. Now I choose what's most important: the band. We'll finish a tour and get involved in a new album. Then we'll promote it, release it, and go touring for a year or two.

My life slowly begins to revolve around a new album. I've got ideas for songs ready and they sound … different, but painfully honest.

Do you want to climb another few hundred metres to the top with your new records?

We've worked with the best people available on the market. Ted Jensen, who normally works with Madonna or Metallica, mastered our last album. Colin Richardson, who produced *Evangelion*, is the number-one guy in metal when it comes to switches and buttons in the studio. Only Rick Rubin and Bob Rock are higher.

Do you have their phone numbers already?

I'm working on it, but I'm rather looking in another direction, where I see people like Steve Albini, Andy Wallace, Ross Robinson, Matt Hyde … someone who could give us more unpredictability and let us escape stiff solutions. I dream about asymmetry and added dirt—all within reasonable limits of course. After all, we play music that's a bit complicated and aggressive so there has to be some selectivity in it. Steve Albini produced a few Neurosis records, and Robinson is responsible for the great sound of Slipknot's *Iowa*. It's not a simple equation, though, and it's not a matter of going with the same settings on the console and the sound will be similar. Some people advise me to play safe, but I don't want that. I *want* risk. That's what my intuition tells me.

You talk about risk, but there have long been accusations that you put into your music what's trendy at any given moment.

I've been hearing this for years. We supposedly abandoned black metal to play death metal, then we somehow turned into some kind of 'religious' black metal … but what the hell is 'religious' black metal? Funeral Mist? We don't sound like Funeral Mist. We've never sounded like Cannibal Corpse or Suffocation either, and they are pure death metal.

Maybe something like Morbid Angel?

That's a timeless inspiration. Their music is in my genes. You can see the similarities. But we never were and never will be their copy.

Are you original at all?

I hate that word; it's not in my dictionary. The guitar has twenty-four frets and six strings, sometimes seven. All sounds have already been played many years ago. You just can't make any new ones; everything's been played. We can play music but we can't play anything revelatory. I focus on emotions, on honest messages. My friends from God Forbid once admitted to Dimebag that they're actually playing his riffs, and he said, 'Listen, we don't steal riffs from each other, we just borrow them, bro.' He was a guy who really created something in metal; he's a real guitar hero.

Did you steal the main riff to 'Conquer All' from Anthrax? Or did you just borrow it?

I went up to them after one of their shows, introduced myself, and told them that I thought I had accidentally covered their song. They burst out laughing; they knew exactly which Behemoth song I meant.

How was it possible that a riff almost identical to the one from 'Be All End All' could appear in one of your songs?

I remember the day when I played that riff for the first time. It's not identical but it is very similar. I started writing 'Conquer All' with the solo, and then we wrote the rest of the music to fit the solo.

I played the solo to the guys in a rehearsal and told them, 'Guys, it's got to be here!' I started humming: *Ta dam … ta da da da da dam*. I found these sounds on the fret board; they joined in, and we felt horrific power. The music carried us away. I knew that the riff of all riffs was just about to be created.

Suddenly, Zbyszek said, 'Ner, I think I've heard this before.'

I just muttered, 'I don't give a shit! The song doesn't exist without that riff!' And it stayed that way.

How did you find out that somebody had played that riff before?

I didn't want to hear it, but a lot of people told me that 'Conquer All' sounded like Anthrax. When I was twelve or thirteen years old, I loved *State Of Euphoria*, so maybe it was coded in my subconscious? But I didn't want to listen to that record, because I felt that our song might be a little bit of a plagiarism.

It was only on tour when somebody played that song to me, without warning. I couldn't run. Besides, I remembered a similar story …

What story?

In one of early Behemoth's songs, I subconsciously smuggled a fragment of Goblin's music that they had composed for the movie *Suspiria*, directed by Dario Argento. His surreal images of horror are cult objects for many people.

As a child, I would sit with my friends by the bonfire. Someone once told us what *Suspiria* was about and hummed the theme tune from the movie. I was terrified. This melody must have rooted deeply in my mind. I won't tell you what song the melody was from. Let Behemoth fans watch the movie and find it themselves. And to all those who don't like our music—I recommend the movie.

So what about your originality generally? You often say that Behemoth has its own character.

I'm like a sponge. I absorb everything that surrounds me. Music, film, conversation; when you squeeze a sponge, the water that squirts out of it is not the same as the water that was absorbed. You filter everything through your experience. Recognition? I'm all for that! Own character? That too. But it doesn't have to mean complete originality. I'd prefer to be secondary but still honest.

There was a band called Aspergillus Flavus in Gdańsk. These guys were obsessed with trying to be original. When someone told them, 'Guys, this sounds like Voivod,' they just threw the song away. They never released an album; they played a few concerts. It was just unlistenable.

Why do you still paint your faces before going onstage? You've resigned from a lot of things, but not from that. Isn't it childish?

Is makeup a privilege of children? I don't think so. Alice Cooper, Kiss, and Celtic Frost still paint their faces for their shows, and they're not neophytes. I don't know where the suggestion that mature artists should not use any additional eccentric gadgets, like costumes or paint, comes from. My opinion on that is exactly the opposite: every artist has the right to do anything if it is to help him achieve his artistic goal and manifest his own vision.

Of course, our corpse paint has its roots in the aesthetics that have accompanied black metal since the very beginning. The pioneers of the genre used paint and military images on their bodies. We continued the tradition, but we added a lot of our own elements to it. Today, Behemoth looks like … Behemoth. Besides, it's not just about aesthetics. Painting faces has a broader sense for us. It's like alchemy. Makeup transforms us, introduces us into a new role, functioning in another space: the stage.

I often describe the stage as the battleground. We go to war and we paint our faces. It's obvious.

But people judge you by this theatre.

'How do you know how an apple tastes, if you're only looking at the tree? How do you know how honey tastes if you only watch the bees? Don't judge me, because I may look like a hillbilly, but I'm a badass motherfucker.'

That's from a song by Maciej Malenczuk, isn't it?

Exactly.

He likes to dress up, too. How did your paths cross?

I used to watch *Idol* on TV. In one of the episodes, Maciej was wearing Behemoth's *Zos Kia Cultus* T-shirt. I didn't peg him as a fan of this kind of music, but the main theme of this T-shirt design was Baphomet, an occult deity. At that time, Maciej was playing Woland in a play based on *The Master And Margarita*. I deduced that the T-shirt—designed by a friend of ours, and a great artist, Tomasz Danilowicz—fitted his image back then. Anyway, the seed has been sown, and I … got interested in his band, Homo Twist.

You didn't know them previously?

I knew the name and a few songs … I'd heard the *Demonologic* album, and then I gave up. A few years passed, and then I spontaneously created the song 'Lucifer' to accompany Tadeusz Micinski's poem. Right before going into the studio, I immediately thought about Maciej. I heard in my head how he recites fragments of the lyrics. I called his manager and made an offer. Five minutes later, he called me back and told me that Maciej would love to take part in the project. 'How much?' I asked, and what I heard in the receiver was, 'For free, of course, it's an honour for him.'

Did he come to the studio?

No. He had only an hour for the recording in his rehearsal room, because he was about to leave for a longer tour. My friend Kikut was supposed to send the music to him. Kikut has his own studio, and he's good at all these switches and buttons. So I'm waiting impatiently for the recording when suddenly Maciej's sound engineer calls me and says that the recording is going rather slowly because the track they have is ... strange.

'What the fuck does that mean?' I asked. As it turned out, Kikut somehow sent them only the tracks with the kick and the French horn in the background. In short, there was NOTHING! No guitars, no bass, no drums ... I was furious.

Fortunately, Maciej also got the metronome track to which we recorded the whole song, so he sang the vocals to that. We had to edit them a little bit, but ultimately everything was perfect. 'Lucifer' is one of the moments on *Evangelion* that gives me goose bumps.

We can also see Maciej Malenczuk—singer in Pudelsi and Homo Twist—in the video to the song.

It was a natural development of our co-operation. I invited him to the set, he said yes ... and I didn't tell the guys. Imagine their faces when we're standing there with this beautiful lady with a camera, and she's interviewing us for *Eska* TV. And then this black Subaru drives into the yard where we shot the clip. The car stops, and Malenki steps out ...

You sang on his album, the one you mentioned before. Was this a return of the favour?

A few months after shooting the video, I met Maciej at the *X-Factor* finals.

Kuba Wojewódzki announced his band and their guest: the singer Gienek Loska. He also mentioned that Adam Nergal Darski was present in the studio, and that he would surely appreciate the performance. And they did indeed play great.

In the dressing room, Maciej shared his idea of recording a country album and invited me to do it with him. I thought for a long time about the idea. I like that sound. I'd been listening to Johnny Cash for years, and I also liked younger artists like Steve Von Till, Bjorn Berge, Wino and Conny Ochs, or Jeff Martin of The Tea Party. The form might be simple—guitar and voice—but this music is very close to my nature. The reflective and calm one, I mean.

I had an epiphany while jogging. I was listening to *Highwayman*—the original version—and then … eureka! Everything was clear. I got home, picked up the phone, and called Maciej to tell him about my vision. You can hear the effect on the album. I'm proud, because this song is close to my heart and my life story. There was supposed to be a video to this song, but there won't be.

Problems with the schedule?

It's hard to say. We'd been discussing the video since the beginning. When I mentioned the idea for the song, I also said something about my vision for an accompanying video. It could have been a video that everyone would talk about. Everything was going smoothly, up to a certain moment. I was driving to the set when I got a phone call to say that Maciej had called everything off. Why? I don't know; I didn't even manage to talk to him directly about it. The only thing I know is that I was very disappointed with him. It's too bad—we could have done something really special.

And how did you get to work with jazz pianist Leszek Mozdzer? That guy is from a different planet.

We bumped into each other at the Radio Gdańsk studio. We were recording *The Apostasy* at that time, and he was doing some of his stuff. He knew Behemoth existed, and I knew who Leszek Mozdzer was. It was all very nice. We were from two different worlds but we spoke the same language.

It was an impulse, too. We were working on 'Inner Sanctum'; I walked out from the recording room and I saw this guy. He stared at me, I stared at him, and everything was clear. It was like I cast a spell and he appeared. I told him that I needed a piano part for a song that we were working on. He agreed practically on the spot: 'You know what … why not?'

We agreed he would visit us in a few days and record everything. When he showed up, he asked about the lyrics before he even sat by the piano. I showed him the words. This was some very honest stuff, taken from deep inside, but its undertone was rather far from Catholicism. But he didn't mind. He didn't want to play music; he wanted to play words.

'I may see darkness in tunnels of light'—he stopped after reading this line, thought for a while, sat by the piano, and played a short intro. We were amazed; he played like a virtuoso. After a while, he asked if we could start recording, and he recorded his part. It was practically four sounds, which was exactly what the song needed.

Do you like jazz at all?

I hate it! It's elevator music. Literally. These songs have no point. They never begin and they never end. I listen to jazz only when I'm staying in a hotel and I'm using an elevator to get to my floor. Or in some little bar in the middle of New Orleans where a jazz trio plays for you while you eat the best-in-the-world steak. I only like this kind of accompaniment when the context is right.

Wasn't that an obstacle in inviting Mozdzer to record with you?

Absolutely not! I feel huge respect for this man. I think that musicians, actors, and people of the stage have this kind of universal code. They understand each other no matter what kind of art they each do.

Imagine this situation: I'm resting my head on the bar in the Radisson Hotel lobby in Warsaw. I'm more tired than drunk. It's May, so it's warm.

I order another espresso, trying to energise myself, then I see this guy and I'm sure I know him. *I know this face!* He looks at me and I can see that he knows me, too. I don't know him personally, but he comes up to me and shakes my hand like we've been friends for years. We started talking … and that's what it is about.

The other night, I was shopping in some supermarket. Suddenly I'm back-to-back with some guy. We turn around, there's a moment of consternation, and then we both laugh. We've never had the chance to talk before, but now we do a high-five. This time it was the Polish actor Borys Szyc.

Do you stay in touch with people you meet this way?

It depends. With Borys, we went to a few parties and danced all night. He's a very sociable and rock'n'roll guy but I think I'm glad I'm not his neighbour or I wouldn't get out alive. I have sporadic contact with Mozdzer. He was at our show in Gdańsk some time ago. Or, rather, he turned up prior to the show. He couldn't stay but he brought us presents. I got underwear.

Are you joking?

He was in Brazil for a long time and decided to bring us something from there. It's a beautiful pair of briefs—pinkish in colour. On the waist there are two two-headed eagles, very similar to the unholy phoenix—the symbol that we often put on our T-shirts. As it turned out, we had even infected Latin fashion.

X

WEAPONS
OF MASS DESTRUCTION

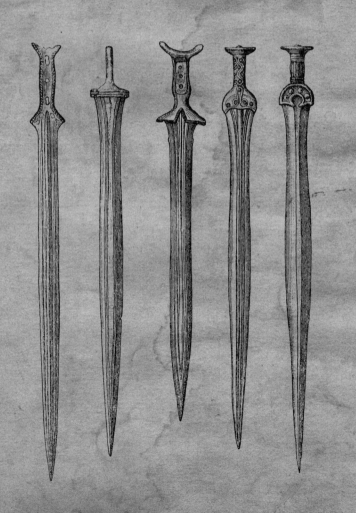

Do you feel robbed when people download your songs from the internet?
No.

A lot of musicians *do* feel that way, though.
I take responsibility for myself, not for other musicians.

But think about it: you record something, you put your heart and a lot of money into it, and then somebody takes it for free.
If someone doesn't know my music, downloads it, listens to it, then decides that it's not his cup of tea and deletes the files, that's OK with me. There will be others who will listen to it, they'll like it, and they'll buy the record. I see a kind of harmony in all that.

And if someone can't afford to buy it but really likes it?
Then let them listen to MP3s. Maybe he will buy it next year? Who knows? And if he doesn't, maybe he'll come to our show and pay for a T-shirt? There are fans like that. The internet is like the radio. I understand it perfectly, and I'm not going to tilt at windmills.

Do you download music from the web?
Of course I do.

But you buy records, too?
I've got a few thousand records. If I'm waiting for something to come out or if somebody recommends it to me and I find it on the internet, then I download it. If it's good, I buy a copy the next day. Or I buy three copies and I give two of them to my friends. If a record is awesome, I will also try to find a vinyl copy. I don't think I cheat or rob anyone.

What do you think about artists who sue their fans?
That's a tough question. I don't want to preach to anyone as to how they are

supposed to build their brand. I guess such artists must have a lot of free time, though, and I'd gladly borrow some of it from them.

So Behemoth fans needn't be afraid of the postman appearing at their door brandishing a lawsuit?

Sometimes things that appear on the web irritate me, but what can I do? Nothing—the world changes. A few years ago, taking pictures at concerts was forbidden; nowadays nobody even thinks about such rules. It's impossible to enforce them, anyway. People have mobile phones so they record what they want.

I go with that flow; I'm not fighting it. I adapt to suit my goals. I treat technical advances as a tool that lets me reach more people. Besides, recordings like that are nothing more than digital bootlegs, and I happen to love bootlegs. I sometimes pay a lot of money for a bootleg on vinyl.

Why don't you upload your records to the internet so that everyone can download them for free, then?

I don't think that's a good way. I'm a musician; that's how I make my living. It's my job and my only source of income. If I put all my heart into something then my prize is my honorarium.

A director spends months taking care of all details of his movie. He fights for quality. Would you appreciate it if you had to watch that movie via a shaky-handed recording somebody made at the cinema? I don't think so. A movie is not just about the plot, and by the same token a record is not only about sounds. It's also about the lyrics, the cover, the photos, the smell of the paper … do *you* like the smell of paper?

But you download music yourself.

And I often battle my own thoughts. I was born in a generation for whom music was a source of wonder. It was physically difficult to get records. For me, the buying of the records was a ritual. You waited for an album; you grabbed it, looked at it from every angle.

Today, the world is faster, there's no place for such deliberation. Before, one had to wait for ages for the release; then we had to physically run to the shop to buy the thing. If it wasn't there, we had to go back the next day. And we would swear, get pissed at the shop owner, at the distributors …

I liked record shops. I loved roaming around the shelves, browsing through the records. I still like it, but I don't do it as often as I used to because I don't have enough time or patience. Today, we have auction websites where you can buy everything in a matter of seconds. It's convenient. Is the world a worse place because of that? I don't know. It's just different. There's less magic in it, for sure, but I won't take any offence at technology and progress.

Did you track down the person who uploaded *Evangelion* to the internet before its release?

It wasn't difficult. It's common knowledge that journalists receive watermarked files. We quickly established where the leakage occurred. I knew this person well. I wasn't as pissed as I might have been; I just spread my arms and sighed. Shit happens. It turned out that the person who was the chief editor of *Terrorizer* magazine at the time accidentally shared our recordings. She simply put them in the wrong folder, and off they went …

So it was genuinely an accident? Do you believe that?

Maybe I am being naïve but yes, I do believe it. It doesn't matter much now anyway. She apologised to us. Besides, she's made it up to us many times over. It's in the past.

Did you follow the fuss concerning the signing of the ACTA (Anti-Counterfeiting Trade Agreement) Treaty?

I did look into it. I was closer to the protesters than to the people who supported it. I always feel closer to people who fight for freedom.

But you didn't take a public stance on the issue?

I didn't feel strongly enough about it. I have no legal knowledge, and I didn't know if the deal would change anything. Most of my friends were against

ACTA. They claimed that signing it might limit freedom on the internet. But there were people who thought that introducing these regulations would be profitable for artists.

Like Zbyszek Holdys, for example? People on the internet almost ate him. They attacked him like wolves attack wounded prey.

I like Zbyszek very much. For me, he's an icon. And I'm not just talking about his life or music. I have a personal debt of gratitude to him. When the media started attacking me, he would always defend me. I didn't ask him to do it; he helped me because he believed that everyone has the right to say what they want. So if someone bashes a person like that and makes an enemy of freedom out of him, is it normal? I don't think so.

You disagree on a lot of issues—piracy being one.

Great! And this is what freedom is all about. He's got his opinion and I've got mine. And we can both express them aloud. We don't have to fight each other. And yes, the internet crucified Zbyszek. And people who supposedly fought for freedom tried to gag him. I don't get it.

Let's leave Zbyszek for a while. Weren't you surprised how internet users mobilised themselves and conducted a global protest?

The range of the action surprised me—in a positive way. It showed how much we all love independence. The internet is a space that represents independence; information lives in it uncensored. Manipulation and distortion appear where the information is to be transmitted by someone. On the net, transmitters are unnecessary. You put information on a website and anyone can read it. Nobody manipulates the content. People see it and they defend that space.

Can anyone deprive them of it?

I don't think so. It's a revolution. It's in progress, and it's gone too far for anyone to say 'stop'. Read the papers—the serious ones, not the tabloids. They've started to reflect what's happening on the internet. Someone tweets something and the media tell you all about it, even the serious media. They've already sensed where the information is really born.

When we talked about the world of glossy magazines, you mentioned Zygmunt Bauman's essay in which he compared modern forms of communication to 'tweeting'. He meant the internet, didn't he?

That's right. The virtual revolution has its dark sides, too. Anyone can tweet 'I just ate my soup' or 'I'm finishing work in an hour' or 'Look at my new haircut'. We're being showered with pieces of information that have no meaning whatsoever. It's difficult to pick out the things that are important in all this mess. We're used to the fact that when we refresh the page, there is always something new.

The lifespan of information is getting shorter, too. When I update my Facebook status, on the first day it gets two hundred comments, the next day there might be twenty, and by the third day nobody comments at all. Everybody is waiting for new posts; the old ones are quickly out of date and dead. It's not about the quality but more about the tempo.

So is the internet a good thing or a bad thing?

Neither. It's just a tool. People forget what it actually is. Their lives take place on the net, not in the real world. One of my friends broke up with his girlfriend. First she removed him from her friend list, and only then did she break up with him in real life.

When I hear about situations like that, I'm really glad that I was born in the generation when there were no computers. Look: today, it's even said that Facebook and Twitter will kill off email.

The traditional letter is obsolete. To sit down and write a multi-page letter—who would do that? But I *did* write letters like that. I know that sense of deeper relations. I appreciate the internet, but I always keep one foot outside of it.

The band's official site, YouTube channel, Behemoth's profile, your fan page, your private profile on Facebook, the web shop, the blog … that's quite a lot. Do you have enough time to take care of all this with only one of your feet in the internet?

The band's site and the shop are managed by my friend and our webmaster, Marcie Gruszka, aka Manticore. I help him, of course, and I co-ordinate everything. I take care of the rest myself, but only when it comes to posting stuff because IT is a closed book for me.

Weren't you interested in getting to know the world from a technical perspective?

I treat my computer like my car. I know how to drive a car and that's enough for me. I don't have to analyse the structure of the engine.

When did you first recognise the power of computers?

I recognised it quite early on, but I started using it quite late.

You don't like technical gadgets, then?

I like them very much, and I usually catch up instantly. Sometimes, my inner gadget-geek comes out in me. When mobile phones were introduced for the first time, I wanted to have one. It didn't matter that it was the size of a loaf of bread. I had it, I could talk, send messages. At first it was only with two or three other people, because only a handful of my friends bought these thingies for themselves.

Communicating has always been important to me. But with computers, I admit that I overslept. At the end of the 90s, I would go on my bicycle to read emails. Manticore—who back then had already tried to convince me to go online—was always ahead of me in these matters. He had an email account; I didn't, so I gave everyone his address. When somebody wrote to me, he would call me and say stuff like, 'Ner, there's an email from Metal Blade Records for you.' So I would get on my bicycle and go to his place to read the message from the label. If I didn't have time, he would read it to me over the phone, and I would tell him what to say in reply. I just didn't get it back then; I was still in the Stone Age. I was sending faxes at the post office.

How long did that last?

Eventually I opened my own email account, but I still didn't actually own a computer. I went to internet cafés. A lot of my friends already had their own PCs, so I would spend hours at their places, taking care of correspondence and even doing a few interviews. A few years passed before I actually got one of my own. I remember I was terribly proud of it when it finally took its place in my apartment.

How much of your free time is absorbed by computers today?

I use one every day. I check my emails in the morning; I visit a few news sites also. I don't have to go to a newsagent to get a bunch of papers; I've got everything within arm's reach. But I try not to overdo it; I don't forget about real life.

Do you treat your internet presence more like having fun or work?

More like having fun with a weapon of mass destruction.

The posts you publish on your personal account are also mirrored by what you write on the fan page.

Don't be surprised by that. My band is my life, 24/7.

Your emergence on Facebook was more private or professional?

I came there out of perversity. Before that, also out of perversity, I avoided that thing like the plague. People told me, 'You're not on Facebook? Then you don't exist!' I promised to myself that they would never see me there. I was proud of it.

You shouldn't have wasted your words.
One day I just accessed the site. I didn't want to log in. I just wanted to check something out; I was looking for information. Then, when I saw how many Nergal profiles there were, something broke in me. I thought that it was high time to rectify the situation and give people the real Darski. And I was quickly drawn in. I like how Facebook dethrones me and diminishes the distance between my fans and me.

Do you often reply when they message you?
I do.

The attractive female fans, too?
Also them …

**Virtual love, flirting over the internet—
are you turned on by that?**
Sometimes I flirt. But it rarely happens with my fans. It's not ethical, anyway. After all, if I were a gynaecologist, I wouldn't try to fuck all the girls.

One in five, maybe?
There are always exceptions. But I prefer to keep a tight rein on my balls. I often meet fans that are willing to do this kind of thing. They're young and attractive, enchanted by me, but also naïve. I try not to abuse it. I'm not particularly turned on by having that kind of advantage when I first meet someone. I prefer women who know who I am but, more than anything, they see a person in me, not just the leader of their favourite band.

**When you talk to people on the internet, you
can never be sure who is on the other side.**
I realise that. I always keep my distance. I am popular, so people sometimes try to trick me. That's not exclusive to the internet, either. Various people call me. I might be on the phone with a journalist, and I can't be sure if he really works for the paper he says he does. I've been burned a few times so

I always try to verify such things. There are lines I don't cross before I make sure that it's the right person at the other end. And that applies to every aspect of life. It doesn't matter if it's flirting, a business conversation, or an interview. I'm very careful.

What is your attitude to journalists generally? We heard that some once called you a buffoon.

Sometimes I actually am a buffoon. Deliberately. I like talking to journalists whom I know and respect. I value reliability. There are people like Tomasz Lis who represent quality. When I get a message from him, asking for an interview, I don't decline, because I know he's going to do a great job, and I will read what I actually said, not some bullshit that's seemingly appeared from outer space.

It's the same with Jarek Szubrycht, whom I've known since the time when he was a singer himself. I trust people like them—even if they were to ask me tough questions and press me a little. That was the case with Piotr Najsztub. He interviewed me for *Przekrój* magazine. When it was published, I had some reservations. I didn't like the way he pitched the whole conversation. But there *was* style in it. And quality. So when he asked me for an interview for *Wprost,* I agreed, and the result was much better than before.

They're all people with big names. Do young, less fashionable journalists ever get the chance to interview you?

It's not about names. I've been burned by a few of them, too. One guy called me, asked me about the tour, the band, and the album, and then an article appeared about me showing off at parties. I am not going to make the same mistake again. As a rule, I avoid the glossy media. Their journalists like to camouflage themselves and pose as somebody else.

But they still call you?

Some time ago, a woman from one of the TV breakfast shows called me. I think that's what they are called. These shows where they broadcast lifestyle bullshit and speculate on who sleeps with who.

Right …

Yeah, so she called me. It was spring, the end of March, and she wanted me to appear on the April Fools' Day episode of the show. I was supposed to smile to the camera and make this bad joke that I'm actually done with metal and that I'm soon to record a new reggae record or some other bullshit.

Suffice to say, I kindly declined. But she wouldn't let go. She kept calling me.

Eventually I told her that I would do it if they met my conditions. I came up with some stupid ideas on the spot: that I wanted to be naked on air, wearing only an American flag, and I wanted a bunch of altar boys dressed as SS soldiers singing the anthem of the Vatican.

Did she give up at that point?

Two hours later, she called me and said that the producer was delighted with my idea. I baled.

But you did appear on these shows a couple of times?

Twice, to be exact. The first time was right after I left hospital. I promoted bone-marrow donation for the German Bone Marrow Donation Centre (DKMS). And the other time, I had promised an appearance to the producers of *The Voice Of Poland*. It was a gentlemen's agreement, and I always fulfil my duties.

Do you get any financial benefit from appearing in these programmes? And we don't mean the one where you promoted leukaemia awareness.

No. At least I have never asked for any fees. I do my best to avoid such things, though. I don't feel the need to publicly vivisect myself in front of two million viewers at seven in the morning.

Right. You appear on the air much later in the day, probably because you swear a lot.

Swear words are a part of our language. Everyone uses them. They're like exorcisms; they let the bad energy out. Sometimes they stress an important message. But one has to know how to curse.

I've got this friend in Olsztyn; her name is Monika. She's the world champion in cursing. All those bad words sound like a symphony in her mouth. They're like chives in perfect scrambled eggs. They just have to be there.

It's worse when someone does not know how to swear. You meet girls like that. Their volleys of abuse make your ears wither. They do it very mechanically, with absolutely no grace whatsoever. I look at them, hear what they say, and in my head there is only one thought: 'For fuck's sake …'

'Nergal caused another scandal!' 'Nergal faked orgasms!' Do you read articles like that?

One in twenty. For entertainment. I prefer serious media.

Entertainment is one thing, but articles like that constantly show up on the internet. Doesn't that irritate you?

It rather tires me. I don't get pissed easily.

And when the media says that you are in hospital again?

There was an article like that some time ago. That was too much. My phone kept ringing, and my friends and colleagues wanted to know if I was OK. I had to explain to everyone for two days that I was alive and well.

You also made a statement saying that the whole of Poland was dumb because they read this bullshit and believed what tabloids say.

The reaction was consistent with the information. In situations like that, there's no point in playing the diplomat.

Some people were offended, though.
The ones who were are stupid.

Do you like to provoke people like that?
I like provoking strong emotions. It makes people think.

**And do you read the comments made about you
on the internet?**
Never. Why would I need that? The internet gives you anonymity. I don't
know the authors of these opinions; I don't know what they stand for, and
I have no idea why they write it. I can take harsh criticism from a friend of
mine. I don't get offended. But from some strange guy who has never met
me? What can he possibly know about my life?

**We'll cite a few for you. They're from an article
about your second hospital visit:
    'Thank you dear lord, I always believed in you and
I always will, and thank you for listening to me'
    'You fucker Nergal asshole, die and rot in hell, prick'
    'Let this Lucifer die'
    'He had it coming, he should have a relapse,
this would cure his brain'
    'Where is this fucker, I'll visit him with Pavulon'
(one of the drugs used in lethal injection).**
A beautiful example of Christ's love in a nutshell. It's like that every time. I
don't have to read these opinions to know what I can find in them. Half of
these people would happily send me to the moon; the other half will send
priests there. The internet is so very predictable.

**'This Nergal guy is cool, I like him, but why does he
fight God?' People express opinions like that, too.**
And I hear them all the time. I don't have to go online to do it. I just need
to walk down the street.

Do people recognise you in the streets?

It happens. Usually they're very nice, actually.

And what does Nergal tell them? Why
***does* he fight God so much?**

I don't get into discussions. I keep calm. I always thank everyone for their good words and I shake their hands and keep walking. I know that people's view of me is completely distorted. The computer or the TV screen—these are false mirrors. They lie. I'm not talking exclusively about my appearance in pictures or on the TV. I mean the full image of a human being. People have a problem because the media paint me as a 'vulgar Satanist' and make a monster out of me. Then, on the other hand, they present a nice guy who will tell a joke here, cite a philosopher there—a guy who smiles nicely and kisses ladies on their palms.

And what is he really like?

He likes to stir things up. So he also likes this media disharmony in his image. He doesn't want to straighten it out.

Aren't you afraid that, one day, people will
want to lynch you for stirring things up?

I'm not made of glass. I've been punched in the face a few times. But I don't think anybody would want to lynch me, at least not literally.

'Hitler was nice to his close ones, too.' That's how
Marcin Meller, former chief editor of the Polish
***Playboy*, replied to Malgosia Domagalik and**
Zbyszek Holdys, who defended you from the
attacks by the conservative media and claimed that
you are a nice and kind guy. Did that hurt?

It made me laugh. A guy who publishes a magazine with naked chicks in it should have a more liberal attitude toward reality, shouldn't he? I will not insult him in public; I will just say that he is not credible in my eyes anymore. Nevertheless, this whole situation turned out well for me. I ended up being in a movie because of it!

As Hitler?

Close. A few days after this wretched TV show, I accidentally met the film director Juliusz Machulski and his wife, Ewa, in Warsaw. They were walking out of their tenement, they recognised me, smiled at me, and we started talking. We went for lunch together and spent a few hours discussing life, the media, and our favourite TV shows. At one point— just when Machulski commented on the situation with Meller—Ewa asked me to turn my head to the right, and then she said, 'Julek, look, he would make for a perfect Ribbentrop.' And I was offered a role in a movie: a comedy about Nazis.

Did you know Machulski previously?

We had only exchanged a few texts. When my interview for *Newsweek* was published, I got a message: 'Mr Darski, my heart grows when I see young Poles thinking like Gombrowicz, not Sienkiewicz—Juliusz Machulski.' I was speechless. I quickly replied to him and asked if it was *the* Juliusz Machulski. He assured me it was, and he invited me for a coffee.

You were serious about playing a part in a movie?

I've had offers like that before. But they were usually for bad-guy roles in horror movies. That would be just too predictable. It would be a much bigger challenge for me to play someone I don't really relate to. To play a Nazi, a zealot, or a priest—now *that* would be something. My old friend Bartek Krysiuk, when he found out about the movie, told me I was headed straight to Cannes. I wrote back to say that a Golden Raspberry Award was much more likely.

Do you get offers for roles in commercials?

I do. I did a commercial for an energy drink once. But that was an exception, because a beautiful idea stood behind it: I could support the

DKMS Foundation, which did a lot for me. This way, too, I'm repaying my debt to them. And I plan to do it until the end of my life, because it's thanks to DKMS that I still have it.

**Did you take any money for the commercial,
or did you give everything to the foundation?**
There are details of that contract that I can't disclose, so I will hold my tongue on that subject. For me, something else is important: the fact that business can carry with it some altruistic values. I give my face to a company, and thanks to that, a percentage of every drink goes to people who really need it—not to bums who will just buy more booze but instead to the people who, if they live, may enrich the world. Besides, there is a message here: there are never too many donors. This kind of information goes out to my fans, and each of them is a potential donor.

XI

OUR EARTHLY
EDEN

Are you a hedonist?

I'd like to think so.

But you don't *look* like a glutton.

Are you suggesting I look malnourished? Unfortunately, I can't cook. I can only make scrambled eggs. It's a narrow specialisation, granted, but one that I've truly mastered.

Do you like to eat?

Definitely, yes. But I put quality ahead of quantity. That's the philosophy I came up with. Or, rather, I borrowed it from a wise man who once said that we are what we eat. I have even expanded this motto to fit other aspects of life. We are what we watch, we are who we love, we are what we listen to; we become what we spend time with.

So you're rather picky?

It comes with time. When we're young, we absorb everything, and we eat whatever they give us. That's normal. A young body needs fuel and doesn't care what it puts in its mouth. Selectiveness comes with age.

When did yours come?

It's still coming, gradually. I still discover and grow it. I think it's the best thing that maturity brings to you. We're talking about food, but it really applies to every aspect of life. Friendships, women, music, art …

I'll give you an example—a very simple one. I'm a coffee lover. I absolutely love caffeine. The taste and aroma of this beverage is one of the most wonderful things in the world. For years, I had been a fan of large and sweet coffees: milk, sugar, caramel, and other flavours. I would pour these inside myself all the time. But eventually I had enough. Nowadays I will occasionally consume a calorie-bomb like that, but only very sporadically. I found the real taste of coffee behind all that sugar. I started experimenting. I tried out different types of coffee, and I tried different methods of making it. Sometimes I use an espresso machine, sometimes a French press; sometimes

I mix different kinds of coffee, and you know what? I taste the difference every time. Coffee does not have to be large and sweet anymore, it can be stronger, and it can have just a little bit of milk.

A coffee purist would consider even a little bit of milk a sacrilege.

I don't go to extremes; I'm not a purist. Besides, a bit of sacrilege is good for you. I know that from my own experience.

Are you addicted to coffee?

Before I went to hospital, I couldn't imagine a single day without a large, sweet coffee. The milk-free diet was the worst for me.

No milk was the worst thing for you?

Leukaemia and culinary adventures do not go hand in hand. They told me that I couldn't eat any fried food for the next few months. I thought, 'OK, it's not a tragedy, I don't eat fried food that often anyway.' But when they told me that I couldn't enjoy my favourite daily caramel macchiato, I realised that I really had a problem.

The first days were hard. With time, my body withdrew from caffeine, and I got used to not having it. I missed coffee but I didn't need it.

Didn't you break at any point?

There were occasions when I could drink coffee, but only without milk. I would then ask my friend to bring me soymilk, and I added it to my caffeine beverages. It tasted awful, but I was content, anyway, because I knew that soon I wouldn't even be able to drink even this kind of coffee. I was still on a milk-free diet: barren, boiled food with no spice. It was all about not overloading the liver, which was heavily bashed after each round of chemo. When I got chemo, my diet was even more restrictive.

When you recovered, did you go mad for milk again?

I reintroduced it gradually into my diet. A large, sweet coffee became part of life again. But I started re-evaluating some things. I felt that pouring half a litre of a sweet liquid into my body was pointless—particularly as I don't really like other sweet drinks. I changed and I like that change.

So it's not just about coffee?

No, it isn't. I like making authoritarian judgments, and I like claiming that there are things in life I would never touch. But I do realise that these are only words. In a year or two or ten I will probably try this or that thing out. It's almost certain that I will. Changes are inscribed in my life. Mystery is, too. I get a boost from what is just around the corner.

So the culinary gusto in Nergal does not exist?

It does, but only for the day. The acquisition of gusto—like everything in life—is a process. It's evolving all the time. Some people don't accept it and they draw a map for themselves. They put it in their reality and they're surprised when, a few years later, something is not right. I do exactly the opposite—I enjoy the fact that everything flows. I compare it to the biblical apple …

You're quite drawn to the Bible aren't you?

But it's really a good comparison. There's the story about the apple of knowledge—of good and evil. I interpret this story in such a way that reaching for the apple means resignation from a regular and unchangeable system of meanings. In such a system, everything has its place and value. Nothing changes, not even by a millimetre. That kind of fun is not for me. I choose the change, the movement, and the riddle.

So you take the apple, and then what?

And then we have the smorgasbord. Imagine if you ate the same balanced dinner every day. It's not as if it's bad at all. It's an old, traditional recipe, tried from generation to generation and deeply rooted in tradition. Meat, salads, and spices—everything your body needs is there. There are vitamins, carbohydrates, and proteins.

The first time you eat it, it's delightful; the second time, it's delicious; the third time, you revel in the harmony of taste. But what do you feel when you eat it for the *ninety*-third time? Now imagine that you are to eat the same dish until the day of your death. Each day it's the same, made in the same pot. Do you like that vision? I don't. I want to decide what to put on my plate.

And what if somebody chooses your favourite salad? Will you reach onto his plate and take it?

Why not? I often take delicious bites from other people's plates.

And when somebody tries to take something from your plate? Do you growl at him?

I treat him to it. Of course I don't run around restaurants stealing food from people, and I don't just toss my food to everyone in the room, either. But when I'm with friends, it's natural for each one of us to share our food both ways. It's actually beautiful. When we're on tour with the band, we always order so that everyone can taste everything. Instead of one pork chop, everyone has four smaller but different dishes.

Do you eat a lot?

I eat enough to live through the day and have enough strength to do all that I do. And I do a lot.

So you eat to live, not live to eat?

I eat to eat, but enough to live. People tend to go to extremes. Pleasure or energy? I choose both options in one package.

You never overeat?

Overeating is our national tradition. We tend to eat hearty lunches and square dinners. We don't eat anything the whole day, and then we get an XXL-sized plate. It took me a while to abandon that kind of lifestyle, but I've been eating in a different way for years. I eat often, but not a lot. And I don't believe in myths. It's not a problem to eat after midnight as long as it's not bread with sausage. In the evenings I will go for snacks like vegetables, fruit, and yoghurts. During the day, on the other hand, I try to eat foods that will give me energy, so dishes containing carbohydrates and proteins. I also eat a lot of fish.

What about red meat?
No more than two or three times a week. But it's difficult to generalise. Sometimes I don't eat meat for three weeks and sometimes I just feel I need it. Sometimes it's an impulse. I walk by the butcher's and suddenly I feel like eating a turkey. That's the way it works.

You don't have any ideological reasons, though?
I'm a predator. When someone tells me they don't eat meat because it's not right to hurt animals, I don't understand it. But I wouldn't eat a dog, or a horse, because a horse, to me, is like a dog.

And a pig isn't?
No. But I would never say a pig is not intelligent. They're shrewd and clever. I don't touch them for other reasons. It's the worst meat there is: it's unhealthy, it's fat, and it contains a lot of toxins.

And cows?
I eat beef from time to time, but it has to be well prepared. I have a few trusted places where it's made and served well. Then it's definitely worth trying.

Do you fight with your vegetarian friends?
On the contrary, I often defend them. Whenever there is a conflict between them and the meat-eaters, and the latter claim that you need to eat meat because it's the source of strength, vital energy, and other important elements, I take the vegetarians' side—partly out of spite, of course, because I love playing devil's advocate, but also because I love freedom. Besides, I've never met a person who could tell me why the biggest mammals—elephants and whales—are not carnivorous.

Well, you are, and you don't get the point about our animal friends.

I believe that you can't just take a race, a nation, or even a group of people and tell them that they need particular things. Be it a god or a cow. It doesn't matter. *You have to believe in God, because God is good; you have to eat cows, because cow is healthy; you have to do sports, because it's healthy … it's all bullshit!*

I knew sportsmen who died young and I know smokers who lived for many years. I know vegetarians who are as fit as a fiddle and I know some who are anaemic. I have met a lot of wonderful and good people who have never been to a church and I've had the misfortune of meeting a lot of Christians who are fucking assholes. I could go on like that forever. Eat what is good for you. Don't give a fuck about the guys who try to persuade you otherwise.

And isn't it the truth that obesity doesn't serve anybody well?

Obese people are usually those who don't care what they put on their plates. They just stuff themselves with whatever unhealthy crap is within reach at a given moment. There is no awareness in that. They *devour* food; it's mechanical. Besides, obesity is often the result of laziness, of which I am a fierce enemy. People who eat consciously rarely get obese. And even if they do, then they probably need it, as that's what their priorities are dictating. Maybe if they ate less they would be unhappy?

There are different cultures, different models of beauty, and different models of health. We tend to think that some things are universal, but they seem universal only here and now. I don't want to compare and judge them. I choose my own model, but I don't want to impose it on others.

Since we're talking about different cultures, do you think that the culinary tradition can tell us anything about the place it comes from?

Of course. I travel a lot and I always try to eat food that's synonymous with that given region. It's very educating. There are people who go to Egypt or Mexico on holiday. They just lie on the beach and eat exactly the same stuff as they eat at home. For me that's pointless. Wherever I go, I like to go outside, see the people and get some inside information about the place. And I like to find a bar where they serve regional food. Although I feel a bit reluctant to try such food sometimes …

You mentioned that you wouldn't eat a dog …
There's this guy on TV called Anthony Bourdain. He goes to *the* most bizarre places in the world and eats *the* most sophisticated dishes. When I see how they cook a reptile's tail or some other animal's genitals for him in the jungle, I feel comfortable with my limitations. But that doesn't mean I don't admire the guy. I really like his radical, anarchic hedonism. His shows are a real feast—for the eyes.

**Aren't you inclined to break your
culinary taboo sometimes?**
There are aspects of life in which I try to break all limitations, but there are also ones where I knowingly limit my impulses.

Do you eat fast food?
At four in the morning, after a lot of alcohol … then, it might happen. But to eat this shit, sober, in plain daylight? When I see people stuffing themselves with large buns with a lump of meat inside, it's like watching pigeons feasting on vomit or rats rummaging through waste. There's emptiness in their eyes—like watching hens about to be slaughtered. I feel sick at the very sight of it.

**What about stimulants? Do you put good alcohol
alongside your plate?**
I don't drink much, but a dinner with good wine is advisable.

Do you know anything about wine at all?
I prefer white, so I obviously don't. I choose what suits me at a given

moment. I usually eat fish rather than meat, so white wine suits fish better. Besides, I feel better after it; it doesn't seem to overload your liver as much. It's a question of preference.

What about other alcohol?
As I said, I don't drink much. And I seldom drink spirits. I just don't feel the need.

Drugs. Do you take them? Do you like them?
I've tried, but I was never sucked into it.

You seem to break the mould of the typical rock'n'roll musician …
Thankfully. I don't like clichés.

… who doesn't drink much, says drugs are bad …
I didn't say that. There is nothing wrong with drugs—each to their own. We just have to know how to use some of these things. Sometimes I smoke a joint or eat a hash-cookie, but it happens rarely, and only when someone treats me to it.

And cocaine? Have you tried it?
It has happened. I liked it even more than marijuana or hashish. But I would never buy it myself.

Because it's illegal?
No, that's irrelevant. I am all for the legalisation of drugs, especially soft ones. Poland would benefit from the taxes, and the police would get more time to take care of serious stuff.

Let's face it: chasing kids with weed in their pockets is not serious. It's the same with prostitution. I would legalise that, too. Everyone would benefit from it. It doesn't mean that I have to go to a brothel every week or stuff myself with drugs every day.

Are drugs dangerous, in your opinion?

A lot of things are dangerous. I'm convinced that vodka and cigarettes kill many more people than drugs. The law should be built on cold calculation. If we ban drugs, why do we let people buy alcohol and smoke tobacco?

Would you support a ban on them, then?

I think that adults deserve the right to decide about their own life choices. If they want to poison themselves, let them do it. It's not my business.

What about kids?

It's difficult for me to place myself in the position of a parent. Recently, we've been talking about it among friends. Some of them have kids, and we were discussing how to protect them from addiction. Alcohol, drugs, everything that's attractive to teenagers—the fact they're forbidden is a factor, too. If I ever have children, and I hope I will one day, I would rather they taste the forbidden fruit at home than on the street. I'll have a joint myself and smoke with them. I'll drink their first beer with them; I'll explain how it all works.

But you won't inject heroin into their veins?

You're kidding. I'd be afraid of heroin myself. I've seen heroin's effect on people, and that's enough for me.

You mentioned you're all for the legalisation of prostitution. Have you ever used these services?

I don't have to pay for sex.

But did you ever try it?

Twice. My attitude toward reality is strictly empirical. I have to try something before judging it. It happened for the first time in the late 90s. I could barely make ends meet back then; actually I was quite poor, and I couldn't afford that kind of entertainment. But after one party I found myself in my friend's house in Warsaw. Today, he is a respectable man; he's got a wife and kids. I won't mention his name. He worked in the drinks business and he earned quite a lot of money. After some heavy drinking, he offered to take me to a brothel. We went there, we picked two girls, he paid for them, and off we went. My girl was, at first glance, not bad. But when I looked at her closely, my vision returned …

There are no ugly women; sometimes you just need more wine?

Too much wine was the problem. 'Beer goggles', I think it's called. Drunk as I was, I couldn't help notice that this was one nasty women standing in front of me. The walls were decorated with mirrors. I looked in one of them and all I saw this jerk with a cheap hooker. It was really bad.

Suddenly there was a knock at the door. It turned out that my friend had a problem. The other girl came to our room and informed us that my friend had fallen asleep instead of getting horny. She started moaning that it was a brothel, not a hotel, and that I should wake him up. I called a cab and we went home. But he wouldn't let it go. He pulled himself together and tried to say that it was a bad agency, and that he'd show me where the real cats were.

Did you agree to that?

I was drunk. But I do remember that he got his phone and called girls. I'm there, sitting next to him, dying of laughter. Completely off his face, but very polite and to the point, he explained to someone on the phone exactly what kind of girls we wanted: sizes, hair colour, everything in detail. Eventually, he says, 'You know, please don't disappoint us.'

Were there any available?

Two ladies with stretched sweaters and greasy hair came to us. They were very disappointing. I was tired of it all and more than a little embarrassed. I politely declined and went to the other room.

Was your friend up to the task?

I heard the frame of his bed bashing against the wall, so I think he was content.

That was your first time, what about the second?
What happened then?

The second time, I fell in love with a hooker. It was during our tour with Carpathian Forest in 2001. We had a day off and we were spending it in Amsterdam. Of course, we went to see the red light district. It was winter, but the ladies in the shop windows didn't seem to mind. They were flexing, smiling coquettishly, alluring us. And then I saw this brunette—a dark-haired version of Venus of Milo. She was Greek, and she looked like a real goddess. I told the guys that I just had to have her, and I told them there was no stopping me. I won't go into details but I was disappointed again. So I got hookers out of my head for good.

The goddess didn't meet the expectations?

We've talked about it already; I'm an idealist. I value intimacy and conversation, not just sex.

Do you have any sexual fetishes?

I am a fan of shapely butts. I am one of these guys who think that a woman does not necessarily need large breasts if she has shapely hips and something to sit on.

Do you have many erotic fantasies?

Of course I do. But I'm not about to confess them in public. When I meet a girl that I am interested in, I try to check out what her attitude to sex is. If she can talk about intimate situations with ease, it's a signal that she's open. And this, in turn, means that we can do some crazy stuff in bed and let our fantasies carry us on. That's great! Openness in bed also means the same attitude toward other things, and I like brave women.

Do you prefer to make love during the day
or the night, as a real devil should?

I'm a day creature. I love mornings. Good exercise, good coffee, good sex … my potency is at its peak in the morning. I used to date a girl who wouldn't wake up before noon. Our biological clocks were completely off. That's something you just can't help.

Do you like porn magazines?

Pornography is healthy. It can't replace real sex but it can help bridge some gaps. It develops imagination, makes you experiment. Sometimes it even educates.

Porn in schools?

Let's not get carried away. Besides, young people know what's going on. They will find what they need. I read *The Art Of Loving* as a kid.

You once said that if you hadn't become a musician, you would have been a porn star.

It was a joke, of course. But I don't have any problems with getting naked. The guys from the band will tell you that.

Do you get naked in front of them?

Sometimes I run around naked in the dressing room after the show. But, to be honest, I don't think I could handle the porn business. Even if I have sex for fun, I still feel strong emotions. I'm not a robot.

You can't separate feeling from sex?

I can, but only to some extent. When you shoot a good, high-budget porn movie, the actors screw in the company of a few or even a dozen people. I don't think such circumstances would be ideal for me.

But you often talk about porn stars. Have you met anyone from that field?

Many times, but mostly in the States. Some of them are our fans. There was this guy in a Behemoth T-shirt at our show. He was from the I Love Vagina label. It was funny. I met the icon of that scene a few times, Ron Jeremy, and he was always accompanied by busty, plastic-looking blondes. It looked great, because his height and general appearance are quite lousy. He looks like a moron, wearing flip-flops and stretched sports clothes. But he can sell himself perfectly. I'd like to meet porn director Rocco Siffredi one day. His accent is hilarious. And he appears quite relaxed: a guy with perspective.

What do you like about his movies?
I like their naturalism. These are real documentaries. I think he sees beauty in every woman. I envy him because I don't see women that way.

What about actresses?
I love Belladonna. She's the absolute top. She's got this certain *Pulp Fiction* Uma Thurman look. She's wildly perverse and open.

A lot of porn movies are pure craft, like watching a guy hammering nails into a fence. No finesse, no passion, no spark in the eye. Belladonna's movies are different. This girl does crazy things; she's always full of passion and not only that; there is no taboo for her. Her pornography is art.

Do you see any boundaries for such 'art'?
Child pornography. In that case, it's zero tolerance.

Psychologists say that every kind of pornography falsifies reality.
I'm sorry, but I like false reality.

So maybe you will change your mind and appear in a movie? With Belladonna, maybe?
I don't think so, but you already know how it is when I swear I would never do something in my life. Never say never, right?

Seeing what you wear makes it obvious that you are volatile. You like good clothes?
I do, because I value quality. Always and everywhere. We talked about food earlier; it's the same here. When I was a student, I ate sausages and I washed

them down with curdled milk. It was tasty, but with time I discovered that you could eat differently and better.

It's the same with clothes. A leather jacket and combat boots used to be enough for me, but not today. Italian shoes made of good leather; something exclusive, one of a kind: that's what I need. You may say I'm vain. Maybe, but just a little, because I seek quality in every aspect of life. You couldn't call me vain if I surround myself with quality *people*, so why would surrounding myself with quality items and wearing quality clothes make me vain?

The proverb says beauty is only skin deep.

Bullshit! Everything we choose knowingly is a part of our beauty. Disdain for carnality is a result of 2,000 years of waiting for the kingdom that only comes when we die. I reject that fairy tale, and I reject the disdain for temporality. What we wear is what we are; it shapes our image in the eyes of people.

Do you feel like you look good in what you wear?

I feel comfortable, that's for sure. Besides, I play with my clothes. I think that's what fashion is all about. It's not about following any particular trend but about having fun. And sometimes it's about provocation, too. Of course, I won't wear something that I don't feel good in. That would be the overriding rule. Other rules? There are no other rules.

Some people say that you look a bit metrosexual.

Should I look like a typical metal caveman instead? Should I be dirty and stinky? I still consider myself a metal-head, but I never signed a pact with the devil and I never promised that I would run around in combat trousers until the end of my life. In my dictionary there is no such word as 'should'. It's exactly what we discussed before: eat meat, it's good for you … I am the one who knows which trousers look good on me. I don't force anybody to wear them. Besides, let people talk about me and say that I'm metrosexual. They can even say that I'm gay if they want. I don't have a problem with it as long as women tell me that I look like a man.

What do you think about gay people? Metal isn't very welcoming to them, is it?

In Poland it's not, but in the West that's in the past. I have a few gay friends. I like to make jokes with them, but not because I'm homophobic. I do it because I love joking. Besides, I think our nation is slowly becoming open to homosexuals and accepting them.

Some time ago, we went to a party with *Voice Of Poland* contestant Damian Ukeje. It was the middle of the night and we were leaving a bar on Plac Zbawiciela in Warsaw. We had the munchies, and we had to eat something. We went into another bar and some guy comes up to us—I think he was gay—and tells us they're closing down and we won't get anything to eat. We're about to leave when Ukeje screams, 'Then fuck you in the ass!' The guy smiles at him and says, 'Oh! That would actually be a pleasure.'

We could get seriously beaten for saying something like that in a smaller city. But Warsaw is already a bit different. My friend's excess was met with humour—even with a bit of playful perversion.

So when you have a homophobe and a homosexual in front of you, you'll take the side of the latter?

Of course. And I would take the side of a Jew, a black guy, a mason …

Like Jesus. He always defended the persecuted, right?

Stop kidding me.

What about feminists?

I like to make fun of them, too. I don't consider myself a sexist pig. I like strong and independent women, and sometimes I even admire them, but I don't get some of their posturing. Why would your gender decide whether you're going to be hired or not? Shouldn't it be about your skills and predispositions? Every woman and every man has potential, and gender has nothing to do with it.

So you're not a eulogist for political correctness?

I am tolerant, but political correctness, especially in the Unites States, is the peak of the absurd. A movie could be deemed racist there because there was no black actor in it—or if there is, he plays the part of a criminal. Come on, that's total bullshit.

Should homosexual marriages be legalised?

Of course they should. Recently I read an interview with Clint Eastwood. This guy has been associated with rather conservative views for years. But, as it turns out, his attitude toward same sex relationships is liberal. He said, 'Give everyone the chance to live the only life they have, the way they want to.' So if a guy like this says something like that, what can I possibly say?

What about the adoption of children by homosexual couples?

I would lean toward saying yes there too. Why would two nice lesbians give a child less warmth than a heterosexual family where the father drinks and beats his wife? Sexual orientation does not influence my judgement of a person. But Poles have terrible theories lodged in their heads, both in terms of sex and of fashion.

Do you like to break schemata?

I bought some trousers in London: they're red, with Scottish tartan and torn patches on the knees. They look like they were taken from *Gangs Of New York* or *A Clockwork Orange*. The previous day, I had seen a theatrical production of *The Master And Margarita*, and Azazello was wearing similar pants himself. I went back to Poland wearing them, and I met a friend who shouted at me from a distance, 'What? So Punk's not dead?' So, because they're red, and because they have patches, that makes me Johnny Rotten? Pathetic.

Wearing sunglasses after dark and inside is breaking the rules, too, isn't it?

I love sunglasses, and I do put them on my nose quite often, even when the sun is not out. I have my reasons: I'm dazzled by people's stupidity. Also, I can stare at girls' legs with impunity, and I can stay anonymous in doing so.

Have you had any offers to endorse a clothing line?

I am a patron of just one: the Behemoth brand. I design our T-shirts and hoodies. I don't do this on my own: it's a collective effort, but I do have an influence on what our fans wear. This is creative, too. Our shop's assortment is huge, and it's not enough for us to put our album cover on a black T-shirt. Of course, it's business—this is how we make our living—but we're not afraid of brave things. Besides, looking at our fans' preferences, I see that a lot has changed. A few years ago, a metal-head would never buy anything other than a black T-shirt with the band's logo on it. Nowadays white, red, and sports-type T-shirts are quite popular.

OK, so: you're not a good boy, but you won't go to the Rock'n'roll Lovers Of Destruction Hall Of Fame, either?

Because hedonism is not the way to destruction—at least not my type of hedonism. If somebody swims and loves swimming, he doesn't jump in the water to drown. It's about the happiness that you get out of the activity; the very fact that you're challenging yourself to swim a greater distance than the last time. I believe that you can consume life and not choke on it. I just like to control myself and my own fate. In fact, I like to control everything.

There's a name for that: control freak.

There is some truth in that, because when I lose control, I become afraid. I think there's only one exception: I love flying. I was talking about that with Rinke Rooyens recently. He's a typical control freak. We both came to the conclusion that there's nothing that relaxes us more than flying. You get on a plane, and it is the only moment in your life when you have absolutely no control over what's going to happen. You just stretch your legs, pick up a book or a newspaper, and all responsibility vanishes. You have to trust a machine and the man who controls it. It's beautiful.

Some people might get stressed out by that.

Not me. I'm calm even when there's turbulence.

Do you clap when a plane lands?

I hate that! It makes me furious to even think about clapping on a plane. You should have your hands cut off for that. What the hell is that supposed to mean?

'Oh! We made it this time! We're alive!' Is that what it's about?

Nobody else in the world claps after landing, only Poles. You will get your head smashed by a brick on the street sooner than you'll die in a plane crash. So why would you thank the pilots so ostentatiously? They landed because it's their job. You might as well clap the bus driver whenever he stops at a bus stop.

There's not a lot of space for risk in your life, is there?

I like to feel adrenalin, but only to a certain extent. It's like spice, and you can't overdo it with spices, because they might spoil the meal. And, equally, there can't be too few of them, because the meal would then be insipid. Besides, let's face it, I love life, and I want to enjoy it for as long as possible.

Maybe that's why I don't stuff myself with drugs, why I drink with moderation. I like to be conscious, and I want to set the tempo of the journey myself. Sometimes I run, but I want to also have the luxury of stopping, thinking, and resting from time to time. I'm not saying it's better than rushing through life. It's just the way I want to taste the world. Someone wants to do it differently? Go right ahead.

And if someone close to you chooses the path of destruction? What would you do?

You're asking if I moralise? It happens, but subtly. I hate being preached to myself. It's OK when it's a friend, as I know he cares about me and wants to give me good advice. I don't have to accept it, but I do appreciate it. It's worse when someone takes on a mentor's tone and goes on to explain to me how I should live. I can't stand it; I just resist and don't listen. So I approach my close friends carefully. I advise but I don't impose—like a friendly ghost. Or like an offscreen voice of reason.

When you were in the hospital, fighting leukaemia, did it occur to you that you should have lived more dangerously and taken more risks?

My thoughts were quite different. I saw my whole life before my eyes, and I realised that I had walked through it just as I had wanted. I'd experienced a lot of things; I'd visited almost every place in the world; I'd met thousands of fantastic and inspiring people. I also met a lot of idiots, but that's how it goes—you reach for the apple from the tree of knowledge and you get the full product in a package. You get what's nice and also what's a pain in the ass. I don't feel old, but I think I experienced more than a statistical John Smith would if he had five lives.

You take a lot from life. What do you give in return? Does a hedonist want to give anything at all?

Because someone is a great journalist, that doesn't mean he's also a great mechanic or a tightrope walker. Let's not demand omnipotence from ourselves. I believe we can become masters in one or two branches of life. There's just not enough time for more.

Yes, I take a lot from life, but I'm not a parasite. I give the energy back by creating, by being a musician. I make my dreams come true and I feed thousands of people with my vision. Some people identify with it; some people draw strength from it. I believe there's a balance between what I give to the world and what I take from it. Besides, there's nothing wrong with being hungry for life.

XII

OUT OF THE LAND OF EGYPT, OUT OF THE HOUSE OF SLAVERY

On June 18 2012, you committed apostasy. You've been playing black metal for twenty years; why did you make the decision so late?

Out of laziness. In reality, I made the decision many years ago. There are things that you are sure are going to happen sooner or later but you always put them off. It's usually obvious stuff and things that are very easy to do. That said, the process of apostasy is actually quite complicated. You can't sign out of the church just like that. In my case, it could take up to six months. Of course, that's all in an attempt to discourage even the biggest antichrist.

When did you visit your rector for the first time?

In the winter. I went to the church that is only about fifty metres from my house. It's funny, because I've lived in various areas of Gdańsk over the years but, eventually, I ended up in a place that was very close to the church where I was christened. I always end up close to the cross, it seems. That's karma coming back to bite me, I guess.

Anyway, I showed up in the sacristy and was received by a nice, elderly lady. Unfortunately, she was unable to give me all the information I needed. The rector has a monopoly on that, and he was not there at that moment. So I went back a few days later.

Did he await you with holy water?

I was there before him. He had some kind of a problem with his car, and he was a few minutes late. He turned out to be a very friendly and matter-of-fact elderly man with grey hair. We shook hands and he invited me to his place.

Did he recognise you?

Instantly. Our conversation took a few minutes. He explained to me what I had to do to commit apostasy. Most of my knowledge about it was gathered from the internet. There are a few websites that describe how to leave the church. Besides, a few of my friends had been through it, so they gave me a few tips, too. I was convinced that I had to go to the church where I was christened. But the rector told me to go to the church in the district where I was registered.

Did he try to convince you to change your mind?

He didn't try to convert me, and nor did he attempt to indoctrinate me. When I was leaving, the only thing he said was that whenever he saw me on TV, I looked like an intelligent and well-behaved man. I smiled and thanked him for the help, and we shook hands again.

Did you have to wait long for the meeting with the next rector?

That's where it all began to get more difficult. I went to the church many times. The rector worked in the diocese, too, so his secretary justified his absences with an excess of duties. Finally, I asked her to give me his telephone number. I called a few times, but each time someone else picked up the phone. It took me a few months to finally hunt him down.

The right person eventually answered the phone one Sunday. The conversation wasn't too pleasant. I had the impression that I was talking to a dense boor. He just didn't get anything, even though I was speaking calmly and factually. I politely explained why I was calling. Each of my arguments was met with negation and verbal aggression. He finally told me that I couldn't commit apostasy if I wasn't a member of the parish, and obviously I couldn't be a member of the parish because I didn't attend mass or receive the priest at my house each year. He tried to tell me that the very fact of being registered in his parish meant only that I live in a given district, and not that I'm a believer. And only believers can leave the church …

It was all even more absurd because I was only registered there, but I lived somewhere else.

But you did manage to meet him face to face?

Somehow I did. I was afraid of the meeting. I knew it was going to be a battle. But I was prepared for a war. Besides, I felt that I had been preparing for it for years. I remember that it was going on at the time when the politician and activist Janusz Palikot committed apostasy, too. He nailed his form to the doors of a church like Luther. It was very ostentatious, but why not? I thought maybe that was the way to do it. I promised myself that if they tried to make it hard for me, I would provoke the third world war.

One phone call to a journalist friend, someone like Monika Olejnik who loved that stuff, and the whole of Poland would be talking about it the next day. I also consulted my lawyers, but there was nothing they could do. Church laws have nothing in common with civil laws. So, armed to the teeth with a pile of documents, two witnesses, and two recording machines, I set out to the sacristy.

But there was no scandal in the media?

The guy who stood in front of me didn't resemble the moron on the phone at all. He was quite coarse and talkative, but in a peaceful mood. He asked me inside and offered me something to drink. At the very beginning he said, 'Are you recording this conversation?'

'Should I be?' I asked.

'I don't know,' he replied.

Today, I know that it wasn't necessary. It was an hour-long conversation that went precisely nowhere.

So you couldn't commit apostasy just like that?

The priest went by the rules that he had printed out on a piece of paper. He had also prepared for this meeting. He informed me that I couldn't commit apostasy on the day when the first conversation took place. He admitted that it was a rule to keep the potential apostate among the sheep in the flock.

I did understand his points, but I couldn't comprehend how one could look at the world so one-dimensionally. Every time a word like 'good' or 'evil' or 'sin' came up in conversation, I felt like he was talking about some distant galaxy. He just didn't get that there might be people who look at world in a different way than he did. Nevertheless, the atmosphere was calm—at times, even facetious.

What was his argument?

He told me, for example, that there must be something to the fact that people have believed in Christ for 2,000 years and stuck to the Catholic doctrine. I told him that I have a druid friend who still sticks to a tradition that is much older than Christianity, and it's still alive and kicking. So, because of that, what? We should all wear Celtic robes?

Did he acknowledge that you were right?

He just mumbled that they had told him it would be no easy ride with this guy, Darski, because he's quite clever. But he didn't give up; he tried to convince me, sometimes very seriously, sometimes by telling jokes. I would argue, but most of the time I would just smile and nod my head. As I said, I had committed my apostasy in my heart a long time ago anyway.

I think he eventually grew weary of the conversation and, looking into my eyes, he said, 'There they are, two stubborn mules.' He knew he wouldn't achieve anything, but he kept suggesting that maybe I should think about it all again. He expected a miracle. At the end, he added that apostasy would not change anything, because I couldn't erase my actual christening.

So what? I still wanted a symbolical cut of this umbilical cord. He proposed a meeting, but he didn't want to commit to a firm date. He wanted to give me time to think—but I didn't need it. I insisted, and he finally gave up. We arranged a phone call for two weeks later.

Did he answer it?

The onus was on me. I called him on the eleventh of June, the day after my thirty-fifth birthday. The priest changed the subject to football. It was Monday, and on Tuesday there was a match between Poland and Russia. He asked me what I thought the score would be. I don't know anything about football—I don't like the sport, and besides I'm no Nostradamus—but for the sake of it I told him that Russia would kick our ass 4–1. He jokingly offered me a bet. He wanted to postpone the apostasy if I was wrong by three goals—he was a little gambler.

Did you get the score right?

I was at the Polonia Hotel in Wroclaw when the match was taking place. By the way, it's not a very interesting place, quite dingy … anyway, I heard the voices of supporters all the time. Loud shouts of happiness, so I felt that I was losing the bet. Right after the match, the rector called me. He asked for the hundredth time if I hadn't changed my mind.

I told him that it was quite the contrary: that with each day my determination was getting bigger, and that I couldn't guarantee what my behaviour was going to be like in the next few weeks. We agreed to meet on the eighteenth of June.

Did you have any problems with finding witnesses?

No problem. My friends Maciej and Agnieszka were with me—a married couple. They came with their eight-month-old daughter—and before you ask, no, she wasn't christened. She won't have problems like that in the future, either; she will choose her own path.

What were your last moments as a member of church like?

It was not a good day. In the morning I had morphology tests, then I had to give some marrow for more tests; I also had to drink one and a half litres of a disgusting liquid, because I was having a tomography test of my stomach and chest later. I was short of sleep, in pain, and pissed. I needed sleep. At times like that, I'm a friend to nobody—far less a priest. I wanted to get it over as fast as possible.

The rector asked me to read my will aloud in the presence of the witnesses. Then he signed the document. He told me that the document would first go to the diocese and later to the parish where I was christened. And there they would put an appropriate note in my certificate of christening. At the very end, he pointed at my T-shirt and said, 'I used to listen to AC/DC too.' Even then he didn't want to let go: 'Just remember, Mr Darski, you still have three days to call it all off.'

'I will sooner believe that you can rise from the dead after three days than change my mind on this,' I jokingly replied.

Do you think that day changed anything in your life? Did you lose anything? Gain anything?

It was all, of course, very symbolic. My whole life was proof of what side of the barricade I was on; I just wanted to dot the 'I'. It might seem like a small detail but it bothered me. Like a little thorn: almost invisible, but very irritating. I had to get rid of it. Just for myself.

During one of my visits to the church, the priest mentioned, en passant, that apostasy does not change anything. That it only causes the church sadness. I asked him if it occurred to him that maybe it's that grief that I was concerned with?

Leaving the flock was not just a PR gimmick, then?

I didn't run to the media with it; I didn't call reporters to come to the church. Actually, it was this book that gave me the pretext. At the very beginning of our conversations, you mentioned you wanted to talk about apostasy. So I thought, 'If so, then I have to commit it; I can't find any better reason to move my ass to the sacristy.'

Apostasy is a departure. What place did you leave that June afternoon?

I left a very small, dark room, where, at least formally, I had been enclosed for my whole life. The very word 'apostasy' is fascinating. It's like a keyword or, as I sometimes put it, a 'power word'. By that, I mean that the words or symbols carry a clear message with them: a message that has a lot of content. There is a whole philosophy behind it. You don't have to explain it because it speaks for itself. That's why I chose that title for Behemoth's *Apostasy* album. And this is also one of the reasons I felt it was important for me to commit it and buy my own ticket to the forest.

The forest?

When I think about the church, I see a zoo in my head. Everything is in order; there are cages everywhere. In one cage there are monkeys, in another there are huge elephants, then some giraffes in another, and so on. Church activity revolves around the process of putting things in cages, of ordering the world by force. The only difference is that zoos are usually quite small, whereas Christianity is an ideology that tries to put the whole word behind bars. Of course, I'm referring generally to all forms of institutionalised religion here, but I can only talk specifically about the religion I know, because I live in a country where it dominates. 'Dominate' being the operative word …

The church talks about free will, though.

The presumptions of a religion may be beautiful, but 'by their fruit you will recognise them'. Free will is a clever trick, anyway. Catholics say, 'Do what you want; we're not here to judge you'—and then they turn their backs on you and judge you. Then they make a fuss that they're being hurt because someone has different views from them. The next step is lobbying for laws that are there to impose their own rules on absolutely everybody.

When someone mentions freedom of belief, then publicly cries and laments the tragedy of the believers, attacked by aggressive minorities, like how Poland was attacked by Bolsheviks … all that just to dominate the people with different beliefs and to impose their own worldview on them.

'John Smith fucks girl after girl, and my religion forbids me to do that! So let's forbid him from doing it too! In fact, let's forbid *everybody* from doing it. Let them all be sad like us! And then, let them thank the Lord for that privilege. Besides, they should be happy that we're so generous, because Islamists would have killed them long ago!' I despise this.

So you're saying that there is no freedom of belief in Poland?

We live in a wonderful democracy that gives us an illusion of equality. Unfortunately, we're equal only in the material sphere. With finance and the economy—there are no superstitions there. And the rest? It was only recently—during the twentieth century—that the world was actually freed from the feudal system. People have been exploited by this system since the Middle Ages and the church was always supporting feudalism. For ages, the princes and bishops have shouted from the pulpits that a good peasant is an obedient peasant. And they were invested in that, of course. Affluent life among the nobility meant affluent life among the clergy. The system changed, the church … not so much.

The priests don't propose serfdom nowadays, though.

But they persuade people to vote for particular political options—to maintain the status quo and prevent changes. To concretise reality. The Church's structure is based on precise and unshakable hierarchy. It's all about keeping its position and influence. So you can see the importance of every sheep. Or maybe, I should say, every scapegoat …

Why do you call believers names?

How would you describe someone who takes the burden of slavery and tries to force others to do the same? Faith has nothing to do with it. It's a system that imposes a spiritual totalitarianism. If we were born before the seizures and annexations, most of us would do anything to throw off the chains. But when we're dealing in the spiritual sphere, we give up before we even start.

For a long time, religion in Poland has been treated like air. When you breathe, you don't think about why you do it—you just do it. The church managed to inscribe religion into our tradition—to the point where nobody even questioned it.

It seems like this is changing.

Because there's corrosion at work. The main foundation of Catholicism—a statistical believer asks questions, often very inconvenient questions. It's hard to stop social change, and people start using their heads. They often turn their backs on the institution, but not the faith itself. They feel that religion is turning into politics. It's actually funny because Jesus, who was a rebel fighting with the order of the world, became the symbol of all that's conservative.

What do the rebels do today?

They flee from the zoo I talked about before. It's not the whole world, but it's a big area. In Poland, it's most of the country's territory. When we look at a map from above, we can only see a few places where there are no cages, and where animals live according to their nature. For example, in Bieszczady: there is a pack of wolves there. They are people, who—just like me—love freedom. It's easier to kill a wolf like that than to catch it because, even if you do catch it, it will die longing for freedom. Apostasy is my ticket to this forest.

Is that how you see yourself? As a wolf?

I don't want to make up any forced or incoherent definitions. I would rather quote the words of the free-jazz composer Tomasz Stanko, inspired by the poet Witkacy. They stuck in my mind, and it's difficult to come up with something better. 'I am Particular Being. PB. No union or group or patriotism. I am a Pole, I was born here, that's the language I speak, but I really feel that I am Tomasz Stanko. I am an inimitable collection of atoms, there is no one like me in the world, in the space.' Replace the word Stanko with Darski and you've got the answer to your question.

We've talked at length about what Nergal does not believe. What *does* he believe?

I think that emerges from our conversations. I believe in change and that everything flows. Reality never really 'is' but it rather 'is becoming'. I don't know how the process started and I don't know where it's going. And I will probably never know that, so I don't bother myself with it.

Relativism?

Call it what you want. These are just categories. The meaning of words also changes with time.

If everything flows, maybe in a few years you will draw a conclusion that apostasy was a mistake. What then?

Just like a man can harness the flow of the river, he can also steer his own life. We build a dam to make the water flow in a given direction, and I burnt a bridge so that my life would not go back to wrong tracks. I was driven by instinct, intuition—something very strong and primitive.

What did God do to you?

In 'Chant For Eschaton', I sing, 'Remove all gods from my way.' There is no place in my life for any powers of nature superior to men. I absolutely decline the belief in a personified God. I also decline the belief that our fortunes and misfortunes are dependent on some force majeure. We take responsibility for our own lives. Knock God off the pedestal and you will take his place. *Deus absconditus*. That's my philosophy.

Is that why you often quote Austin Osman Spare, the English occultist, at your concerts? He said that he has never met a man who wasn't God.

A man created God, and he even gave him his own features and personified him; then he fell to his knees before something he created—as if he had taken everything that's wonderful, creative and good out of himself and put it on a pedestal, while at the same time seeing himself as a pile of rotten manure. Why? I have no idea. What I do know is that with our attitude, creativity, and expansive relation to the world, each one of us can develop their godly element—without the help of figurines on walls and without prayers to golden calves.

Pride … one of the deadly sins.

I was always arrogant and insolent. I embrace these features. Just like my secret love for anarchy and chaos. Nietzsche once said that you need to have chaos in you to give life to the dancing star …

You want to incite riots?

I treat it metaphorically. Revolution, first of all, is just a state of mind. A thought that turns the system upside down and provokes, is always useful. It has nothing to do with politics. I'm not interested in coups; I am interested in human and his godly potential.

You decline religion, but you often refer to occultism. Can't you see a contradiction?

The fact that I assume that God does not exist does not mean that I'm automatically deprived of spirituality. There are a lot of things that happen to us and manifest themselves and are not quite explainable by science.

The world is magical. As children, we look at it in a very simple, often very naïve, but pure way. We notice the magic. Only later do the definitions and concepts in which we close down the reality appear. We tame it and describe it. With time we treat descriptions as unchangeable and ultimate. That's how organised religions work. People are drawn to it because they want to feel safe and get all the answers to their questions. We fear what we don't know. This fear kills curiosity and the will of cognition. I don't close my door to something I can't touch, name, and define.

You take Crowley's or the aforementioned Spare's books, read them, and accept them uncritically?

I am very sceptical. That's my attitude toward everything. On the other hand, I am an empiricist. I don't negate anything before I digest it. I don't decline an idea because of labels that somebody decorated it with.

What Crowley, Spare, and I have in common is a conviction about the existence of a hidden potential in human nature. They look at the world like a constantly curious boy. And I'm buying that. I'm not running around with a magic wand; I don't do rituals with candles, and I'm not a student in any school of magic. But there are things in occultism that inspire me. I take a lot from that legacy, like I do from many others.

I've got a tattoo on my back of the whole Hieroglyphic Monad by John Dee, Queen Elizabeth I's astrologist. Does that mean I walk the same path as he did? No. I can't; that's not me. My nature is extreme eclecticism. We've talked about the smorgasbord. This is what it is about. I am interested in philosophy, counterculture, and also occultism, for sure, but I don't want to follow a path that somebody else walked first. I avoid categories like the plague. I decline all kinds of universalism in a natural way.

Of course, I read with passion; I get inspirations and I borrow and steal ideas—anything! I'm like a sponge soaking up water. This knowledge is my fuel, but the creator of the system that allows me to live and function is *me*.

You often refer to polytheism. Is there a place for many gods in the world, and not just one God?

I use them as tools. That's what they were made for. In pre-Christian religions, whole pantheons were needed to explain natural phenomena. People didn't understand them—they couldn't justify them—so they were given godly features. It's naïve but beautiful.

I'm not interested in trying to recreate antiquity. I prefer to use that legacy by giving it a new, up-to-date meaning. I translate polytheism into a language that is modern and closer to me. Gods are metaphors. Pantheons of pagan idols just give a bit of colour to our black-and-white reality. When thunder roars outside, no one says that Thor is having a fucked up day. The reason? A storm is an atmospheric phenomenon, perfectly described and explained by science. But when I'm attacked by a Christian, I proudly respond, 'Your God was nailed to the cross, and mine has a hammer in His hands. Draw your own conclusions!'

Nature versus God?

If nature is chaos and change, and God is an ordered world of illusion, then yes. The old gods were not perfect. On the contrary, they were described as being chimerical and capricious. They were with the world, not against it.

Humans fear space and the fact that they will end up in nonexistence, and I can understand that. That lack of sense is terrifying. What I don't understand, though, is why people are so naïve to think that by keeping order in this chaos and placing God against it, they will harness nature. It's like standing eye-to-eye with a huge tornado or a ninety-metre tidal wave, waving your fists, trying to show the element that it's not in charge ... nature will easily take care of this kind of thinking.

Nergal: nature's ally.

I just fight sickness effectively. It doesn't matter if that sickness is cancer or religion.

XIII

WHAT LIVES
WILL NOT DIE

There's no sign of your sickness anymore. Behemoth is back onstage for good. How tough has it been?

I did it, but the beginning was difficult. We began with some one-off shows in the fall of 2011, then in the spring we went for a bigger tour of Europe. Coming back to playing music was quite stressful for me. Sylwia Gruchala—the Polish fencer who won a silver medal in 2003 at the World Championship and a bronze medal in 2004—told me that when sportsmen and women go to competitions, they are so tense that it is much easier for them to get injured.

It got to the point where some federations even forbade their athletes from meeting each other before competition, so as to avoid getting any infections through a handshake. It's amazing, because this is exactly the same kind of stress that I get before a tour. Being aware of the fact that I need to be in my best shape for another month makes me think about whether I can even make it. Especially nowadays. Three days before departure I had some problems with my lungs. I got myself examined, it was nothing serious, but my stress levels went a bit higher.

How did you cope with that?

I kept a positive attitude. The first concert was to take place in Hamburg. We played the show—even though I was literally coughing my lungs out before, during, and after it. Then we had another two shows and I was already counting the days to the end of the tour: twenty-two, twenty-one, twenty …

I finally got rid of all the tension somewhere in the middle of the tour. I felt that it was my natural habitat. The rhythm of the tour straightened me out both physically and mentally. Then one day I just felt good. I started exercising; the back problems that I had for the first few days suddenly let go, and there was also no sign of the cold and cough …

You're back in rock'n'roll mode, then?

I feel responsible for the band. Now, after the illness, I feel it even more.

Besides, I am the front man; I use my vocal cords. A guitarist will be OK even if he has tonsillitis, but the singer? I've been through times when I couldn't even speak and I would go onstage regardless. Sometimes I was even spitting blood—my own blood. If we cancel a show, we lose money, and we just can't afford that. You don't earn, but you still have to pay for everything, starting with the bus, the production, the gear, and finishing with hotels. It's a damn difficult and demanding profession.

So the party images that one can see on your *Crush.Fukk.Create* DVD are all in the past?

Our natural clocks are unrelenting. Today, we are more driven by routine. But I like it. More sleep, proper amounts of vitamins and minerals, some relaxation, a nap before the show, some exercise, and then some rest at the hotel—it's all good! Of course we still party, and the guys can still drink quite a lot. After the shows, of course.

What about you?

When I got more settled, I danced my ass off a few times. But I'm a good boy. We're good friends with white wine. I could drink a bottle or two a day.

Isn't two bottles of wine quite a lot?

Tours have their own microclimate. What you drink during a tour is not equal to what you might drink at home. It's the same with holidays. You wake up in the morning and you don't even feel hung over … but if you drank the same volume at home, you'd find it difficult to get out of bed the next day.

Have you ever thrown somebody out of the band because of drinking?

No. I've stopped being the nanny. I'm their partner. It's a question of trust and respect for the rules we established ourselves. The priority is the tour, the band, and the show. Partying is in the background. If somebody goes over the line, they usually apologise and behave themselves. Everybody here knows that making a living in music is a privilege, just like the parties after the shows are. Throw all that away? What for?

What if somebody does not apologise?

Then the rest of the band straightens him out. But we're tolerant. What's important is that everybody must be sober before the show. Before and after that, they can be off their faces. We had such a situation not that long ago. The European Tour was really great socially. We toured with bands that we know and like—Cannibal Corpse, for example. They are our old buddies. For the first few days, George Fischer, their lead singer, was drinking with Pazdzioch, our guitarist.

At the beginning, they were drinking equally. I would wake up at 11am and they would still be sat there with beers in their hands, completely drunk. They went to bed and woke up just before the show. Then they did it again and again.

The show was over, and George would come to our bus again and drink with Seth. He was doing all right until he got so drunk that he shat his pants. From this day on we stopped calling him George 'Corpsegrinder'—as he is officially known—and changed it to George 'Shitmaster' instead. We would make fun of him until the end of the tour. But it was very friendly. We, musicians, are like a family. We can really talk a lot of shit to one another, but these jokes are not aggressive.

Don't your groupies miss you?

I guess so, but I didn't ever take advantage of it. Touring is hard, dirty, tiring … and then fucking some broad in the toilets on top of that? I'm too old for that. Besides, as I said before, I'm not really interested in my fans from that perspective.

What about when you were younger?

I'm not the Holy Ghost. There are conditions that are more or less appropriate for such situations. The latter ones occur more frequently. Also,

I never felt the urge to break the record for nailing girls in combat boots. But that's just one side of me.

What's the other?

There are places where circumstances are good, more often. But we don't go there too often. South America is a real Eldorado for a guy. Their women have a totally different temper—a different approach to life. There are fewer boundaries for them. They really like to have fun. It's the same case in Russia. Man-woman relations are much simpler there.

Russian girls are like Polish ones. They are bohemian.

I have the impression that Russian women are much less calculating. Besides, when we play a show in Moscow, I am much more anonymous than I am in Warsaw. In Russia, I know that a girl who wants to spend the next few hours with me will then disappear from my life, but in Poland? I have to consider it five times before I even think about going into an intimate situation with a girl.

Polish women are calculating?

Sometimes. Very often I have the feeling that they have ulterior motives beyond sheer fun. It seems that it's sometimes about my social status, and that, naturally, makes me reluctant.

Is there anyone in the band who is not so reluctant?

There is, but I won't say anything more.

Did you notice any changes in your audience after you started showing up in tabloids and on TV?

There were voices at our shows that had changed. One of my friends even refused to come to one of our shows. I thought that he understood me and knew how honest I am when it comes to the music that I make. But he said that memories are very important to him, and he wanted to remember us as a band playing for serious people—not for 'one-season' fans. That's his right.

Yes, but is he right?

We conducted some sociological experiments with the guys and we checked what kinds of people show up at our shows. It turned out that the audience still mainly consists of true metal fans. Maybe they are a bit younger, but that's only natural. It's a shift of generations. Of course, there were some busybodies looking for cheap stories who only came to see the guy from the television. But they constituted only a small proportion of the whole audience. Anyway, our attitude hasn't changed: we play for our loyal fans.

Were the Polish shows successful?

Most of them were sold out; people were hungry for Behemoth. But we were regaining our form slowly. We started pretty well. The European tour was very good, and in the States, where we went later, we got better still.

But then America greeted you with a concert that was cancelled on 'religious grounds'.

The club that booked it, three months earlier, cancelled the concert. The owner agreed to a concert by Behemoth, Watain, and The Devil's Blood, and then he changed his mind. If I were a God-fearing Christian, I would probably look at these names and say, 'Oh, no, no, you will not play at my place.' Ultimately, I viewed it as good promotion. A kind of a gift for Easter.

Have you had situations like this before, in the States?

We've had to cancel a few shows, but only because of technical issues. That was the case on the *Evangelion* promo tour. We were driving through North Dakota in winter when we found ourselves in the middle of a snowstorm. We were in some fucking backwoods place, like in *Fargo*. All we needed was a pregnant police officer …

We stopped at a gas station. We knew that the gig was fucked. There was no chance we could get there on time. But that wasn't our biggest problem: the heating on the bus had failed. It was fucking freezing. The gas station crew let us inside. We bought some blankets. It was a night of living like tramps …

A few other people were in the same situation; the police were out in the streets, directing everybody to the gas station. The next day we were supposed to play in Chicago, a few hundred miles away. In the morning we were in really bad shape. We slept on the floor, shivering, and it's not easy to rest in such conditions. Finally, the highway was reopened. The bus's heating system still didn't work, but we were on our way, even though the temperature inside was well below zero. We were driving in silence, muffled in blankets. Road conditions were difficult, so reaching the nearest city took us a few hours.

No matter what we did, it would have been impossible to get to Chicago by bus, so we called our promoter. We found the nearest airport and caught a plane to Chicago. We only took our instruments and the most important gear. Before the show we only just managed to take a shower and went onstage right afterwards. American winter *versus* Behemoth: 1:1.

The next time you went to America was in the spring, so you couldn't complain about the weather.
It was beautiful. I really took advantage of it—I jogged every day, I exercised a lot …

At least you didn't have to hide from paparazzi.
I met one in New York City. I was wandering around Manhattan with my two friends Julka and Kinga. We were checking out local boutiques. We were sitting in a Rick Owens shop in South Village; I'm trying on this new pair of shoes when I look out the window and on the other side of the street there's this guy with a huge smile on his mug, taking pictures of me. The shop's staff noticed it, too, so they curtained the window off. But the guy just wouldn't go away.

When we walked out, he still took pictures of us. I whistled to him, he obediently approached us, smiled, and—before I had managed to say anything—apologised for disturbing our privacy. He was a Pole, and he'd been working in the States for five years. He promised not to follow us, wished us a nice day, and was soon on his way. His behaviour was extremely different from what I knew from the streets of Warsaw or Gdańsk. He didn't anger me. I even wished him good luck with selling the pictures …

They were published in the tabloids, so he probably earned something. The weather was good; the mood was good; how did the shows go?

The reception was amazing. People knew what I'd been through during the last couple of years. They supported me. During shows, I like to watch the people in front of the stage. I always do that. Seeing my fans gets me going. That was the case on one of the first shows on the tour. At one moment I saw this guy holding his T-shirt high above his head so that I could see what was printed on it. It said '*Fuck cancer*'. Wow! I felt strange … maybe even a little moved.

Another time, I saw a fan in a T-shirt that said, 'Nergal *versus* Leukaemia: 1:0'. That gave me an awesome kick. Things like that create a bond. You just realise how important your fans are to you. Sometimes they're even like family. The more you respect them, the more you feel like unstitching yourself onstage for them.

Were there more stories of this kind?

Our second last concert was in the Palladium club in New England. The venue was packed. I look at the audience. On one of the balconies I see an older, skinny guy. I have the impression that I know him from somewhere. He watches me closely. A few times our eyes meet, but I am absorbed by the show, I drift away on the stage …

An hour later, I'm taking a shower. Suddenly our tour manager knocks at the door and says, 'Nergal, hurry up, there's somebody who wants to meet you.' I get dressed, walk in the room, and I see the guy from the balcony. He introduces himself.

'Tom Hamilton, nice to meet you.'

He points at a boy who was with him and says it's his son, who is our big fan, and the pieces fall into place; I match the face with the name. 'Fuck,' I think to myself, 'the guy from Aerosmith brought his son to our show, what a blast.'

In the meantime, Tom starts to share his thoughts on the show. He talks about our music, and I am amazed at how much fun he actually found in it. He could easily be my father! Besides, he is one of the pioneers of hard rock. I stand face to face with a legend, and I try very hard not to show that I feel very small. When he mentions *his* band, I try to make a joke, and I ask, 'You play in Bon Jovi, right?'

'No, Aerosmith,' he replies, equally seriously. He's absolutely unfazed by it. It turns out that he knows my name, he'd heard about my sickness, and tells me how happy he is that I managed to overcome it. A moment later, he points to the side of his neck and shows me the mark where he had his tumour cut out. More time passes; we talk, take some pictures. Another exceptional day in a wonderful life.

Is the support of other people from the music industry important to you?

I take pride in the fact that I work with many people with whom I am connected not only by business but also by friendship. In twenty years, I have learned that if you're doing business, you need to have eyes in the back of your head. There is always someone who will try to fuck you over and stick a knife in your back.

Fortunately, I also meet exceptional people and I try to keep them close. Michał Wardzała—our Polish publisher, and the boss of the Mystic record label—is a great example. It all started simply enough: he offered to release our album and I agreed to that, even though I was still careful about my every move. My trust grew over time, and today I trust him like I trust my own mother. He's my friend. The chance to work with this kind of person is a real treasure. Their support was and is priceless for me.

Do you feel fulfilled?

The life of a musician is a peculiar one. It's easy to become too big for your own shoes. Each evening you get on the stage and you hear a thousand throats scream the words of your songs. After the shows you get alcohol and other things for free, girls are just waiting to lock themselves in the dressing room with you.

There have been a lot of guys who thought it would be like this forever. Many were quickly out of the game. There are thousands of people who are just waiting for your one bad move. And then they will force their way into taking your place. If you want to make your living in music, you have to remember that.

Do you remember?
Our bus stops in the middle of the Alps; I can see mountaintops bathed in sunlight. I get out of the car and go to stretch my legs. Everything around me is so beautiful that it takes my breath away. It is in this kind of situation where I realise what a wonderful surprise my life had for me. I keep on telling myself: 'Darski, don't fuck it up.'

Do you sometimes feel writer's block?
Often.

Do you fight it, or do you just wait for it to pass?
I fight. I try to overcome it but then I get doubts. Should I be fighting? Is that honest? Shouldn't it come freely without this fight? Is what I create still authentic?

Well, is it?
At moments like this, I think about mountain climbers—guys who climb 8,000 metre peaks. It's not easy, nice, and cosy. Or, I think about women.

Women?
The emotions that accompany you when you fight for a woman might be compared to those I feel when I try to write. When a man conquers a woman, it's not always easy, is it? You conquer her, you fight for her;

sometimes she reacts and sometimes she ignores you. It's like a dance. And this is how I dance with my guitar all my life. It's my *utensil*.

It seems easy: you just grab it and play.

It depends how you approach it. A utensil—as its very name suggests—is supposed to be utilised. I'm not talking about playing for its own sake or the sounds themselves, but about something much bigger, more complete. I find it hard to say the word 'art', because it's quite a big word. There's a wholeness attached to it. You have a vision—a picture in your head—and you want to express it in a particular language. In my case, this language is the language of music. That poses quite a few problems, because I am no virtuoso. Of course, I keep trying to get better at what I do, I work hard, but some things are just insurmountable for me. So I have to realise my vision with the skills I have at my disposal. But they are only one side of the story. There is also imagination, which is like a motivational power … but that is limited as well.

Young Nergal's sorrows …

It does look a bit like that, because music is often born out of pain. A carpenter takes a piece of wood, works on it, polishes it; he cuts it, he saws it, but he works according to a particular scheme. He already sees in his head—and sometimes even on paper—the chair that he's supposed to make. I create differently. I take a piece of wood and I carve it with a hit-or-miss method. I look for an accurate form. Sometimes it takes weeks. But it makes you even happier when you manage to find the right shape, even if it's still quite gnarled, heavy-handed, full of splinters.

All this creating is quite painful?

The inability to create is especially painful. And extremely tiresome.

How do you overcome it?

I need to be alone. It may be a cliché, but loneliness motivates you when you're creating. When I think that I'm about to take my guitar in my hands when somebody is walking around the house, I feel nothing would come out of it. Even if it's somebody close … the very sound generated by somebody's presence may well be an obstacle.

So you're home alone …
Just like today, I looked out of the window. As you know, I live close to a church, so I saw a huge cross in splashes of heavy rain. I suspect that most people would get really sad when seeing this view: because it's raining, because it's cold, because it's just another day and you have to keep doing all the same things. But I was cheered by it. And this emptiness in my house, this silence—all that worked as a soundboard. And it was THE moment. I took my guitar, I strummed a few chords, and all the pieces fell into place. Everything matched.

And if it was sunny, and a loving wife was in the house?
It would be difficult to play the right chords.

Isn't that a bit like a creative masochism? People say that artists make their best works when they suffer.
That's what they say.

Is it true?
I wrote *Evangelion* after breaking up with a girl I'd spent a year with. I really felt terrible. It was the only moment in my life that I sought help in pills and antidepressants. That and the fact that I started creating like crazy made my total breakdown fade into nothing. That record turned out to be our biggest success, and not just in commercial terms.

It's quite brave to say, but don't you think that admitting to have been taking antidepressants collides a bit with your artistic image? You're always so full of vitality and strength.
I am not embarrassed by it, and I don't have any problem with it. When you

get your ass kicked by life and you can't even get out of your own bed, why would you be reluctant to get an antidote, even if it's chemical? It's a method just like anything else, but what matters is that it's effective.

If I am supposed to get into a building, it doesn't matter what method I choose in order to do it. It just needs to work, that's all. I can be like Spider-Man and climb up the wall, I can be a sprinter and run up the stairs, or I can be a cat and try to jump from roof to roof … besides, do you know why the turtle is hard? Because it's soft.

So the shell of a hardcore metal-head hides a sensitive soul inside?

It's not just about my psyche but about me as a person, including my body. It's like you've tried to combine a child and a titan into one character. That's how I am constructed. With time, I get more aware of my soft spots—areas where I feel defenceless. And I feel authentic fear that one day one of them will stop working. On the other hand, my attitude is like armour that enables me to walk through life like a soldier.

What is the music in this case? Your sword?

It's more like a soundtrack to my journey. Don't get me wrong, sometimes a good soundtrack contains a lot of silence. Lately there has been quite a lot of that in my life. Sometimes it has to be silent, so that sometimes there is an orchestra playing.

There are quite a lot of opposites in your life, aren't there?

I think so. I must fall in order to rise and go up.

Just like Sisyphus?

It's funny you should say that. I was thinking about Sisyphus not long ago when I was reminiscing about what has happened in my life during the last few years. I remembered this situation we talked about earlier. Once, after breaking up with my beloved, I felt like I had fallen down—like I'd hit rock bottom. My armour was broken, and I just couldn't fix it myself. That's when I reached for the pills. It was a major kick. On the one hand, it was superficial, external, but on the other hand I imposed strict discipline on myself and started climbing up again.

For a few months I lived like I was in barracks—the only thing missing was the daily drill. I started each day with heavy training, then I worked a lot with the guitar in my studio at home. In the evenings I would read or go to the cinema. It was the end of December, and I was really amped by the thought that, all around me, this Christmas Eve show was taking place. People sitting, watching their TVs, stuffing their stomachs, and then me, muffled in three layers of clothes and a scarf, running through snow in the forest.

Like Rocky Balboa?

I've always been fond of movies where the protagonist gets really fucked in life, then gets a grip, gets up from his knees, and moves toward life's adversities with his eyes open. That is what really impresses me about American culture—programming yourself to win.

Did you beat your demons, too?

All the time there was this feeling in me—the feeling of being seriously wounded by the breakup with someone I loved. But I also felt it healing. I started putting this feeling into words and sounds. That's how the *Evangelion* album was created. I think it's the best album that I have recorded to this day.

When Sisyphus reaches the top, he falls. You fell in a big way. You were close to death.

It's difficult for me to assess this. I don't know any appropriate measure that you could apply to such events and categorise them in any way. I really don't know if a terminal illness is a bigger fall than breaking up with a woman. All this is extremely individual and dependent on thousands of factors.

You beat terminal illness, but you've been through many more breakups.

In a way, I even learned *how* to break up. Still, that does not make it any easier, I just know how to heal my wounds. In situations like this, a human being feels like a child in the middle of a forest. It's dark, and you don't know which way to go. And that feeling stays with you.

But I keep learning. I know that, instead of running wild, I must wait until sunrise. Light always comes, but never immediately. Honestly speaking, I can't be sure if—whenever I find myself in such a situation again—I won't just panic and start running blindly ahead. You never really know that until you're there, do you?

PICTURE CREDITS

The photographs used in this book came from the following sources. If you feel there has been a mistaken attribution, please contact the publisher. Many of the images used came from Nergal's own archives, and we are grateful to him and to Maciej Szymanowicz, who designed the original Polish version of this book, for their help in assembling this edition.

Jacket front and back, 3–6 Ivo Ledwożyw **81–3** Nergal **84** Damian Kramski **85** *top left* Agnieszka Krysiuk, *top right* Nergal, *bottom* Martin Darksoul **86** *top left* Charlene Tupper, *top right* Nergal, *bottom* Natalia Kempin **87** Nergal **88** Ivo Ledwoż **201** *top* Natalia Kempin, *bottom* Agnieszka Krysiuk **202–3** Nergal **204** Rafał Szyjer **205** *top* Agnieszka Krysiuk, *bottom* Krzysztof Wiktor **206** Nergal **207** *top* Jan Bogacz TNP SA, *bottom* Charlene Tupper **208** Mike Savoya.